THE UNIVERSITY OF NORTH CAROLINA
SOCIAL STUDY SERIES

WILLIAM GREGG

THE UNIVERSITY OF NORTH CAROLINA
SOCIAL STUDY SERIES

ODUM AND JOHNSON: *The Negro and His Songs* . $3.00
PUCKETT: *Folk Beliefs of the Southern Negro* . . 5.00
ODUM AND JOHNSON: *Negro Workaday Songs* . . 3.00
ODUM AND OTHERS: *Southern Pioneers* 2.00
POUND: *Law and Morals* 2.00
GIDDINGS: *The Scientific Study of Human Society* . 2.00
ODUM AND WILLARD: *Systems of Public Welfare* . 2.00
BRANSON: *Farm Life Abroad* 2.00
ROSS: *Roads to Social Peace* 1.50
WILLEY: *The Country Newspaper* 1.50
JORDAN: *Children's Interests in Reading* . . . 1.50
ODUM: *An Approach to Public Welfare and Social
Work* 1.50
NORTH: *Social Differentiation* 2.50
KNIGHT: *Among the Danes* 2.50
STEINER AND BROWN: *The North Carolina Chain
Gang* 2.00
CARTER: *The Social Theories of L. T. Hobhouse* . 1.50
LOU: *Juvenile Courts in the United States* . . . 3.00
BROWN: *A State Movement in Railroad Development* 5.00
MILLER: *Town and Country* 2.00
MITCHELL: *William Gregg: Factory Master of the
Old South* 3.00
METFESSEL: *Phonophotography in Folk Music* . . 3.00
WAGER: *County Government in North Carolina* . 5.00

THE UNIVERSITY OF NORTH CAROLINA PRESS
CHAPEL HILL, N. C.

THE BAKER AND TAYLOR CO.
NEW YORK

OXFORD UNIVERSITY PRESS
LONDON

MARUZEN-KABUSHIKI-KAISHA
TOKYO

WILLIAM GREGG

WILLIAM GREGG

FACTORY MASTER
OF THE
OLD SOUTH

BY

BROADUS MITCHELL, PH.D.

ASSOCIATE PROFESSOR OF POLITICAL ECONOMY
IN THE JOHNS HOPKINS UNIVERSITY

CHAPEL HILL
THE UNIVERSITY OF NORTH CAROLINA PRESS
1928

PRINTED IN THE UNITED STATES OF AMERICA BY
EDWARDS & BROUGHTON COMPANY, RALEIGH, N. C.

To Bobs
With Love

FOREWORD

This essay undertakes two things—first, to set forth the main facts in the life of William Gregg, and second, to record in some detail the operations of the Graniteville Factory which he built in South Carolina.

Possessed of a sense of humor, resourceful beyond other Southerners of his day, uniquely successful, and forever buoyant, Gregg was nevertheless a tragic figure. The advocate of industry and the advancement of the average man, he opposed an economic system built upon agriculture, in which a landed aristocracy was dominant. Southerners would not, could not, act upon his example. The social scheme against which he worked had entered the phase where it was not to be argued with. Many of his contemporaries got their costly reward in civil conflict. Gregg, the servant of material improvement, died in the dark days of after-war collapse, a generation before the fruition of his hopes.

He was the South's first great bourgeois, the forerunner of a new era. The reader may feel that the pages which follow contain too much praise of him. I can only say that the evidence which I have been able to collect lends little support to an unfavorable view of the man.

Now that industry, and particularly the cotton manufacture, is growing so conspicuously in the South, it is interesting to try to picture rather minutely the development of the most important early factory. As a justification I have had in mind Professor Unwin's painstaking description of an English prototype in his "Samuel Oldknow and the Arkwrights." Though the manufacturing enterprise which Gregg founded has continued to expand and is today notably prosperous, I have not followed its history beyond the period of Gregg's lifetime.

It is a great pity that a dozen years ago an outsider, ignorant of the interest attaching to Gregg and to Graniteville, destroyed many of the mill records. The minutes of the directors' meetings especially would have been of use in my work.

Many have helped me, and cordially. I owe first thanks to Mrs. R. C. Chafee, Gregg's only surviving child, who has assisted me by her vivid recollection and has lent me what she has of her father's papers. Talks with her have been the most charming part of a pleasant undertaking. Miss Rena Chafee has also been kind in placing material in my hands. I could not have done the work without the assistance of funds made available by Professor Howard W. Odum, of the University of North Carolina, and his kindly interest in the project has encouraged me. Mr. August Kohn, of Columbia, to whom any student of the economic history of South Carolina must have recourse, drew my attention to William Gregg originally; he has helped me with suggestions from his rich knowledge of the subject and has allowed me the use of many pamphlets from his unique collection. Officials of the Graniteville Manufacturing Company have coöperated with me to the fullest extent. Mr. Lanier Branson, president, and Mr. George H. Leit-

ner, vice president and superintendent, have cherished
an affectionate interest in the history of the company
and have trusted me with records that have been indispensable, besides giving up much time to my questions.
Mrs. Dexter Otey, of Lynchburg, Virginia, came to my
rescue with a rare report which saved me from "the
tyranny of the unread." Miss Elizabeth Merritt, of
Goucher College, furnished me a finding list of Gregg's
letters to Hammond.

B. M.

SWEET BRIAR, VIRGINIA
August 25, 1927

CONTENTS

CONTENTS

WILLIAM GREGG

CHAPTER I

THE JEWELER'S APPRENTICE

The first of the family in America, the great-great-great-grandfather of the subject of this essay, was William Gregg, who "settled on a tract of 400 acres of land in Christiana Hundred, New Castle County, Delaware, [at that time in William Penn's grant] surveyed to him 3 Mo. 11, 1685. He died 'ye 1st of ye 7th month and was buried on his own plantation 1687.' "[1] It has been recorded that he was a member of William Penn's original party which arrived with the Proprietor on the ship *Welcome*, October 28, 1682.[2]

William Gregg seems to have been a native of Scotland, a member of the clan of McGregor (the names being really the same), who, settled in Ireland, met with Penn at the lead mines of the latter and was so converted to be a Quaker.[3] The second of the family in America was John Gregg, born in 1668. He married Elizabeth Cook, at Concord Meeting, in 1694.[4] He must have been the John Gregg among those taxed in Kennett in 1715.[5]

William, the son of this marriage and the great-grandfather of the William Gregg of this essay, married in 1725 Margery Hinkey, daughter of a German astronomer of some note.[6] William became a miller, his father John having bought a tract of land for him on Red Clay Creek ten miles from Wilmington, and built there the only grist mill within a wide radius of country. Herman, son of this marriage, was born May 10, 1730. He married Mary Dixon in 1750, and built near the mill, to which he undoubtedly fell heir, what was described as a fine house. As late as 1879 it was recorded that "The old house is still in pretty good preservation, and has his name and his wife's (Herman & Mary) inscribed with dark colored bricks over the front entrance."[7] Herman died in 1773.

William Gregg, the father of our William, was born in the Red Clay Creek house September 13, 1756. He represents the first connection of the family with South Carolina. He "settled in Virginia, and during the Revolutionary War took up arms in behalf of his native country, and was among the troops who fought in defence of Charleston." At the surrender of the city he was taken prisoner by the British. "Whilst on the road to Ninety-Six, with other prisoners, he managed to make his escape in one of our swamps, and found his way back to his native state."[8] Upon his return to Delaware he married Elizabeth Webb, of a Philadelphia Quaker family, moved to South Carolina, and settled in Newberry District. He subsequently removed to what is now Monongalia County, West Virginia, and established himself near Muddy Creek at a point above Carmichaels.[9]

Here William Gregg was born, February 2, 1800. Monongalia County, which was formed in 1776 from the old District of West Augusta, was at this time primitive frontier. In 1782 Morgantown was made the county seat, court being held at Zackwell Morgan's house. The town's charter required that within four years every lot owner should build a house at least 18x18 feet, with a stone or brick chimney; however, extensions of time were granted, due to Indian attacks and difficulty in obtaining material. About the time the Quaker immigrants were arriving, pioneer clearings began to widen into farms; at first the settlers had sent peltries, ginseng, and bear's grease by pack horses over the mountains to the East, but now the treaty with Spain stimulated commerce on the Ohio, and potatoes, apples, pork, and flour began to go to New Orleans. It had been a country of blockhouses and roads that followed the ridges to afford warning of Indian attacks, but by the time of Gregg's birth the traveled ways ran through cultivated fields. The county had more than 8,000 settlers.[10]

William's mother died when he was four years old, leaving him the youngest of several children. A kind woman neighbor of the Greggs took the little boy to live with her. She brought him up to the age of ten or perhaps older, when he was placed with his uncle, Jacob Gregg, of Alexandria.[11] A very pretty story is told of Gregg and his foster mother. Years afterwards, when he was a prosperous merchant in Columbia, South Carolina, he set out with his wife and child, in a coach and four, to visit his sisters in Iowa. One night in the western country the family halted at a farm house to ask for a lodging. To Gregg's complete surprise, the elderly woman who came to the door recognized him and embraced him, calling him by name. He was of course

3

delighted to find her, and when he left gave her a handsome check.[12]

Jacob Gregg had accumulated a considerable fortune as a watchmaker, and also "engaged largely in the manufacture of spinning machinery."[13] At the time Jacob Gregg took William to start him in life, Alexandria was the entrepôt for the northwestern part of Virginia, and the productions of the frontier were marketed through the Potomac River town. It was particularly the center for the grain trade. Removal from the farms of distant Monongalia to Alexandria meant that the boy was put in the way of an active commercial or industrial career.

William did not remain long in Alexandria, for his uncle, abandoning watchmaking for textiles, moved to Georgia, where he established "one of the first cotton factories in the South. It was situated on Little River—Whatley's mills—midway between Monticello and Madison."[14] Here William got his first taste of the industry which was to inspire his later life, and for which he did so much in return. Hargreaves stumbled over his wife's spinning wheel and began the Industrial Revolution. William Gregg happened on his uncle's tiny plant in Georgia, and became the father of the cotton manufacture in the cotton States.[15]

The equipment was largely of Jacob Gregg's own manufacture. The enterprise was doubtless inspired by the anti-British feeling which preceded the War of 1812, and during the continuance of hostilities the mill prospered, but with the return of peace was ruined, along with other like establishments, by the flood of importa-

tion from England. Apparently Jacob Gregg lost more
than this particular plant, having investments, perhaps
in the form of credit for machinery, in other small mills,
all of which were depreciated by the swamping of the
business after 1814. Unable to carry on in cotton manufacturing, Jacob Gregg had to find a new trade for his
nephew, and naturally chose that of watchmaker and
silversmith. He placed the boy with a fellow-craftsman
and old friend of his at Lexington, Kentucky, to begin
his apprenticeship. Here William remained until 1821,
when he went to Petersburg, Virginia, "to perfect himself in his profession."[16]

His education was thus a practical one of manual
dexterity. It is not known that he ever went to school
a day in his life.[17] It is interesting to think that his
trade of jeweler and silversmith gave him a sense of
precision and a love of beautiful things which were
abundantly shown in his later career. At the workbench
was nourished the creative capacity which distinguished
his life. Gregg's master in Petersburg was named
Blanchard, and with him Gregg must have formed a fast
friendship; a decade later, when he was returning from
his carriage trip to the West, he stopped to see Blanchard
at Louisville, to which place he had removed. At
Blanchard's bench Gregg made a silver pitcher of the
treasured first coins he ever earned, and this interesting
heirloom has since been handed down from first son
to first son in the Gregg family.

In 1824[18] he was a full-fledged workman, and resolved to establish himself in business at Columbia, the
capital of South Carolina. This was a decision which

carried great importance for the future. Had he remained in Virginia he probably would never have been as deeply impressed as he was in South Carolina with the economic one-sidedness which was ruining the South; he would not have been drawn to the rescue of the Poor Whites, nor been in any way identified with cotton manufacturing.

Gregg must have been the model apprentice, for it was said that he "commenced business at Columbia with a limited capital which he had accumulated by untiring industry, economy, and assiduous attention to the duties of his profession."[19] It was probably Gregg himself who said that by faithfulness and punctuality he gained the confidence of the community, and prospered. Before long he enlarged his business to include "an extensive European correspondence and direct trade," to effect which he visited England and France in 1837.[20]

In April, 1829, Gregg was married to Marina Jones, of Edgefield District, whom he had met in the course of his business travels in the State. It is well here, at the outset, to know something of William Gregg's appearance and manner. He was a large man, tall and broad-shouldered. His physical vigor was inherited from a line of pioneering Scotch-Irish ancestors. Throughout his life, with the exception of a short period after quitting his business in Columbia, he was capable of sustained exertion of mind and body without exhaustion. He must have been an impressive figure—in the streets of Charleston, in the halls of the legislature, in the village of Graniteville. When a young man he

6

regularly rode horseback, but in later years he stoutened and found his buggy more comfortable.

He had a fine head, with unusually high forehead and regular features. His brown hair was inclined to be wavy, and was worn in longish locks. He had no mustache, but at one period of his life wore a short beard, only on his chin. His eyes, under heavy brows, were very perceiving, and yet held a smile. His expression was one of strength and a self-confident reserve, but of a winning kindliness, too. All of his pictures show this. Those who knew him speak of his double virtue of logic and humor. His was a nicely poised intelligence, recalling Hazlitt's phrase descriptive of Charles Lamb, that "his jests scald like tears, and he probes a question with a play upon words." Living in a period of extraordinary controversy, sectional self-righteousness and bitterness, in which men were flying off on tangents, he kept his balance. There was a spiritual quality about Gregg which showed in his face; his love of his fellows put him at peace with himself, and this gave a harmony to all he did. Loyal to his own purposes, he drew people to him—the wealthy and influential, and the poor and neglected. He did not have to unbend. Rollicking with children came natural to him, and he was the friend of dumb animals. At the same time, his manner owed something, in conviction and dignity, to his Quaker forbears.

The Gregg family lived on Lady Street in a house that was burned in the great fire of the Civil War. Gregg's income must have been good when he had been

7

established in Columbia only a few years, for he set out for Iowa with a white coachman and four horses.[21] The three oldest children, Mary,[22] William, and James, were born in the Lady Street house.

Gregg had been in business in Columbia only a decade when he decided to withdraw from active commercial life. He said later that he "retired from a very lucrative business in Columbia on account of ill health. . . ."[23] The nature of his ailment is not known; afterwards he was exceptionally robust. Nor is it known what became of the business, except that Gregg apparently had all his capital free for other uses. He probably went with his family to his wife's home in Edgefield, or to the town of Aiken near by, in either of which places he found a better climate than that of Columbia.

One of the most interesting spots in the countryside was the little village of the Vaucluse Manufacturing Company, and being possessed of a restless mind and unemployed funds, Gregg bought into this enterprise. He seems to have had no deliberate plan at this time to take a leading part in cotton manufacturing. His first shares in Vaucluse were acquired rather casually, and he did not investigate the affairs of the company closely, much less make any general inquiry into the prospects of the industry in the South, until some time later.[24] His health had not sufficiently improved to persuade him to purchase the establishment when it was sold late in the same year, though he had previously become its active manager. The Vaucluse episode will be returned to later in this story. In a review of this period of his life he

8

was praised for not standing idly by while his money accumulated in bank investments, but for departing from the rule in South Carolina at the time by placing his means at the service of commerce and industry.[25] In 1838 he moved to Charleston, where he resumed the business of jeweler and silversmith in the firm of Hayden, Gregg & Co., successors to the old house of Eyland, Hayden & Co.[26]

This change of scene to Charleston was of the first moment in Gregg's later activities. He had become familiar with Virginia, Georgia, and Kentucky, and had had a view of Europe. He had been a workman at the bench, and had won independence through his own hard exertions. He knew well the central portion of South Carolina and the upper portion about his wife's home, besides having traveled all over the State, probably, in the early years of his business in Columbia. In his capacity as a jewelry merchant he had been in touch with the wealthy part of the population, and at Vaucluse he was in intimate contact with the Poor Whites of a rural district. He had participated in commerce and in a pioneer adventure into industry. Now he went to live in the cultural, political, and financial center of the State and to a less extent of the South. In Charleston, possessed of his previous experiences, he found South Carolina at a focus. It was now that his public life began. He saw represented in Charleston what was most hopeful and what was most retarding in the State; he discovered a forum for his preachments and financial backing to carry them into execution.

In the firm "the terms of co-partnership were such as to afford the senior partner of the house entire leisure from the active labors of business."[27] He gave range to his thoughts. "Naturally possessed of an active temperament, with a mind to which knowledge of every kind was easily accessible, his time and advantage were not suffered to pass unimproved. . . . He sought for information from all quarters and intuitively applied it to practical purposes, and in this way laid up a fund of useful knowledge which he from time to time communicated to the public."[28]

The family remained in Charleston for most of the time during the next sixteen years. The large, square, cypress clapboarded mansion, with great porches at the front and side, is now numbered 274 Calhoun Street. When Gregg bought it and lived there, the yard was almost an island, Calhoun Street being a creek. Most of the houses now standing near are built on made ground. An old oil painting[29] shows the Gregg house surrounded by blue water and embosomed in trees which further envelop it today. The family used a boat a good deal for exit and entry, and crabs used to nibble at the bare toes of the children when they came down to the brink of the yard. Two large palmettoes stand at the sides of the front walk, and carry a peculiar Gregg association, for Mrs. Gregg raised them from seed indoors and set them out. The garden in Gregg's time (he always took a pride in gardening—in Charleston, at Kalmia and at the Graniteville Mill itself) was a show place of the city, and drivers from the Charleston Hotel used to bring visitors to admire it.[30]

William Gregg's factory at Graniteville, for which he will always be chiefly remembered, was an outgrowth not only of his philosophy, but of his romance. A century ago in South Carolina a merchant eager to extend his sales was likely to be his own "drummer." Thus Gregg went about the country on horseback carrying his wares in saddlebags. Among the customers whom he visited was Colonel Matthias Jones,[31] who kept a store at Ridge Spring, in Edgefield District. Here the young man met Marina, the eldest daughter of the house, and they were married in 1829, the bride being seventeen years old.

It is altogether likely that the association thus formed with Edgefield District determined Gregg, when he retired from his jewelry business in Columbia because of ill health in 1837, to buy into the Vaucluse Manufacturing Company, which had its small cotton mill near by in Barnwell District. The locality was his wife's home, the region was healthful, Gregg had sufficient means unengaged, and he had already for some years been inquiring into the business of cotton manufacturing and was anxious to try his hand at it.

The Vaucluse cotton factory close by was completed in 1833, by a chartered company of which George McDuffie and Mitchell King were two of the principal stockholders.[32] Gregg later used this venture as an illustration, together with the Saluda factory near Columbia, of how cotton manufacturing should not be prosecuted in the South. Particularly he visited strictures upon McDuffie, who, influenced by his failure in Vaucluse, counseled against attempts at industry in South Carolina. McDuffie and his associates failed to give the enterprise sufficient preliminary investigation; "they only looked across the waters, at the promised land—they fitted out their bark for the voyage, but went to sleep at the helm." The company, Gregg said, "was no doubt stimulated to action by the disposition that pervaded this State about that time, for manufacturing, bringing into existence the Marlboro, DeKalb, Saluda, and two or three smaller mills, and it is truly unfortunate for this State, that such mistakes should have been made."[33]

The first owners of Vaucluse chose a president and five directors, and wrote to Paterson, New Jersey, for machinery suited to the manufacture of both cotton and wool, fine and coarse cloth and several counts of yarn. "They committed the same error, ["which wrecked the Saluda Company"] of not looking beyond the supply of the immediate neighborhood, and so complicated their machinery as to render it impossible for it to produce profit, except by the nicest and most skillful management."[34] The directors never had a meeting to receive the factory building and operatives' cottages from the hands of the contractor. The factory, thus neglected, ran for two and a half years and accumulated a debt of $6,000. It was at this point that Gregg's association with Vaucluse commenced. It is best to give his own words from the *Essays on Domestic Industry* (writing under a *nom de plume*, he spoke of himself in the third person):

"Fortunately for the company, an individual undertook to purchase some of the shares, and after possessing himself of a number sufficient to excite some interest, he looked into matters and found the mill in charge of an ignorant Englishman, who received $5 per day. He knew nothing of the business, and as was afterwards proved, had never before had charge, even of a single department in a mill. He was, in fact, only a common operative, with neither truth nor honesty in him. This gentleman immediately determined to apprize the company of their real condition. It was with the greatest difficulty that a sufficient number of the stockholders could be brought together, to form a quorum, in order that measures of relief might be taken; and but for the debt of $6,000, which was about to go into judgment, it is very questionable whether a meeting could have been obtained. The result of this meeting was, that the property was offered for sale. The gentleman alluded to above, who had purchased into the company, took up his abode at the factory, as a summer residence—discharged the English overseer and took charge of the establishment in person—made the Factory turn out double its former product—purchased the cotton and other supplies—sold the goods, &c., and in eight months previous to the sale made a net sum for the owners of about $11,000. This paid the debt and left a surplus of about $5,000, and but for this circumstance, the establishment would have sold for a mere song."[35]

This practical experience at Vaucluse produced in Gregg's mind "a settled conviction . . . that manufacturing is a business that ought to engage the attention of the two Carolinas and Georgia."[36] The mill continued to make money under the individual owner who suc-

13

ceeded the company, though his affairs were so complicated that he could not give the factory the special
attention which one of its sort demanded in order to
flourish.[37] However, the Vaucluse factory came into
Gregg's possession "in connection with Gen. James
Jones" in March of 1843.[38] The investigation into the
possibilities of cotton manufacturing in the South,
prompted by his ownership, and twenty months of active
operation of the plant, confirmed, Gregg said, "my
previous impressions, and I am now prepared to stake
my reputation as to the issue."[39] Gregg and Jones sold
the woolen machinery and remodeled the rest, but
Gregg believed it would have to receive many additions
in new machinery before, even with the best management, it could turn out the production per hand of the
Massachusetts mills.[40]

CHAPTER II

AN ARGUMENT FOR MANUFACTURES

William Gregg was superior to most of his contemporaries because he had the capacity to see the South's economic problem not in sections, but as a whole. He had thought it through, and went to the root of the matter. He quoted from the *Southern Quarterly Review* words which he himself might have penned: "An exclusively agricultural people, in the present age of the world, will always be poor. They want a home market. They want cities and towns, they want diversity of employment." And he added sentences that should have undone the philosophy of the leaders of his time: "Suppose the protective system, to be wholly abandoned by the country, how will the change affect our condition as a State? Will it bring back the rich treasures that have left us? Will it bring back the enterprising citizens that have removed from our State to settle in others? Will it be the means of resuscitating our worn-out soil? Shall not the sound still continue to be rung in our ears, of ten bales to the hand in Mississippi, and three in Carolina? So long as we make the culture of cotton our chief employment, will not the same causes continue to exist, that are now depopulating our State?"[1]

Gregg might have remained in a life of leisure in Charleston, as others did; his money was well invested, he had a beautiful home, and interesting friends aplenty.

But he could not be idle. His experiment at Vaucluse being still in his mind, he went North on a tour of inspection of the textile districts in 1844. In order to bring the subject of manufactures before the South, and to pave the way for launching a cotton mill which should be an object lesson, he prepared a series of papers which he published first in the *Courier*, Charleston. The first of his articles appeared on the editorial page of the issue of September 20, 1844, with the heading, "Encouragement of Domestic Industry the True Policy of South Carolina," and was signed "South-Carolina." It began without formality: "It must be apparent to all men of discernment that whether a tariff for protection is continued or not, our only safety lies in a change of our industrial pursuits." The next day the second article appeared with the heading "Domestic Industry," and so they continued, with the same signature, for ten installments at intervals over the period of nearly three months.[2]

The articles awakened an immediate response. Some of the seed, it is true, fell upon stony ground, for one reader wrote the paper acknowledging the sorrows of the South as springing from too much cotton, and proposed agreements, to be entered into in solemn honor, to curtail the acreage by one-fourth.[3] But others embraced Gregg's advocacy. The editor of the paper was glad to know that a memorial was in course of signature by many citizens asking of the city council "the removal of the very unnecessary restrictions now imposed on the erection of steam mills in Charleston." No other city thus crippled its own industry. "The little inconveniences . . . are trifles when compared with the magnitude of good in prospect."[4]

It has not been recognized that Gregg was influential in the inauguration of cotton manufacturing in Charleston with the organization of the Charleston Factory, of which his friend James H. Taylor became the agent. The editor of the *Courier* was delighted that such a movement was on foot in the city. "Much of public gratitude is due to the author of the admirable essays of 'South-Carolina' in our paper, for the patriotic, practical and happy manner in which he has urged this vital matter on our citizens. . . ." And with a view to giving additional impetus to the rolling ball he asked general attention to an article, printed that day, about the superior cheapness of steam over water power for cotton manufacturing, by C. T. James, engineer of the steam mills in Newburyport, Massachusetts.[5]

Early in the new year[6] the *Courier* announced the publication of the *Essays on Domestic Industry* in pamphlet form from the press of Burger and Jones, Broad Street. Gregg's identity now first became known: "The author is William Gregg, Esq., of this city, a gentleman, by his connection with the Vaucluse Factory . . . and his recent examination of the Northern Factories, qualified to speak on the subject with all the weight due to practical experience and an enlightened judgment. . . . The influence of his essays has been already beneficially felt in our community, and is about to result in the commencement of a new era in our industrial pursuits. We are authorized to say, that the subscription to the establishment of a cotton factory in this city, is now so nearly filled up that the enterprise will certainly be carried out."[7]

The *Essays on Domestic Industry,* in originality, grasp of economic fact, amplitude of acquaintance, and earnest simplicity of statement, as well as in practical influence, rank first among the writings of William Gregg; though his name is identified with no half efforts, his place in the economic history of the South rests primarily upon these *Essays* and upon the Graniteville Factory which was their counterpart. Both bespeak the man of strong sense, of ingenuity, and practical energy, and the lover of his fellows.

It is questionable whether any other single piece of writing proceeding from the South holds so much of interest to the economist as these observations of a Charleston merchant. Those about him, nourishing the suspicion and hatred that ended in civil war, were confused as to causes and remedies. Gregg went directly to the point with his economic analysis. While others tried, with extraordinary if short-lived seamanship, to beat against the wind, Gregg brought his craft full into the breeze and loosed all sail. This took him in the opposite direction from his contemporaries. South Carolina's political statesmen of the day engaged their attention principally in accusation against the North and excuse for the South; Gregg accused the South, and promised a satisfying future by patterning after the industrial pursuits of the North.

He wrote in the preface to the pamphlet that it was particularly the active management of the Vaucluse Factory which had confirmed his old belief in the ability of the Southern States to succeed in the manufacture of coarse cotton fabrics; moreover, he had made a tour of inspection in the textile districts of New England, and prepared a part of the manuscript on this trip. He begged to be released from imputation of "unfriendly feelings towards South-Carolina. To be in the midst of the scene, which surrounded me, when I commenced writing these essays, and to compare them with the existing condition of things in our State, would indeed require some philosophy to write or speak on the subject without using reproachful epithets."[8]

There can be no doubt that William Gregg knew Henry C. Carey of Philadelphia, and was familiar with his advocacies. Gregg's mother had come from Philadelphia, and he visited that city, both on business and with his family. He must have attended some of the weekly gatherings at Carey's house, where there was animated discussion of economic theory and policies. It is difficult to say whether Carey molded Gregg's thought. It is certain that he contributed importantly to it. The similarity of the ideas of the two men is striking—the economic and social value of association, the necessity for a diversity of pursuits, particularly the linking of manufactures and agriculture, the deploring of soil exhaustion by export of staple crops, the virtue of the introduction of handicraft industries in small towns, elimination of useless middlemen, dislike of

England's industrial domination, and the desirability of such great works as the draining of swamp areas appear in the arguments of both. Gregg's final avowal of protection may have been due to Carey's influence. There is evidence that Gregg was in turn useful to Carey, because he was in position to give practical demonstration of their principles.[9]

In Gregg's eyes the contrast between North and South was essentially that between conservation and waste, economy and exploitation. The seaboard South, with cotton raising unprofitable at the prevailing low prices, was poised for flight to the new lands of the Southwest. This gave to every institution a quality depressing and impermanent. This irked the author of the *Essays on Domestic Industry*. He wanted a society firmly rooted and growing vigorously. He described the scrupulous care with which the people of the North utilized their resources, and compared "this state of things with that in our State, in which a man hesitates about building a comfortable dwelling-house, lest the spirit of emigration deprive him of its use—in which the cream of a virgin soil is hardly exhausted, before the owner is ready to abandon it, in search of a country affording new and better lands,—in which our forest lumber cutters fell, with ruthless hand, the finest timber trees on the face of the globe, selecting those portions which are most easily turned into merchantable lumber, and leaving the balance to rot on the ground. . . ."

"I now commit the whole subject of Cotton Manufactures," he wrote, "to the people of the Southern

States, especially of South-Carolina, hoping . . . that
my attachment to the State will be best shown, by my
efforts to promote her welfare, even at the risk of offending, by too much plainness of speech."[10]

Gregg was capable of scorn, not less devastating because delivered with dignity. In his opening pages, he
visited his reproaches upon the public men of the State
who ran counter to his convictions. McDuffie, Hamilton,
Cheves, and Calhoun were in his mind when he declared: "It would indeed be well for us, if we were not
so refined in politics—if the talent, which has been, for
years past, and is now engaged in embittering our in-
dolent people against their industrious neighbors of the
North, had been with the same zeal engaged in promot-
ing domestic industry and the encouragement of the
mechanical arts."[11]

With dire apprehension he asked: "Are we to commence another ten years' crusade, to prepare the minds
of the people of this State for revolution; thus unhinging
every department of industry, and paralyzing the best
efforts to promote the welfare of our country?" And he
appended a prophecy which came true with startling
accuracy, namely, that secession from the Union would
find the South helpless to provide herself with manufactured goods, for nations which had bought her cotton
would have become her enemies. Gregg dreaded disunion, speaking of it as the "greatest of calamities."[12]
"A change in our habits and industrial pursuits," he
said, "is a far greater desideratum than any change in
the laws of our government, which the most clamorous

21

opponents of the tariff could devise." He knew that in arguing for industrial development in the South he immediately raised the tariff question, which was a red flag to a bull. Sectional politicians of the time cried down all attempts at manufacturing on the ground that these would dilute Southern enmity to protection, and that protection was the source of all the wrongs and disabilities of the cotton States. Nullification was a recent experience to South Carolina.

Gregg was wise enough to see, first, that "whether a tariff for protection is continued or not, our only safety, in this State, lies in a change of our industrial pursuits," and second, that the manufacturing greatness of the United States, and of commonwealths with the resources of South Carolina and Georgia, was to be independent of tariff policy.[13] Gregg at this time did not favor a protective tariff any more than his opponents did.[14] But his emphasis was totally different from theirs. "Laying aside the vexed question of a Tariff for Protection, which I don't pretend to advocate, I cannot see how we are to look with a reasonable hope for relief, even from its abandonment, without a total change of our habits. My recent visit to the Northern States has fully satisfied me that the true secret of our difficulties, lies in the want of energy on the part of our capitalists, and ignorance and laziness on the part of those who *ought* to labour."[15] And again: "We want no laws for the protection of those that embark in the manufacture, of such cotton fabrics, as we propose to make in South Carolina; nor does it follow, as a matter of course, . . . because we advocate

22

a system which will diversify the pursuits of our people, . . . that we wish manufactures to predominate over other employments."[16]

Gregg was trying to persuade an agricultural people to embark on manufactures. One of the first questions that would arise in their minds was, where are the skilled operatives to come from? He answered here, as in the case of capital, that home resources would answer amply. Those who knew the hand processes of spinning and weaving could learn the power processes. Of the two classes from which labor was to be drawn, slaves and Poor Whites, he was inclined, in the *Essays*, to prefer slaves.[17] Since at his own Graniteville, started so soon afterwards, he employed only whites, and since Negroes have been a negligible factor in the industry which Gregg did much to found, this view at first seems strange. Four circumstances go far to account for it. Slavery was the prevalent labor system, and he was appealing in large part to slave proprietors; he was urging the establishment of coarse-goods mills requiring the minimum of dexterity; not a few successful cotton factories were using slave labor; and lastly, the Englishman Montgomery, with whose treatise he was particularly acquainted, saw great promise for the Southern industry in the use of slaves. Gregg believed blacks preferable to whites for two main reasons: "First—you are not under the necessity of educating them, and have, therefore, their uninterrupted services from the age of eight years. The second is, that when you have your mill filled with expert hands, you are not subjected to the change

23

which is constantly taking place with whites. In the Northern States, these are inconveniences of no small moment."

Though from an economical point of view he preferred slaves, considerations of humanity moved him to enlarge upon the advantages of converting Poor Whites into cotton mill workers. It is proper to quote a complete passage upon this point, because it must indicate that Gregg had made up his mind to use whites when he should build his Graniteville Factory, as was done at Vaucluse:

"I would ask, shall we stop at the effort to prove the capacity of blacks for manufacturing? Shall we pass unnoticed the thousands of poor, ignorant, degraded white people among us, who, in this land of plenty, live in comparative nakedness and starvation? Many a one is reared in *proud* South Carolina, from birth to manhood, who has never passed a month, in which he has not, some part of the time, been stinted for meat. Many a mother is there, who will tell you that her children are but scantily supplied with bread. . . . These may be startling statements, but they are nevertheless true. . . . It is only necessary to build a manufacturing village of shanties, in a healthy location in any part of the State, to have crowds of these poor people around you, seeking employment at half the compensation given to operatives at the North. It is indeed painful to be brought in contact with such ignorance and degradation; but on the other hand, it is pleasant to witness the change, which soon takes place in the condition of those who obtain employment. The emaciated, pale-faced children, soon assume the appearance of robust health, and their tattered garments are exchanged for those suited to a better condition; if you visit their dwellings, you will find their tables supplied with wholesome food; on the Sabbath, when the females turn out in their gay colored gowns, you will imagine yourself surrounded by groups of city belles. How easy would it be for the proprietors of such establishments, with only a small share of philanthropy, to make good use of the school fund in ameliorating the condition of this class of our population, now but little elevated above the Indian of the forest. The cause of this degradation and poverty . . . is an interesting subject, and one that ought to engage the attention of every philanthropist and Christian. It is, perhaps, not generally known, that there are *twenty-nine thousand* white persons in this State, above the age of twelve years, who can neither read nor write—this is about one in every five of the white population."[18]

The prospect which Gregg here held out contained much of the utopianism of Robert Owen, and more significant is the recollection that Graniteville fulfilled dreams as certainly as did New Lanark.

If labor was calling to be employed in manufacturing, capital was no less seeking opportunity. "It is only necessary," Gregg said, "to revert to the fact, that lands and negroes pay but *three* per cent when engaged in the culture of cotton, and to name the price of 5 and 6 per cent State stocks."[19] Gregg was continually impressed with the drain of South Carolina capital to the

North and to the Southwest. "There is no lack of capital in South-Carolina; Charleston, herself, possesses all the requisites, and it is only necessary that public attention should be properly directed to those vast fields, for profitable investments, in this State . . . to bring it out, and to stop the millions which are being all the time transferred from the South to the North. . . ."[20]

If these passages reflect a dark side, there is also sufficient suggestion of hope: "The period is fast approaching in South-Carolina, which shall produce a great change in these matters. Many persons are now looking to the subject of manufactures with intense interest, and it is believed that many men of capital would at once embark in this business, could this field of profitable enterprise, be laid open before our wealthy business men of Charleston, . . . and these . . . gentlemen see that it is only necessary that Georgia and the two Carolinas engage in the manufactory [sic] of coarse cotton fabrics, in order to monopolize the trade in those articles."[21] And his experience in the Horse Creek Valley, gained from summers at Aiken and working months at Vaucluse, made him recommend to other retired merchants the upcountry of South Carolina as a locality for investment and recreation.[22]

How richly Gregg's visit of inquiry to the textile districts of New England bore fruit, is evident in every page of the *Essays on Domestic Industry*. He remarked in his preface that "I have always been a close observer of things, but when I visited . . . Connecticut, Massachusetts, Vermont and New-Hampshire, . . . I could not but notice, with surprise, the effect which this branch of manufactures had produced."[23] That his admiration stimulated his zeal in pushing his investigation is manifest in the particularity of his findings and in the eagerness with which he applied New England experience to opportunities existing in the South.

In Chapter VI he described broadly the two main systems of cotton manufacture which he found—that of Massachusetts and New Hampshire characterized by extensive establishments owned by joint stock companies of retired merchants, and devoted to coarse goods; and that of Rhode Island, exhibiting individual ownership of small plants turning out a finely wrought product. William Gregg the manufacturer was captured by the dexterity and close calculation of the mills centering about Providence, but William Gregg the economist saw clearly that the Massachusetts system of coarse goods fabrication was the wise one for the South to pattern after. He rightly realized that nothing but a tradition of manufacturing could accomplish the ends which he had ultimately in view: "Merchants and retired men of capital may erect factories, and work them with white hands, or purchase blacks for the purpose—our wealthy planters may engage in this business and turn their young negroes in for workers, but it will be long before the Southern States shall have a set of manufacturers similar to those in Rhode Island; they must grow up among us. . . ."[24]

He gave the labor cost and gross profit of typical mills in Lowell, Massachusetts, and took pains to point out the

opportunity for success of similar establishments in
South Carolina. Particularly he showed the gain to the
entire community from the addition of about 20 cents
to each pound of raw material through the manufacturing process; the Lowell mills represented to the town
and vicinity an annual income of $4,000,000—equal
to the value of the entire cotton crop of South Carolina.[25]
He mentioned especially two towns in New England
which had accomplished in manufacturing no more
than his own State could duplicate. These were Manchester, New Hampshire, where a thriving center was
built up in the forest in just the way that Gregg's own
Graniteville and its neighbors were constructed later,
and Newburyport, Massachusetts, which, in replacing
a waning shipping interest with a vigorous industrial
development, pointed the way to Charleston.[26]

He next directed attention to the foremost spinning
mills in his own State, the Saluda and Vaucluse factories. The failure of these ventures, which were the children in 1833 of the Nullification controversy, Gregg
complained was "brought to the view of every one who
turns his attention to the subject, and the effect is, to
dampen ardor, and wither all such enterprises in the
bud. These two establishments stand like rocks in the
ocean, to warn the mariner of the approach of danger;
but it is hoped, that on nearing the objects, they will
be found to be mere delusions."[27] He believed he could
prove that no approach to a fair experiment had been
tried in South Carolina. In the two instances in point,
he brought out many evidences of inexperience and

neglect. Both mills undertook to manufacture over a wide range of products, from coarse to fine, instead of restricting themselves to a standard cheap grade. Both tried to dispose of their output in the locality, instead of reaching out to national markets.[28]

The immediate management in both cases, but particularly at Vaucluse, was as bad as possible; Gregg declared they should have sought advice at the North, and hired experienced New England overseers at the best wages to instruct the native workers.[29] Though Gregg did not emphasize the fact, the failure of these companies was due basically to the self-same "patriotic motives" by which "they were stimulated to action." They were offshoots of political pique, rather than of genuine industrial incentive; they were born in a contracted sectionalism which turned its back upon the rest of the country. It may be said that they were set up in spite, and they lasted a shorter time than the jealousy which inspired them. Thus Gregg wrote in another connection: "Let us endeavor to bring about such a state of things as shall invite the industry, if not capital, of other countries, to our State. Let us try to cultivate a good feeling among our people, for our Northern brethren. We have no lack of trading men from among this class of persons. Let us offer inducements that shall bring their workingmen to our delightful climate. . . . They will teach our children lessons of industry and economy. . . . They will teach us lessons in agriculture that shall prove to us, that the money expended for an agricultural survey, [that by Edmund Ruffin] has not been spent in

29

vain; and above all, they will give some of our wise
men, practical lessons in Political Economy."[30]

Following the principle already laid down, that manufactures embodying large quantities of material and requiring only cheap labor were the best for the South at
the outset, Gregg reviewed the profitableness of making
cotton bagging to enter into competition with the hempen
article then largely produced by hand processes in Kentucky. Not without important reservations, he recommended that the South should exploit this manufacture.
Northern mills would not be able to compete with the
South in such coarse goods, since in osnaburgs, the next
finer material, they had been largely supplanted by the
Southern production.[31]

The manufacture of cotton bagging was at best prob-
lematical, since no machinery had been specially constructed for the purpose, but in urging that the South
erect yarn spinning mills, Gregg was on certain ground,
and pleading only for the extension of an already successful business. "Previous to 1833," he said, "there
were many Cotton Factories about Philadelphia and
throughout the North, engaged in making Cotton Yarn,
to supply the hand and power-loom weavers; but since
the erection of mills at Petersburg, Va., Fayetteville,
N. C., and in South-Carolina and Georgia, the result
has been, to drive most of these Northern spinners to
weaving. . . . The home trade in this article, may now
be said to be ours."[32] Southern spinners should look forward to capturing a good part of the continental yarn
trade.

30

In clearing the way for the discussion of spinning, Gregg sought to refute two current errors "which will prove fatal if not removed. The first is, that Cotton Manufacturing is so complicated in its details and requires such nice management to keep . . . in order . . . delicate . . . machinery, that none need expect to succeed in it, who have not served regular apprenticeship at the business. The other is, that the improvements constantly making in machinery, render it necessary to lay aside old, and purchase new, in order to keep up with the age." The assurances which he gave were truer then on both counts than they are today. As to the first, it must be remembered that he was recommending the building of an industry *de novo*. Cotton manufacturing, he reminded his readers, was not to be confused with a machine shop requiring practiced craftsmanship in its control. Cotton factories needed just such wise oversight as was necessary to the success of the planting or merchandizing interests, with which his audience was familiar. Skilled overseers must be placed in charge of the several departments, and their expert efforts well coordinated. "The labors [of the owner] are, however, entirely mental, and just such, as are required to give healthful and pleasant employment, to a retired Merchant. The man who has devoted the greater part of his life to mercantile pursuits, is generally, from his habits, unfitted for literary pleasures; still his habits are so active, as to forbid his living in idleness. The supervision of a well regulated manufacturing establishment,

31

is above all other employments, the best adapted to such a man."[33]

Gregg concluded his work by giving data collected in the North as to sizes and dates of building of New England mills, cost of machinery for a 5,000-spindle yarn mill, price lists from two machine shops, and wages paid in cotton factories in Massachusetts and in South Carolina. He added an estimate of the cost of the smallest amount of machinery which he thought could be run to advantage in the South, a 620-spindle mill to make yarns Nos. 8 to 20.

These *Essays on Domestic Industry* left an afterglow in the Charleston newspapers, in several series of unsigned articles on cotton manufacturing in that city and the South generally. Some of these, among which are articles in the *Evening News* in 1846 and 1847 and the *Mercury* in 1848, have been ascribed to Gregg,[34] but they contain nothing directly to show that he was their author. Some passages sound like Gregg, but others are just as unlike him. He was busy about the practical launching of Graniteville about this time, and it is not probable that he had leisure for newspaper writing, even had he cared to continue it so soon following the publication of his *Essays*. Those in the *News* may have been written by James H. Taylor, who knew Gregg's sentiments, was intimately identified with Graniteville, and became a cotton manufacturer in Charleston; A. H. Brisbane, whom we will meet later, may have been the author, or perhaps they were the work of J. N. Cardozo, the economist-editor of the paper.[35]

CHAPTER III

A FACTORY OF GRANITE

No sooner had Gregg satisfied himself of the usefulness and profit of manufacturing cotton in South Carolina, than he set about organizing a company to build a mill. He meant to practice what he preached. If his argument was powerful, his concrete example was even more convincing. In deciding upon the corporate form of enterprise, he was doubtless moved by considerations of public benefit as well as of private convenience. Limited liability companies held the field in manufacturing elsewhere in the United States, and the South should build on this experience; moreover, he would apply to himself his counsel that it was unwise for an individual to put his whole capital into such an experiment.

Corporations were unpopular in South Carolina at this time, being associated in the public mind with speculations. Consequently, in 1845, in addition to applying to the South Carolina legislature for a charter for the Graniteville Manufacturing Company, the legislature of Georgia was applied to also. It was expected that the former legislature might not act favorably, in which case Augusta would probably have been the site of the factory. At any rate, Gregg set about a new process of education. As in his *Domestic Industry* he had broached the whole subject of manufactures, so now he published a pamphlet, "An Inquiry into the Expediency of Grant-

33

ing Charters of Incorporation for Manufacturing Purposes in South Carolina," signed "One of the People."
A copy was put into the hands of every member of the
legislature, was also published in Georgia and similarly
used there, and was afterwards employed by others in
Southern States.[1] There is reason to believe that Gregg
went to Columbia and worked actively in behalf of the
application.[2]

As it turned out, South Carolina granted a charter,
and Georgia did not. "An Act to incorporate the Graniteville Manufacturing Company in the State of South
Carolina" was signed December 15, 1845, a year after
Gregg's *Domestic Industry* first appeared.[3] The company
was granted sufficient latitude except that, perhaps by
oversight (since this disability did not attach to other
companies chartered directly afterwards) it was not
given the right to increase its capital stock at will. The
incorporators were named as William Gregg, Hiram
Hutchinson, Otis Mills, and Joel Smith; they were made
"a body politic and corporate in law" for dyeing, print-
ing, and finishing all goods of which cotton or other
fibrous articles formed a part, and they might also make
machinery needed for such manufacture. They were
given power to raise by subscription a capital of
$300,000 in shares of $500 each. They might hold land.
The company was not to go into operation until $150,000
of the capital had been paid in gold, silver, or the current bank notes of the State. Members of the corporation were liable jointly and severally for all debts and
contracts of the corporation until the whole amount of

the stock was actually paid in, and no note given by a stockholder was to be considered as payment of any part of the capital. Officers might be elected when half the capital had been subscribed. The Act was to continue in force for fourteen years, and the legislature guarded itself by inserting the express provision that no part of the capital stock nor any of its funds should at any time be used "directly or indirectly in banking operations." Unless directors were to be liable in their natural persons, the corporation must never owe more than the amount of the paid-in capital.[4]

In pleading for the privilege of incorporation for manufactures in South Carolina, Gregg summed up his argument thus: ". . . although it is true, that capital managed by its owner . . . will always produce better results than that which is managed by companies, yet, in manufacturing, where large amounts of capital are requisite, the latter will, in the main, be found more steady in their operations—less subject to fluctuations—better for the individual whose capital is involved—better for the laboring operative as well as for the consumer—more democratic in their tendency, and, being a more certain means of bringing about the changes so much desired in our State, they will be found better adapted to the wants of the community at large."[5]

Because of the prevalent laxity of State banks of issue, and because of his own pronounced disapproval of bank investments for the South (which, to his mind, needed rather industrial upbuilding), Gregg thought it proper to draw a distinction between liberality of the legislature

35

toward financial and toward manufacturing institutions. The State had done well to guard against bank abuses. "Banks live on the credit which the community around extend to them. . . . Banks may be said literally to live on the substance of the community, gathering tribute from every individual who handles their bills. . . ."[6] On the other hand, "Incorporated companies for mining, railroading, and improving navigation, or for agricultural, commercial, and manufacturing purposes," asked for "liability only so far as to exhaust the capital of each individual."

He proceeded to mention achievements which the corporate form of enterprise had made possible, showing, incidentally, how keenly alive he was to the material progress of his world. The South Carolina Railroad was a case in point, and Gregg hoped that by the grant of similar charters, capital might be found to drain great swamp areas in the State. The enterprise of Boston was not due to the city's being wealthier than Philadelphia, New York, or Charleston, but to "the practice of operating by associated capital," which enlisted the resources of all. "The divine, lawyer, doctor, schoolmaster, guardian, widow, farmer, merchant, mechanic, common labourer, in fact, the whole community is made tributary to these great enterprises." The panic of 1837, then fresh in the public mind, had been weathered by the chartered companies of New England, while the private undertakings of Pennsylvania were sold for a song, bringing widespread ruin in their downward course.[7]

The issue of this appeal to the legislature was of deepest moment to Gregg, for upon it hung the possibility of Graniteville's establishment. Large as were his personal resources, and as certain of success as he believed cotton manufactures in the State to be, Gregg knew that he could not found single-handed the sizable plant which alone he believed economical. He planned his own experiment as an object lesson to the Commonwealth, so that unless it materialized, all his proposals were for nothing. "If we shut the door against associated capital," he warned, "and place our reliance upon individual exertion, we may talk over the matter and grow poorer for fifty years to come, without effecting the change in industrial pursuits, necessary to renovate the fortunes of our State. Individuals will not be found among us, who are willing to embark their $100, $200, or $300,000 in untried pursuits; and however favorably we may think of such investments, . . . we do not hesitate to say, that it would be an unwise act in a single individual, to put the whole of a large fortune into a single manufacturing establishment."[8]

William Gregg differed from most Americans of his day, and conspicuously from most Southerners, by favoring internal improvements through private rather than public enterprise. Pennsylvania's system of "public works," constructed by the State in the effort to conserve Philadelphia's western trade after the Erie canal had so greatly increased the business of New York, had better been left, Gregg thought, to chartered companies.

37

Pennsylvania capitalists were seeking opportunities in New Jersey; and so would South Carolina investors, unless the legislature liberalized incorporation laws, put their money in factories along the newly dug Augusta canal.[9]

Having encountered the public discouragement which followed failures in manufacturing, Gregg was eager to see the spirit for industry directed so as to give permanent results. He therefore pointed out, and illustrated by local examples, that whereas an individual enterprise was likely to suffer cessation or great loss of potential on the death or withdrawal of the owner, a corporation was self-renewing, immortal.[10] The community, contrary to the fears of many, was less likely to lose through a limited liability corporation than through an individual enterprise. The corporation was restricted by law to specified operations, while the individual was not; and how often, Gregg asked, did men of large affairs "prove on their failure, never to have been worth even a moderate fortune."[11]

It seems strange that South Carolina, a leader in slavery and ruled by the seacoast parishes, should be concerned lest incorporated companies in their undemocratic influence, "usurp political power and oppress the poor." Still, Gregg had to combat this fear, and did so by referring to the widespread ownership of stock in the chartered company (including operatives themselves), and the greater guarantee of competitive business where enterprise was not restricted to the few rich.[12]

38

Knowing well the vicinity of Vaucluse from the year 1837, and having it in his mind to go extensively into cotton manufacturing, Gregg must certainly have investigated the water powers and the available mill sites in this valley.[13] It is not certain when Gregg, in conjunction with Ker Boyce, bought land which now forms part of the Graniteville tract, but it was probably in 1845, not long before application was made to the legislature for a charter for the Graniteville Company. The Graniteville experiment was surely being mooted by Gregg as early as the summer of 1844; its launching was in his thoughts when he made his "tour of inspection through the Manufacturing districts of the Northern States" at this time. In his *Domestic Industry*, begun during this trip, he said "I trust . . . that if the facts here stated, are not the means of producing a single establishment— to test the matter, and prove to our people what may be done in South-Carolina—they will, at least, awaken a spirit of enquiry. . . ."[14]

The capital of the company was not fully subscribed when the charter was applied for. However, when Gregg began to ask for subscriptions, the enterprise moved swiftly and easily. He wrote a dozen years later that "although such projects had but little of the confidence of the public mind, upwards of two hundred thousand dollars were without any difficulty raised for that purpose."[15]

The first meeting of subscribers to stock of the Graniteville Manufacturing Company was held at Aiken,

South Carolina, January 14, 1846, just a year after Gregg's *Essays on Domestic Industry* had appeared under his own name. Those present besides William Gregg were Ker Boyce, Hiram Hutchinson, Joel Smith, C. K. Huger, and James Jones.[16] Gregg and Boyce had bought land in anticipation of the company's needs, for it was agreed at this meeting that they convey to the company all their land on Horse and Bridge creeks except a portion known as the "Bridge Creek Tract," for the sum of $6,000. Gregg and Boyce possibly had operated a saw mill in the valley for some time prior to this.[17] Perhaps they planned to furnish lumber for the company's construction. In any event, they reserved the right to cut timber for two years "above the Columbia Road," and also the right to set up saw mills at the dam the company was to build on Bridge Creek and to use the surplus water power for four years. At the next stockholders' meeting, however, when the company was formally organized, the directors were authorized to purchase, as well, the Bridge Creek Tract formerly reserved by Gregg and Boyce, and a tract on Good Spring Branch, 276 acres, paying for the entire 7,952 acres $11,000. The title was to be "divested of . . . all . . . privileges and reservations of the said William Gregg & Ker Boyce, whatever."[18]

The first construction work to be undertaken was the building of dams across Horse Creek and Bridge Creek and the cutting of a canal. These operations, to begin as soon as possible, were placed under the charge of Gregg, Hutchinson, and Jones. Additional land was to be pur-

"Charleston S.C. 7th March 1846

We hereby constitute and appoint Robert Martin Esq
our Attorney to represent our Stock Subscribed for in
our name in the Graniteville Manufy Co & to vote for
officers in the said Company, to be elected on the
10th inst.   Howland & Taft "

The meeting then proceeded to ballot for a President
and four members to serve as a Board of Directors,
when upon Counting the ballots it appeared, that
William Gregg had received for President, and
H Hutchison, A R Taft, C K Huger and Samuel
Jones for Directors each three hundred and two
votes respectively, being the whole number given
and were consequently declared duly elected —

The President elect William Gregg was invited
to the Chair by Mr Boyce, and took his seat as
President of the Company —

The following resolution was then submitted and
passed

Resolved: That a Treasurer and a Secretary to
the Company shall be annually elected by the
Stockholders, and that the Treasurer shall be chosen
from the Directors.

A R Taft was then elected Treasurer and Saml Jones
Secretary to the Company —

The following resolutions were submitted and adopted
Resolved.

That an assessment of five per cent upon the
amount of Stock subscribed be now made, and that
the Stockholders shall respectively deposit the amount
assessed upon them in the Bank of Hamburg, in
Cash to the Credit of the Treasurer of the Company —

Resolved.

That the Directors shall not Contract any debt exceeding
Ten thousand dollars, until all the Stock shall have been paid in —

PAGE FROM STOCKHOLDERS' MINUTES

chased for the company—the Hamilton tract from the South Carolina Railroad, and up to 1,000 acres from John Marsh, including Hamilton's Falls.[19]

In the two months that intervened before the next meeting (held the evening of March 10 at the Bank of Hamburg, the time and place doubtless chosen for the traveling convenience of the stockholders from Charleston), subscriptions were being actively solicited. It was reported that 391 shares had been taken, each share being $500, making a total of $195,500.[20] Nine stockholders were present, and two more were represented by proxy; with Boyce in the chair, the meeting proceeded to organize the Graniteville Manufacturing Company. Upon counting election ballots "it appeared that William Gregg had received for President and H. Hutchinson, A. R. Taft, C. K. Huger, and James Jones for Directors, each, 302 votes respectively, being the whole number. . . . The President-elect, William Gregg, was invited to the chair by Mr. Boyce and took his seat as President of the Company." Taft was elected treasurer and Jones secretary, all elections being for one year. It was decided to make right away an assessment of 5 per cent on the stock; the directors were forbidden to contract debts in excess of $10,000 until all the stock had been paid in.

The stockholders first met at Graniteville on March 9, 1847. Gregg reported verbally the progress made in erecting the manufacturing establishment. An old man, born the year of this meeting and a resident of Graniteville from childhood, recalls that before the mill was built the only house at the place was a log cabin under a big poplar tree near what is now "Blue Row." It had a "stick and dirt" chimney, and was inhabited by an old man and woman afterwards buried at the foot of their own garden. They sold their land to Gregg when the Graniteville tract was acquired. The Horse Creek Valley, now humming and clanking with half a million spindles and looms, was then a lovely wilderness, green and silent except for the little Vaucluse Factory above and the slender line of railroad creeping in below. A quarter-mile apart on each side rose the major hills, and between them pleasant knolls were tumbled against each other, the whole thickly wooded with forest trees.[21]

The streams which, in Gregg's day, supplied all the power for Vaucluse and Graniteville, take their rise within short distances of the villages. The main one is Big Horse Creek, flowing in from the northeast. It is soon joined from the northwest by Kines Fork and Long Branch; Camp Branch joins it farther down in its course, after its waters have spread to form Vaucluse Lake behind the Vaucluse dam. Still farther down, Good Spring Branch comes in from the eastward, forming a lake, now used as a reservoir, which discharges into Vaucluse Lake. Between Vaucluse and Graniteville, Sage Mill Branch makes its confluence with Big Horse Creek from the northeast, flowing, since the construction of the dam, into the Graniteville Lake, as does also, from the same side but farther down, Flat Rock Branch. Bridge Creek enters from the east, and behind its dam forms the small-

est of the lakes, out of which the canal leads directly to
the mill. Big Horse Creek flows on down its valley into
the Savannah River. The stream carried more water in
Gregg's time than it has in later years.

Years after this first meeting at Graniteville, Gregg
reviewed to the stockholders the history of the building
of the mill and town. "In January, 1846," he said, "I
took charge and gave the Company's service my undivided attention, acted the part of Engineer and general Agent. . . . I had retired from business with an
ample fortune to live on, and it never was my intention
to occupy more than temporarily, so laborious a situation as I have at G'ville." Before he came to grips with
the problem, he had meant to employ a mill engineer
to accomplish the construction and later a skilled agent
to conduct the business, thus delegating responsibility
as did the Boston manufacturers whom he had visited,
and as, indeed, he had advised mill projectors in South
Carolina to do.[22]

Gregg found, however, that he must be engineer and
administrator both. Specialists in cotton mill construction were "scarce and not to be had at any price," and
he did not want to risk the company's capital by engaging an untried man.[23] "Having made manufacturing a
study from 1837 to 1845," he said, "I felt that I was
fully competent to the task of rearing this work without the aid of manufacturing engineers, a class of men
. . . who would necessarily be strangers to our country,
whose undivided services would be obtained at a high

43

cost, and who might prove to be impracticable, wasteful, or possibly worse, speculative, aiming solely to
make money on their own account, out of us."[24]

His explanation almost at the end of his life of why,
when the mill was completed, he did not turn it over to
an experienced agent, admits of some reading between
the lines. "After the works were completed a series of
difficulties followed one after another, in procuring
competent managers, and I have never felt, until recently, that I could, consistently with my own interest,
as well as that of my associates in the enterprise, resign
the charge of our affairs." The truth is that his heart was
too much in the venture to permit him to "retire back"
into his "former berth of ease and comfort." Further-
more, he was in the prime of life, at the high tide of his
great powers, with a restless mind, an outreaching
spirit, and eager, capable hands.[25]

It was essential to Gregg's plan that his mill should
be a native product—in inspiration, in capital, in workpeople, and in actual building material as well. The blue
granite, of which mill and dams were built, was quar-
ried from beside the stream, a few hundred yards away
from the factory site.[26] An expert judge says that Gregg
must have obtained the plan of the old mill building,
however, from New England; there are any number like
it in the Blackstone Valley.[27] He was undoubtedly influenced by James Montgomery's estimate of the cost of
buildings and machinery for a cotton factory. This contemplated a "brick, or stone-house, four stories and
attic, 142 by 42 feet," 4,992 throstle spindles, and 128

looms; Montgomery thought the building and power equipment could be had more cheaply in South Carolina than in New England, for which he gave prices.[28]

The Graniteville mill was made two stories and an attic, 315 by 55 feet. The plant was more modern than many of its New England contemporaries. Graniteville after a few years was lit by gas, whereas oil lamps were frequently used in the North, some of these old factories, incredible as it may seem, continuing to use kerosene until five years ago. The Graniteville mill shows throughout how solidly Gregg built. The thick masonry walls without have their counterpart within in the great ceiling timbers with their ship-splice and wedge to draw and hold them fast together. In order to add to the rigidity, the stringers at the ends of the building, where the main shaft carrying the power rested, are single giant beams.

Though there is some doubt about the matter, it would appear that the mill was driven at first by a single water wheel; however, evidences of this original arrangement were obliterated by changes in the power system made in 1854 and again in 1866. In the former year a second wheel was installed in a new wheel pit, and a conducting pipe was constructed to serve a third wheel should it be required. In the latter year a new turbine wheel, more powerful than those of 1854, was installed, and what remains to be seen now goes back to both of these periods of improvement. An examination of the wheel pit at the lower end of the mill would indicate that the wheel once housed here was of some sixty feet diameter and twelve feet on the face.

45

The space in which the wheel revolved has now been floored over at several levels, but the hollowed out stones sunk into each wall, in which the 30-inch axle rested, are still to be seen; imbedded in one of them are the stumps of the iron bolts which held the capstone on.[29]

William Gregg must have been a very busy man during those days of construction work. His mind must conceive, his skill organize, and his attention direct every operation.[30] Raw materials were abundant and cheap, and labor was as readily commanded; what the situation required was leadership, the vital elements of purpose and activity. These Gregg possessed and brought to bear. One of his primary objects at Graniteville was the giving of employment to the neighboring Poor Whites.[31] He began with this policy in the work of building the factory and town. Small independent farmers and poor tenants who had possessed few means of earning money came into the valley to fell trees, cut the canal, and quarry stone.[32]

One who saw the first granite blocks of the factory laid[33] described the bustle of those days at the outset. People came eager to get the work. There was no one but found a job congenial to his country training, though it be no better than ditching. Gregg was in the midst of them every day, called upon for a hundred decisions. After dams were built, a saw mill was erected and in two years cut over 5,000,000 feet of lumber; while the mill itself and the warehouses took much of this, the cottages for future operatives took more.[34]

The masonry and carpenter's work on the factory buildings proper was let on contract, and Gregg, insistent upon his structures being erected in first-rate style, soon found that there were to be difficulties with both the contractors. He cautioned his subordinates to avoid litigation with either of them, but the mason abandoned the job before it was finished and sued the company for ten times as much as he got on the settlement. The company sued the carpenter for work which had to be done over again and finally, upon arbitration, he paid within $20 of what Gregg claimed.[35]

Gregg had the operatives' cottages, for the most part, dotted about irregularly on the forested slopes. All of those he built are standing and in good condition, except five which burned.

It should be remembered that Gregg "devoted three years of laborious and assiduous attention" to the construction of Graniteville, and then operated the business for five years more before he accepted a penny from the company for his services.[36] It is true that he was a rich man with leisure to give to any project that took his interest, and certainly all he performed for Graniteville was done *con amore;* it is further true that for a while he did not expect to let the work engross all his time and energies, but his service was nonetheless uncalculatingly generous. No amount of money could have procured from any one else but Gregg the eagerness, the consummate care, the many-sided practical effectiveness which he gave freely. Like the creator he was, he did not

47

set a price on the product of his art. His engineering achievement, particularly considering the fact that he was not a technical specialist, was as remarkable as his unpaid devotion. At the stockholders' meeting at the end of the first year of construction work, it was decided to pay the treasurer $500 a year.[37] There was no thought of paying Gregg.

When Graniteville began to take tangible shape its appeal to investors was more general. After this year of building and digging the number of stockholders had increased from 23 to 30, and the number of shares from 391 to 600, making the capital subscribed ($500 a share) $300,000 instead of $195,500. A manuscript list of share owners, dated March 19, 1847, shows that two former members of the company had dropped out, S. S. Farrar and Alex. McDonald, while nine new ones had been added.[38]

CHAPTER IV

THE RETURN OF THE NATIVE

Fortunately, we have several detailed descriptions of Graniteville at the time of its erection and first completion. These differ in some particulars, but no attempt has been made here to reconcile them. The earliest dates from the spring of 1848, and is by a representative of a Charleston newspaper who was one of a party invited by Gregg to view the rising village.[1] The company began by buying 11,000 acres of land in Edgefield District, embracing Horse Creek. In October, 1846, the foundation stone of the main factory building was laid, and the first works of improvement commenced. "It would inspire the visitor," wrote the correspondent, "to see how much has been done since that time. The rude forest has been cleared, streets laid out, canals cut, and embankments thrown up, malls graded and beautifully laid out, saw mills, machine shops, stores, offices, dwellings for operatives, and factory houses erected; and all put in such a state of forwardness as already to present the appearance of a flourishing and busy village."

The canal was almost a mile long, 15 feet wide at the bottom, 37 on the surface, and about 5 feet deep. It commenced at Horse Creek, where it was protected by a substantial granite dam. Finishing the dam and canal first, Gregg was able to use this power on the construction work. Half a mile from the dam was a saw mill, running three single saws. Mr. Brett, here called the proprietor, had cut upwards of 2,000,000 feet of lumber since its erection in 1846. (As will appear later, from a statement of Gregg's, the saw mill was the company's enterprise.) Attached to the saw mill were a grist mill, a grooving, tonguing, and planing machine, circular saws and other equipment for making sash and blinds. A quarter of a mile farther on was a machine shop 40 by 80 feet, with machinery driven by a reaction wheel erected by the company to facilitate work on the factory buildings. This had paid for itself twice over. Between the canal and the factory was a mall of several acres laid out in evergreens.

The motive power for the main factory building was a turbine wheel under a head of 40 feet of water, conveyed to the wheel in circular trunks of 5 feet diameter running 300 feet from the canal. Adjoining the factory was the picker house, also of granite, 84 by 44 feet and two stories. In the factory yard along the line of the canal was the warehouse for raw cotton, 125 by 45 feet, attached to which was a store; on a line with these was another warehouse, for manufactured goods, 100 by 44 feet.

On the opposite side of the canal, which was crossed by several bridges, ran Canal Street, on which were to be boarding houses; twelve of these were completed—a hotel of about twenty rooms, three houses of sixteen rooms each, and eight others of eight rooms each. "Fronting upon the canal, and having handsome porticoes or piazzas, they afford residences which would not detract from the beauty of any village in the Union." On the street back of this, forty cottages were to be built, in the Gothic order, each with five rooms; of these four had been completed. "Determined to impart an entirely religious and moral tone to the community of Graniteville," the company had granted sites to Baptists and Methodists if they would erect churches designed by good architects. The Baptist church, in the Gothic style, was nearing completion; the Methodist was a modification of the Gothic, by J. B. White, a Charleston architect. A handsome school house was to be erected and teachers employed by the company.

Gregg wanted to do all he could to have Graniteville known by the public. He invited the reporter to the meeting of the stockholders to take notes which might prove interesting to his readers. Machinery, when installed, would be of the best, "and the attendants and operatives are to be selected with an eye to the most approved characters." After the meeting, the correspondent enjoyed an excellent dinner at the hotel, which was in charge of Mr. Brett [perhaps the saw mill man], who was in the employ of the company. He spent the night at Gregg's home, Kalmia. Looking back into the valley from the summit of Chalk Hill, he saw it was dotted with farms; these would improve in appearance and profit as the demands of Graniteville created a market for their products.

The second description of Graniteville belongs to the autumn of this same year, 1848. Thomas Maxwell drove six miles from the inclined plane on the South Carolina

51

Railroad at Aiken to examine the new town, his interest having been excited by the founders' purpose "of demonstrating the perfect practicability of the South manufacturing her own cottons, and diverting a portion of her labor from agricultural to manufacturing pursuits."[2] It was the fashion of the day for newspaper writers to repay hospitality with glowing description. In this instance, however, enthusiasm and truth went measurably well together. "When Graniteville burst upon our view from the summit of the hill," wrote Maxwell, "its main building of white granite, 350 feet long, with two massive towers ornamented at the top, looking like some magnificent palace rising out of the vale below, with an extensive lawn in front, and clean trimmed, gravel walks around, and fountains spouting their crystal waters in the air in fantastic shapes; the neat boarding-houses and cottages for single families, and the handsome little church, all constructed and ornamented in the ancient Gothic style, and each house having its own garden for vegetables and flowers; and the evergreen woods sloping from their garden doors gradually to the summit of the hill where we stood—the whole scene is as though the wand of the enchantress had called it into existence."

To the right, at the head of the valley, lay the pond, the canal conducting from it to the mill. "Turning to the left we descended the hill, crossed a nice bridge over the canal and entered the enclosure of the principal works. . . . a fountain was throwing up a jet of clear water fifteen feet into the air. . . ." Gregg was pleased to show his visitors the establishment. The shafting having just been completed, he had it put in motion. "It ran truly and steadily as possible, not a wabble was to be seen in the whole length." Maxwell was glad that there was enough machinery to fill the entire building from the start. Partial equipment was an error which Gregg "had been determined from the beginning not to commit," and had taken control of the project only on condition that enough capital be subscribed to make a brave beginning. The machinery, "all of the most perfect and beautiful kind," was chiefly from Taunton, Massachusetts.

Exact construction expenses were still somewhat uncertain, but it was supposed that the mill and its contents would cost about $150,000, and that the digging of the canal and the erection of boarding houses, cottages and warehouses, with $10,000 paid for the valley itself, would almost amount to the whole of the capital of $300,000. It was proposed to propel the factory "by a turbin [sic] wheel of one hundred and sixteen horsepower, of four feet diameter, with a tube of three feet, and apparently about twenty feet fall."

"All along the banks of the canal, and facing the factory building, are very handsome houses built with strict uniformity, each having its garden and all other conveniences around it, intended for boarding-houses, and can accomodate [sic] besides the family, some ninety boarders with comfortable rooms. . . ." Nestling among the trees on the hill slope were the cottages for single families, the architecture of which drew special

53

comment. They had then, as today, steep roofs, peaked windows, and eaves finished with turned and scroll-cut woodwork called, with less stretch of the imagination than one would think, "the old Gothic style." "Mr. Gregg told us that these cottages thus ornamented, only cost the company $400 each, and that the ornamented work was only a small portion of that cost; while it was intended to give to the inhabitants a taste for the beautiful, and to encourage among the operatives a pleasant rivalry in making their homes agreeable."

In the fall of 1849, when the mill had been in operation about a year, Gregg himself gave a description of the plant and village.[3] The mill buildings were of hammered granite, and contained 8,400 spindles and 300 looms, "the most improved machinery." "The village covers about 150 acres of ground, contains two handsome Gothic churches, an academy, hotel, ten or twelve stores, and about one hundred cottages belonging to the company, and occupied by persons in their service. The houses vary in size from three to nine rooms each, nearly all built after the Gothic cottage order," giving the place "quite a novel appearance to the stranger." The whole property cost about $300,000.

Solon Robinson visited Graniteville at about this time.[4] His account varies in a few particulars from Gregg's—for instance, according to him there were 9,245 spindles. He testified again to the up-to-dateness of all the equipment, which was turning out "No. 14 sheetings and shirtings."[5] He admired the solidity of the main building of blue granite, two stories high, "with a good room in the attic, equal to half a floor, or more," as also the picker room, two stories, and separate from the main building. He found besides store houses, offices, two churches, a school house, 83 dwellings of wood, "and all the fixings of the neatest kind, with two dams, and races a mile long, 40 feet head, two turbine wheels, a saw and grist mill, a hotel, and 9,000 acres of land, all cost $300,000, or $32.44 per each spindle."[6]

The factory building was heated by steam. Stairways occupied the two projecting towers.[7] A director in the Graniteville Company observed that the village was so laid out that all rain water would run into the canal, thus keeping the place perfectly dry and consequently healthy. The canal was, according to him, three-fourths of a mile long and connected with two ponds covering several hundred acres of ground; under the head of 40 feet there was sufficient power to run 20,000 spindles with their complement of looms.[8]

When Graniteville had been in operation a year, Gregg wrote of the family cottages in the village, which formed a part of the original plan. "Our female help," he said, "is all taken from resident families under the protection and care of parents. This is a great moral restraint, and gives us an advantage over those who have to rely on the boarding-house system for help, where large numbers of young females are collected together from a wide range of country, away from parents' care."[9] Gregg also made provision, however, for operatives' boarding houses such as he had seen in Lowell and other mill towns in New England.[10]

James H. Taylor, who from his practical interest in the Graniteville and Charleston cotton mills, was conversant with every detail of policy, wrote at the opening of 1850: "The arrangement for 'boarding operatives,' as it is usually called, is one of the best yet tried in any manufacturing village. At first, large houses were built, capable of accommodating from 10 to 30 boarders. Matrons were procured and placed in them, and efforts were made to induce the girls, who wished to come in to work, to board in them. But this plan did not answer. Girls were unwilling to leave the home of their birth for strange places; and it was soon found that the boarding house plan would not be sustained. The village had been laid out in broad streets and large squares; and upon these, neat, uniform cottages were built, which, with a large lot of land to each, were offered, at a very low rent, to those who would bring in their families and place them in the mill. This plan worked well. The houses were soon filled with respectable tenants. . . . (The youth of the place are under the watchful eye of their parents—a far better safeguard than rules and regulations of corporations."[11] Gregg had always emphasized the primary importance of good homes, and in his *Domestic Industry*[12] evidently meant that families should move bodily to manufacturing villages built in South Carolina. The change from boarding houses to separate cottages must have been made promptly.

In perhaps the majority of instances the father and mother in the family moving to Graniteville did not work in the mill. Thus Taylor remarked that "while the sons and daughters worked in the mill, the father would engage in cultivating his land, hauling wood, &c., and the mother would attend to the housekeeping department. Thus each found employment suited to their age and capacity."[13] A Graniteville resident whose experience dates from these years of first settlement said that if the "old man" had children in the mill but himself wanted to farm, Gregg would rent him land at a nominal price, on which enough corn would be raised to fatten a hog or two.[14] Another man remembering Graniteville's first decade said that some of the farmers giving up in the country and moving into the village brought their horses with them, and were permitted to clear land and cultivate it free of charge; even poor men living near by, in no way connected with Graniteville, were allowed to sell wood from the company's lands. Not a few families placing young people in the mill preferred to build their own homes adjacent to the town rather than becoming the company's tenants. While keeping a watchful eye on the behavior of these, Gregg was always anxious to extend to them the benefits of his community.

The company-owned cotton mill village is now almost peculiar to the South, where it is well-nigh universal. There is reason to believe that Gregg set a precedent at Graniteville which has been controlling.[15]

Different groups of cottages in the village very early came to be known by familiar names. One of these referred to with peculiar affection is "Blue Row," on the opposite side of the canal from the mill, and up the incline. It is composed of houses less ornamented than the rest, and it was for this reason that Gregg had the clapboards washed with blue. Graniteville was a tight little family any way, but dwellers in cottages near together were drawn closer by the use of common wells. Blue Row, for instance, had five wells in the street, all of which, like the rest in the village, were filled in after Gregg's death, when a water system was installed. Different names were attached to other sections of the place—"Punkin Gully," "Skillet Alley," and "Shake-Rag," but these terms were not used in Gregg's hearing!

As soon as Graniteville was built, families from the country about flocked in and applied to Gregg for work and homes. More came than he could take, but in especially needy cases he made shift to keep them somehow. Once when a man came with his family and chattels there was no other place to put them but the blacksmith shop. Beds were set up there and the forge was used for cooking until a house could be got ready. The story is told of a young woman who took a house so fresh from the carpenters' hands that she swept out the shavings herself. She lived there many years until her death.

Graniteville heralded a new day for the Poor Whites of the South. Of English, German, and Scotch-Irish stock, they were blood kin to the dominant class in the low country; they were only a few generations removed from the frontiersmen who cleared the land they occupied; but, expelled by negro slavery, they were strangers in their own land. The first great cotton mill welcomed them back into the body social. The good beginning that

58

Gregg made would have been more closely followed but for the crescendo of pro-slavery argument, the Civil War, and the desperate decade and a half that ensued upon the conflict. After 1880 Gregg's purpose came to the minds of thousands, and, through the founding of scores of mills and villages, was applied widespread. Reëntrance into the life of the South through the industrial door has brought its hardships to the Poor Whites—in long hours, stagnating routine, low wages, and a paternalism which some think has, through several generations, smothered the divine spark of independence. But it is impossible for a ruling society to turn its back on the mass of the people for long years, without recovery of the neglected being painful. On a despoiled field the first poor crops must be turned under before better ones are raised to yield fruit. Faithful and uncomplaining, the Poor Whites have learned a new standard of living, and in a spiritual as well as an economic sense, are catching step with our times. When they were far, far behind the van, William Gregg placed himself at the head of the moving column. He declared that "it is only necessary to make comfortable homes in order to procure families that will afford laborers of the best kind. A large manufacturing establishment located anywhere in the State, away from a town and in a healthy situation, will soon collect around it a population who, however poor, with proper moral restraints thrown around them, will soon develop all the elements of good society. Self-respect, and attachment to the place will soon find their way into the minds of such, while intelligence, morality, and well directed industry, will not fail to acquire position."[16]

Graniteville was like a feudal village, with the great stone factory substituted for the turreted castle, and the wooden houses in place of thatched cots; the Poor Whites came in for the protection of their overlord just as eagerly as did the peasants of centuries earlier, and if they gave up something of an unmeaning freedom, they gained in the substantial asset of security. Gregg was to be to his retainers' landlord, employer, teacher, clergyman, and judge.

The wages paid seem low to us now, but compared favorably with the practice in contemporary neighboring mills. It must always be remembered that before taking industrial employment these people had handled scarcely any cash, having existed under a credit system which kept them barely even with their obligations or plunged them chronically into debt. The money wages Gregg gave them, coupled with the "rights," (to continue the feudal figure) which they enjoyed in garden and woods, and the privileges of school and church and medical service, undoubtedly amounted to more than they had received in their old country environment.[17] Rentals of company houses ran from $16 to $25 a year. The average wage of the 300 men, women, and children employed at Graniteville in April, 1849 was $3.05 per week. Men made from $4 to $5, women from $3 to $4, and children from $1 to $2. Most of the work was done by the piece.[18] The hours were long—from twelve to twelve and a half—about the same working day as in England and the North at this time. A rising bell was rung from the factory tower, and, it was said, "the system of labor requires the attendance of every one in the mill and office, at the ringing of the second bell in the morning. Work is begun as soon as there is light sufficient for running the machines. The instant the bell ceases to ring the gates are locked, and tardy ones are required to pass through the office." Lateness to work was rare. At 7 o'clock (at least this was the time in winter) the mill was stopped for three quarters of an hour, when the operatives had breakfast, undoubtedly going to their homes. Work was resumed then until 1 o'clock, when three quarters of an hour was allowed for dinner. Then work was continued until 7:30. After dark the operatives worked by solar burners. Nothing indicates a short day Saturday. Under this scheme of labor the workers, it was said, were "as cheerful and well disposed as any in the world."[19]

Only one instance of collective discontent among the Graniteville operatives in Gregg's time has come to notice. In 1857 the slashers demanded more wages, and others joined them. It is probable that they quit work. Gregg was at Kalmia, and on being notified of the difficulty that had arisen, went to the mill, talked to the people, and settled the matter—with what result to their wages is not indicated.[20]

Probably an accurate notion of the composition of the working force at Graniteville may be got from the facts as to Vaucluse near by. Here, of 94 hands, 11 were men, 50 to 60 were girls ranging in age from 10

61

to 25 years, and the rest were boys from 12 to 20 years old.[21] A man who went to work at Graniteville a decade after the mill was started, when he was 14 years old, said he worked normally twelve hours, and that nobody seemed to mind the long day.[22] He received $12.50 a month, and thought he was making big wages. New hands at weaving operated two looms. An important respect in which Gregg was like Robert Owen was in his observance of a minimum age of employment for boys and girls—none could enter the mill at Graniteville unless at least twelve years old. This was an improvement upon Owen's rule of ten years, and much in advance of the general practice of the mills in the South at that day.[23]

The purpose which Gregg had, before building his mill, of making cotton manufactures of assistance to the Poor Whites of the South, carried over into his program when Graniteville was established. After the plant commenced running he wrote with a new pleasure of realization: "We employ in and about the mill 325 persons, and support a village of 900 white people. Our superintendent, and a few owners [others he must have meant] are Eastern men; all the laborers, South Carolinians, said to be equal, in point of industry and efficiency to any set of hands of similar number and age in the Northern and Eastern States. . . ."[24] The equal efficiency of Southern operatives with those of New England is hard to substantiate, if for no other reason than the finer counts on which most Northern operatives worked. Gregg's statement would be perfectly accurate if the lower wages he paid were taken into account—20 per cent lower than in Massachusetts and a fraction lower than in Rhode Island.[25]

"We have a large class of white people in South Carolina," Gregg continued, "who are not slave holders, and who are compelled to work for a livelihood. The good lands are generally owned by the wealthy, and cultivated by negroes, affording but little employment to the poor, who readily come into factory service." A little later he went further in showing that cotton culture, as a profitable occupation, was closed to the unpropertied whites in the State. Cotton manufacturing must be their salvation. On the land $2\frac{1}{2}$ to $3\frac{1}{2}$ bales to the hand, with an allowance of foodstuffs equal to an additional bale, was as much as could be looked for, while in a cotton mill of 300 operatives (he certainly had his Graniteville experience in mind), each worker could produce, of No. 14 cloth, a value equal to 12 bales to the hand, or even as high as 18 or 20 bales, and these workers were mostly women and children at that. "Additional force is given to the argument," he said, "by the fact that manufacturing labor is supplied mainly from that portion of society which cannot be rendered available in agriculture, and this has peculiar force, in reference to the policy of the Southern States engaging in the manufacture of cotton; for a large portion of our poor white people, are not only unproductive, but actually a burthen to us." Even though dividends might be low, the introduction of manufactures in the South would thus bring great advantages.[26]

In the years immediately following the building of Graniteville, and in all probability influenced thereby, many cotton factories were erected in the South and public interest in the industry was stirred. This development was an anticipation of the "Cotton Mill Campaign" which inaugurated the Southern industry on a great scale in the eighties, thirty years later.[27] Daniel McCullogh, of Fairfield District, South Carolina, began erecting a small cotton factory in the spring of 1845.[28] A cotton mill which was a community enterprise, calculated to compensate for the loss of the State capital and the wearing out of agricultural lands, was started at Tuscaloosa, Alabama, a few months later.[29] The spirit of the notices of new mills recalls very much the more active period after the Civil War. The *Atlanta Intelligencer* reported that the foundation was laid for a factory in Cobb County, Georgia, and another had been completed in Campbell County: "Thus the work goes merrily on."[30]

A factory was to be built near Auburn, Alabama, and another at VanBuren, Arkansas, the first in the State. Though this latter was a small affair (1,530 spindles, 30 looms) there was the comment, "This is the way for the South to make war upon the North—better than forty South Carolina arsenals."[31] Catching the spirit, a Mississippi writer urged that a mill be built at Biloxi, a healthful location where labor and materials were cheap.[32] Mills already in operation were listed, as lending encouragement to fresh undertakings.[33] Two recently built plants were of special interest—the Augusta

Factory, which was convincing local skepticism that Georgia girls would gladly take factory employment,[34] and the Charleston Mill, which the *Mercury* regarded as an experiment "not merely to determine whether cotton could be profitably converted into cloth in our city, but an experiment upon the industrial habits of our people."[35] The first subscriptions to stock of the Charleston Mill were made in the winter of 1844, apparently as a direct outcome of Gregg's letters in the *Courier*.[36] A year and a half later the company was about to be organized for the erection of the factory, the stock having been taken mostly in small parcels.[37] In Georgia the Troup Factory of 1,000 spindles was put into operation in the autumn of 1847, and the Howard Manufacturing Company commenced its building.[38]

Reviewing developments, DeBow said: "Every month adds more to the interest which the southern and western States are feeling in the subject of domestic manufactures, especially in cotton goods, for which they enjoy such rare facilities. With the material upon the spot, with an abundance of water power, . . . provisions without stint, and cheap labor, particularly that of the slave, . . . it will be strange if the South and West permit much longer their wealth to be drained away by northern manufacturers. . . . Throughout the States of South Carolina, Georgia, and Alabama, mills are continually in construction. . . ."[39]

Other advocates came in with their arguments to assist William Gregg in encouraging these ventures in cotton manufacturing in the South. Some who followed

Gregg in writing about the new departure—with favor or disfavor, without bias or with it—were General Charles T. James, of Rhode Island, Amos A. Lawrence, of Boston, Hamilton Smith, of Kentucky, and James H. Taylor, of Charleston. The first three of these engaged in a controversy into which Gregg was drawn and which had its echoes in less notable statements.

It is convenient to begin with the case for the planting of the industry in the South as put by James.[40] Born in Rhode Island in 1804, James as a youth learned the carpenter's trade, and later became an expert mechanician. Following some years as superintendent of the celebrated Slater mills, he became the engineer in the building of cotton factories throughout the country. In 1850 it was said that he had erected one-eighth of the spindles in the United States.[41] At the time of appearance of his articles favoring Southern entrance into the business, he had received some commissions from that section and was actively bidding for more. In several respects he may be compared with another mill engineer, D. A. Tompkins, whose important advocacy and work came in the eighties and nineties.[42] Both combined legitimate business objects with unselfish motives. James' articles on the prospects of the industry in the South are much like those of Gregg, but less earnest, less careful, and less interesting. He spoke, after all, as an outsider, and did not have Gregg's native understanding. Though the builder of large establishments, James meant planters to turn home manufacturers, employing slave labor in small units. "Our cotton States have all the facilities for manufacturing purposes," he said, "except, perhaps, skill. That can be readily obtained, at a cost quite trifling, when compared with that of the importation of cotton by the manufacturer of Great Britain. . . . it is evident that, did the planter apply labor, skill and materials, to a business as lucrative as that of the manufacture of cotton, and employ the capital he now does, the product would be worth some $120,000,000, instead of $30,000,000, or less, the market value of his cotton."[43]

Not a few at this time, Gregg chief among them, were trying to show the cotton planter that the growing of the staple was the least profitable part of the business and that he was at the mercy of the great cotton exchanges.[44] Said James on this point: "In the first place, the planter sends his cotton abroad to be manufactured, and thus loses the profits of the process, when it might as well be done at home. In the second place, he produces a surplus of the article every year, sends it to Europe in surplus supplies, has to solicit sales, and hence must submit to have purchasers make their own prices, and give him for the article just what they please."[45] The article of James in *Hunt's Merchants' Magazine* was widely reprinted in Southern journals, and letters of disagreement came to the editor from the North. Hunt himself thought James too optimistic over the probable success of the industry in the South, but nonetheless lent his voice to the encouragement of manufacturing in the section.[46]

The weightiest pronouncement against James was from another New Englander. Lawrence, of Boston, was deeply interested in the Massachusetts mills, and he set out, with accuracy as far as he went, to discourage progress in the South by exhibiting the low ebb of the industry even in the section where long established. Edward Atkinson, likewise of Boston, undertook the same rôle, with no more success, thirty years later.[47] Cotton was so high, Lawrence declared, that coarse goods could not be produced by the mills at a profit. He published figures, the authenticity of which was not denied, showing that earnings of mills at Lowell had dropped off, in some cases to 2 and 3 per cent, in the years just preceding, and their stocks were selling generally at much less than par. The Boott mills, for example, made 18 per cent in 1845, 16 per cent in 1846, 8 per cent in 1847, 5 per cent in 1848, and 2 per cent in 1849. The stock of this company sold for 850, par being 1,000.[48]

This was the negative side, and his contention was largely vitiated by the fact that he mistook a period of depression for a settled condition. The positive arguments which Lawrence adduced against the industry in the South were: there was a "radical defect" in steam power, upon which it was presumed the South, certainly planter-manufacturers, must rely; the South did not possess the requisite labor and skill; there was not enough spare capital at the South to inaugurate the industry; there was already enough machinery in operation to absorb all the available labor and supply the whole demand for goods; planters were making more profit by producing than New Englanders by working up the raw material.

James responded at some length to Lawrence's arguments, the force of his defense of the South being somewhat diminished, however, by space devoted to justifying some of his personal engineering achievements.[49] A warmer contestant in behalf of the South was Hamilton Smith, promoter of the new industrial town of Cannelton, Ohio. "The South Carolina and Georgia mills find ready customers," he said, "for their surplus yarns and brown sheetings in Baltimore, Philadelphia, and even as far north as New York." Southern cotton factories had found capital ready and labor fully equal to the demand. "Very many new cotton mills are now in progress of construction in those States, and for the last two years, one of the most prominent topics of discussion in the newspapers of the South and West has been, not whether cotton mills could or could not be operated at home, but when, where, and by whom, they should be put in operation." He complained that Lawrence in writing on American cotton manufactures made no mention of a single mill outside of New England, thus giving a stranger the impression that "the plantation States had just begun to inquire if there was any natural and inseparable connection between ice and spindles, granite and looms." The hardy people of the Southern uplands could not understand why expense could not be saved by manufacturing the staple at home. "In their simplicity they think, that materials and subsistence, or the chief elements to be combined, should attract the laborers and their tools; that there is but little more reason

69

in taking cotton and food from three to six thousand miles, to be ground in a mill of simple construction into *coarse* cloth, than in taking their soil to the shop of the plow-maker."[50]

In controverting Lawrence's statement that the South hadn't the requisite labor and skill, Hamilton Smith referred to a letter of Gregg's published in the same issue of *Hunt's Magazine* with the first of Lawrence's articles.[51]

Gregg, writing from Kalmia, his home at Graniteville, in October, 1849, began by speaking of Graniteville the accomplished fact, "which many persons are looking to for a clear demonstration, that cotton manufacturing can be made a lucrative branch of industry in our State." Graniteville was not a mere project, something to be guessed at, but was a going concern, turning out goods "according to the judgment of the merchants of Charleston, New York and Philadelphia, equal in point of quality to any of the kind made in the United States or any other country." He had no doubt the mill and village would prove to be a profitable investment, "soon to be followed by millions of our capital seeking similar channels." Gregg brought a further air of actuality to his statement by speaking of the momentary difficulty in the trade, North and South, due to the failure of the price of finished products to rise in proportion to that of the raw material. Here was the busy manufacturer, not the controversialist; but, in addition to his description of Graniteville, he gave reasons for believing in the future of the industry in the South.

The mill workers, he said, "are frugal and economical in their habits," while "our mild climate, cheap breadstuffs, fuel, and other substantials of life, render living much cheaper here than in colder countries." In the interior of the State, cotton was 1½ cents cheaper than in the East and 2 cents cheaper than in Europe. "All these advantages, added to the abundance of labor, must operate for many years so favorably on cotton manufacturing in the South, as to render it only necessary to make judicious outlays in erecting mills, and to exercise tolerable management afterwards, to render profitable results certain."[52]

Gregg came directly into the argument between advocates and adversaries of the new Southern industry with a second letter in *Hunt's Magazine*.[53] "The able essay of Mr. Lawrence," he said, "although true, is, in my opinion, calculated to do us quite as much harm as that of General James. The latter's low estimates of the requisite capital, and his extravagant calculation with regard to profits, may lead a few of our unthinking capitalists into embarrassment, and possibly loss of entire investments; while the remarks of the former are calculated to discourage the spirit of progress, at present manifested at the South.

"I have never encouraged persons," he continued, "to look for more than 10, 12 or 14 per cent, on investments in manufacturing; but the remuneration which capital receives, when invested in such pursuits, is not a criterion from which to judge of the profits derived by a country at large. While we admit Mr. Lawrence's statement relative to the dividends paid, we cannot but notice the fact, that New England has grown rich and prosperous, beyond all precedent, since her capitalists enaged in their particular field of enterprise. No one can for a moment doubt that the manufacturing of cotton goods has been chiefly instrumental in producing the great changes wrought in New England, during the last thirty years."

The low dividends of Mr. Lawrence and the high profits of General James were alike misleading. The results which James pictured were "utterly fallacious," for bad management would dissipate even exorbitant profits. His readers were familiar with the way in which land might produce a fair return or bring the farmer into debt, according to the management of it. The same was true of manufacturing. He was taking his illustration from Graniteville when he said that three hundred efficient hands, mostly women and many of them children, would work enough spindles and looms to make into No. 14 cloth 3,600 bales of cotton per annum, which would be worth two or three times the cost of the raw material; but one must know from experience how seriously gross profit might be diminished in the manufacturing and selling costs.

However, the South, remembering what amounts had been constantly invested in the industry in Europe and America, should fortify herself also with the reflection "that we have labor, both white and black, at least 20 per cent cheaper than in New England, and with few exceptions, as cheap as in any part of the world—that water-power may be had for almost nothing—that our provisions are as cheap, and, above all, that we have the cotton at hand, sound, bright, and unsullied by the rain, mud, smoke, etc., incident to its transit from the interior of our State, to its final destination. This last item alone, is equal to ¼ of a cent a pound in our favor, and explains what the generality of persons do not understand—why southern manufactured domestics are superior in quality to a similar style manufactured in the Eastern States. Fair cotton is a very different article by the time it reaches New England, from what it was when it left the interior of any of the Southern States." This, with home demand and the saving of transportation and charges both ways, made "a difference in our favor, which foreigners cannot overcome by superior skill," provided the Southerner exercise in his factory the same prudence which was necessary to the success of a cotton plantation.[54]

James H. Taylor, agent of the Charleston Mill and close associate of Gregg in the Graniteville enterprise, published an article at the same time as this letter of Gregg's; his arguments for the manufacturing of cotton in the South were directly influenced by Gregg—particularly his insistence that there must be a change in the public attitude toward industry and that Negroes should be used in the cotton fields while the Poor Whites worked in the factories, though he expressed fears, not entertained by his friend, of the results of bringing up a white population which had no attachment to slavery.

The Charleston Mill and Graniteville, he said, "have settled the question of practicability of manufacturing cotton goods in this State, *successfully*. . . ."[55]

Graniteville got under way just at the period of depression in 1850-51; this was particularly a bad time for coarse goods mills, and the new factory was thus given a severe test at the outset. A. A. Lawrence, speaking without knowledge of the special advantages possessed by the new Southern mills, gave a gloomy picture of the situation in 1849. "The production of cotton, for the last five years," he said, "has been 11,323,000 bales; and the consumption has been 11,939,000 bales; showing an excess of consumption of 616,000 bales, which has been supplied by the surplus on hand at the commencement of the time." Middling cotton sold at 11 cents, and fair at 13 cents. "The present price renders the manufacture of all descriptions of coarse goods impossible, except at a loss; . . ." In the coming season there must be a fall in the price of cotton or a rise in the price of goods, or both.[56]

Gregg at the same time gave a striking statement of conditions as they affected Graniteville: "We in common with the manufacturing world are laboring under an unprecedented state of things just now. Cotton has advanced upon us 100 per cent in eight months. The raw material which we are now using costs us at the rate of $65,000 per annum more than it did in February last, while manufactured goods have advanced but a shade; this state of things cannot last, for goods will have to go up, or cotton go down to enable the spinners of the world to continue in operation.[57] A year later a writer in the *Boston Daily Advertiser* declared matters were as bad as before, no profit having been made in coarse goods for the past twenty months; if any small return had been realized it had been in the enhanced value of the stocks of cotton, and not in the manufacture. "In fact, these profits would have been larger, had the same cotton been sold, instead of being manufactured. . . . This source of profit has now ceased altogether. . . . The rise of goods has been three cents a pound, from the lowest point, while cotton has gradually risen six cents." The cost per pound of manufacturing common heavy sheetings was, for middling fair cotton, 13.50 cents; on account of waste, 1.48 cents; for labor, 3.80; for general expenses, 2.08, a total of 20.86 cents —which, at 2.80 yards per pound, made the cloth cost 7.45 cents per yard. The nominal market price of such goods was 7¾ cents on eight months credit, but they really could not be sold freely at even 7½ cents, which price, after necessary deductions, brought the price to the producer to 6.85 cents, or 60-100 under the cost of turning them out. It was figured that a 15,000-spindle mill would lose about $40,000 a year.[58] Lawrence had asserted that 7½ cents was a higher price that had been got for No. 14 or 15 plain or twilled goods for two years past. This was precisely what Graniteville was making.[59]

CHAPTER V

A BENEVOLENT DESPOTISM

Gregg and Graniteville were identical terms. He made the place out of hand, and it reflected, in every department of its life, his affectionate care. There have been mill men in the South since who, while no less despotic over their communities, have been less benevolent. A later generation of managers has maintained welfare programs first for profit, and second for the happiness and progress of the workpeople. With William Gregg the human motive ran *pari passu* with the commercial. He acted, in all his plans for the life of the people of Graniteville, from a profound sense of social obligation, and a finer patriotism than answers to war trumpets. *Noblesse oblige* was his intuition. He set a pattern for the industry which, in our more complex day, can never be quite returned to. The subjects over whom he ruled in his little kingdom were economically as weak as he was strong, and yet no hint of exploitation ever entered his consciousness.

"Mr. Gregg was the boss of this place as long as he lived," said an octogenarian who beamed at the name as he commenced his reminiscences. And another assured me that "his memory is very green at Graniteville now. There is no person of any age in the town who hasn't something to tell you of William Gregg."

76

He presents many similarities with Robert Owen, yet with a difference. Gregg's work at Graniteville was like Owen's at New Lanark in that he meant to make it a type for the whole of society. But Owen reached out into utopian fancies as noble as they were impracticable, while Gregg planned a social reorganization through the steady implanting of industry in an agricultural economy. Owen found an industrial revolution demanding remedy on its human side. Gregg, in the midst of slavery and stagnation, believed that only the introduction of manufactures would lift the Poor Whites into an admirable standard of living.

After 1854, Gregg lived the year 'round on the hilltop overlooking the village and so could give it the closest supervision. Just as at New Lanark, so at Graniteville, the school lay very near the proprietor's heart. When Gregg was working out the plans for his venture it is certain that the teaching of reading, writing, and arithmetic to the children was as definitely a part of his program as the industrial training of operatives, the profits of the company, or the indirect advantages that were to accrue to the community from the manufacturing enterprise. "How easy would it be for the proprietors of such establishments," he had written, looking forward to the planting of industrial villages, "with only a small share of philanthropy, to make good use of the school fund in ameliorating the condition of this class of our population, now but little elevated above the Indian of the forest. . . . It is, perhaps, not generally

77

known, that there are *twenty-nine thousand* white persons in this State, above the age of twelve years, who can neither read nor write—this is about one in every five of the white population."[1]

When he could put his purpose into practice, he inaugurated the first compulsory education system (albeit informal and limited, yet surprisingly effective) in the South, and perhaps in this country. He described it briefly himself: "All parents are required to keep their children, between the ages of six and twelve, at school—good teachers, books, etc., are furnished by the company, free of charge." And he added that this requirement was "willingly acquiesced in by the people."[2]

In 1850 the school already had a hundred pupils.[3] The recollection of old inhabitants of Graniteville is that if every urging of Gregg's did not suffice to secure attendance of the children, the offending family was fined by him five cents a day for every day a child stayed away from school. Not only did he insist that the children of the village proper go to school, but he was anxious to have neighboring families benefit from it. One of the early scholars, now a very old man, told of Gregg's solicitude in this connection with lively appreciation. Mr. Perdue's father was a small farmer two miles from Graniteville, and could not pay to keep all of his children at school at once. Gregg came to see the family one morning, and noting children playing about the house, asked why they were not in the classes. The father told him. "Tut-tut-tut-tut-tut, Wylie," he rejoined (he had a way of doing this when a little provoked),

78

"send them all up to the school, you hear!" And so it was.

The school, at any rate after it had been in operation a few years, had three teachers, two of them ladies from Charleston, and the third a man. Gregg would usually include the school in his daily visits to the mill; when he would drive his bob-tailed horse up at recess time, the children would flock against the fence, and spill through and over it into the road until they blocked the way. Gregg liked this, and would laugh and play with them as they climbed over his buggy. Very often he would go in and talk to the pupils. One of those who sat as a little tot under these instructions told me that "he was always impressing lessons of politeness ('if one of you boys sees a lady drive up, run out and offer to hold her horse'). There was one boy in the school said never to be polite. Gregg would always ask for him, ('if George Crocker is here, let him stand up!'). Then he would lecture directly at George."

Sometimes he would conclude his remarks by telling the boys that he did not take his workman's apron off until he was worth $50,000. "Now go to work, boys," he would admonish them.

Gregg not only had his compulsory school attendance law, but he was his own enforcement officer. If he came across a truant, he would return the boy to school, or, if the offense was repeated, would take him to the office for a licking. Nobody wanted to be taken to the office! One day Gregg learned that a boy who had often fallen under his displeasure for truancy had sneaked off from school and gone fishing. The old man lay in wait for him on the road, and as the culprit emerged from the bushes beside the stream, seized him, lifted him into the buggy and drove to the mill office. Instead of the customary whipping, the boy got a new punishment. Gregg stood him on the high bookkeeper's desk and left him there without a word. He had tipped off the office employees to ask questions, and as each one passed through the room, Gregg would explain, "There stands the boy that would rather go fishing than get an education." After this was many times repeated the little fellow begged to be let down, and he would never run away from school again.[5]

Once when Gregg suddenly appeared at the verge of the swimming hole, buggy whip in hand, the boys were so frightened they clutched up their clothes and, without stopping to put them on, ran right into the schoolroom. He devised still another method of punishment. Once at the end of the war when lead was scarce, the boys ripped the metal from the valley gutters of the schoolhouse to make bullets for their hunting excursions. Gregg was very angry, but calmed down by the time he had got them to the mill. Here he organized a jury and "tried" them.

Though he wanted the children to stay in school in school hours, he was fond of taking them on picnics and giving them all the pleasure he could. Every spring there was a special outing, when the youngsters of the village and the near-by country were taken on the millpond in flatboats. These were equipped with seats run across them. Gregg would be full of fun, explaining that all were as safe as on the deck of a ship going into New York harbor. Once, after thus assuring them, he gave them a scare. He always tried to give repair work about the buildings and grounds to the people of the vicinity when he could. One of his firm friends among these folk was an old Irish ditcher, who had very early come to Graniteville, named Fagin. Fagin was a careless old fellow, in summer never bothering to wear shoes. If Gregg saw him he would hail him, take him in the buggy and drive about to explain what was to be done. Fagin would break stone and throw it in behind the dam, and keep the canal banks in shape. Gregg took an undisguised pleasure in his old retainer; they were called "very thick." Gregg had taken Fagin along on this picnic. When the rest were not looking, and by previous arrangement, he pushed Fagin off the "flat" and into the pond. There was a great scrambling and shouting, Gregg waving his arms in mock dismay, before the old fellow, with much spluttering, was drawn aboard.[6]

Every little episode connected with these excursions is likely to be remembered and treasured by some one in Graniteville today. Once Mrs. Gregg, who was likewise the friend of the village, made gingerbread horses for the picnic, and Gregg threw them into the crowd for the children to scramble after.

I drove a dozen miles from Graniteville out into Edgefield County to see an old man who as a boy enjoyed these outings. Now living in exile, he speaks of Graniteville as home. I caught him at the cross-roads store. He told me he had just had his eightieth birthday. He stood with his back to the tall "chunk stove," his hands thrust into the pockets of his baggy old trousers; he seemed to have on several layers of woolen shirts and sweaters under his salt-and-pepper coat. He was a short, spare old fellow, with a hooked nose, sagging fat little cheeks, a tight red skin, and straying whitish whiskers about his chin and neck. A black felt hat with undented crown and gold-rimmed spectacles completed him. He lighted up at mention of my errand. It was clear in what he said that all at Graniteville formed one family under Gregg. Many intimate ties of work, frolic, fatherly discipline, and mutual gratitude and respect knit them into one uniquely happy little group. Gregg stood out in his mind as maybe the biggest fact in his life, certainly in his childhood.

He told me how in the season Gregg would have a wagon load of peaches brought down from the Kalmia orchard, and put in baskets in the school yard, where the children helped themselves, Gregg sitting back in his chair and enjoying the treat as much as any. At Christmas he would bring more firecrackers than had ever been seen in the county before. Tears came to the old man's eyes as he told how Gregg would have a big fire built and hand out torpedoes to the children as they filed past him. Then he wanted to watch every one as it was lighted and thrown into the air.

Gregg enforced a strict rule of prohibition upon liquor in Graniteville. His Quaker tradition may have influenced him, but more powerful considerations were his regard for industrial efficiency and his sense of responsibility for the orderliness and good name of his village. The mill had scarcely started when he wrote that "The use of alcohol is not permitted in the place— young people, particularly males, are not allowed to remain in the place in idleness. . . ." This restraint was "willingly acquiesced in by the people, and we have one of the most moral, quiet, orderly, and busy places to be found any where."[7] In every lease to property in Graniteville the tenant engaged not to have or sell liquor on the premises. Solon Robinson reported that "if any one is disposed to make a brute of himself over the whisky cup, he must go to some other place, for neither in store or tavern in that village has that curse of the earth ever entered, or can ever enter until owners change."[8]

Gregg's anxiety to keep the town sober comes out in his supervision of the hotel. He wrote from Charleston to the superintendent at Graniteville in the winter of 1850: "I have no doubt but Mrs. West would be as good a person as we could get into the Hotel. Mr. Moses told Mr. Boyce that he would expect to keep wine and brandy to accommodate his fashionable boarders. If he takes the house he must sign the rules and carry them out. We don't want a set of loafing wine-drinkers about the place. Whatever money we spend in buildings for the accommodation of the public must be used for the accommodation of that class of persons called business men or at least those who can restrain themselves sufficiently to conform to the moral rules, the maintenance of which we consider vitally important to the success of our enterprise."[9]

His prohibition measures extended beyond the limits of the village. One inhabitant, Dawse Jordan by name, was particularly addicted to the cup, and tried steadily to get around Gregg's watchfulness. If Gregg, driving up the hilly road from Graniteville to Kalmia, met Dawse coming from Aiken with his jug, he would leap from the buggy, seize the jug, and break it over the wheel. Then he would pay over the cost of the liquor and send the man on his way home. An eye witness to one of these encounters said that Dawse threatened violently when he saw the jug smashed, but Gregg's only reply was that he would follow up his discipline with the buggy whip. Dawse got to be such a chronic offender that Gregg would tell the servants at Kalmia to call him if they heard the familiar tipsy song in the road, when he would put out after his wayward villager.[10]

The strictness of supervision at Graniteville was partly responsible for a freer code in a little community which grew up on the outskirts of the village. It was at first called Wooleytown after a man who came from the North and set up a shop where he made beaver hats. Though Wooleytown was not pleasing to the Graniteville authorities, its founder was a great favorite with the children, for he liked to play with them, and in front of his house he built a small ferris wheel which was their delight.[11]

Individuals could do as they pleased, of course, with their premises off the Graniteville property, but even here Gregg was not without resource. In the spring of 1851 he had gone down to Charleston troubled by the amount of dancing that was taking place. He wrote back to his superintendent a letter that seems out of tune with the present practice whereby mill managements encourage dances in their own welfare buildings. "Further reflection in regard to the Balls," he said, "has convinced me of the necessity of taking some decided steps on the part of the Company to put a stop to them, as I am fully convinced of their injurious tendency upon the morality and good order of the village. I would call on Mr. M. and talk with him on the subject and if he persists in hiring his hall for the purpose of such balls, I would advise him that all connection between him and the company in interest and reciprocity would be severed, and if this did not answer I would have it understood that any girl who attended these balls would have no further employment from the Company." He knew well that most country people likely to become operatives did not approve of dancing. "I consider this course better than any temporizing measures," he concluded, "and not only absolutely necessary for the preservation of our standard of morality in G-ville but also to give confidence to those persons of good character who might desire to become residents of our industrious village."[12]

Perhaps because his relatives were Quakers, who had few Meetings in South Carolina, or from choice, William Gregg had no formal church connection until in his last illness he asked for baptism, which was administered by the rector of St. Thaddeus' Episcopal Church, of

Aiken. However, his daughter describes him as being always religiously inclined. He was punctilious in attending St. Philip's Church as long as he lived in Charleston, and when churches were built at Graniteville, he went regularly to that of the Methodists. He felt that his example was important to the young men and boys of the village, and often with little persuasion he got them to join him. He gave largely to the support of the Methodist church at Graniteville, his daughter conducted a Sunday school class here, and he often spoke to the scholars himself.[13] He contributed also to Mrs. Gregg's church, the Episcopal, in Aiken.

At the same time that Graniteville was building, Gregg erected a house for himself three miles away, which he called "Kalmia" because of the profuseness of the kalmia flowers which covered the hills sloping down toward the village. This was planned first for a summer residence, Gregg at this time intending to live most of the year in the Calhoun Street house in Charleston.[14] Kalmia was begun possibly in 1846, though probably in 1847. The minutes of the stockholders of Graniteville in the latter year record that the directors were authorized to sell to Gregg and his associates that part of the Bridge Creek tract of land (all of which had previously been reserved by Boyce and Gregg from sale to the company), which had been surveyed for them in 1846 for summer residences. This land, about a hundred acres and sold for a dollar an acre, adjoined lands of the railroad company and of J. G. O. Wilkinson. Mr. Wilkinson, apparently, was the first to build a summer home on this hilltop.[15]   Ker Boyce built a house near by, and also Judge Carroll.

The Kalmia house was in the prevailing Southern manner—of frame, large and about square, with a portico in front, the round columns of which rose the height of both storeys. Behind the house, to the east, Gregg had a series of curving terraces constructed, the planting upon which, and in the yard, was increasingly beautiful in his lifetime. Near the door leading from the dining room to the lawn was a small dairy, sunk five feet in the ground, with a vaulted masonry roof, sanded floor and double doors.[16] When the family moved permanently from Charleston to Kalmia in 1854, Gregg made changes to adapt it for a year-round home, among other things adding a wing which contained his study. Here was his desk, a fine mahogany piece at which he had written the *Domestic Industry* and the *Charters of Incorporation* while yet a merchant in Charleston and at which he composed later speeches and letters. Gregg was a poor speller, due partly to the deficiency of his day in this regard, but more to his lack of formal schooling. Consequently, when he had finished a manuscript he would hand it over to his wife to be corrected. His daughter Clara was his amanuensis, copying his sheets which were to go to the printer, and making duplicates, with an old-fashioned press, of the letters he wrote. He was most careful about preserving correspondence and receipts, but none of these papers, in the writer's search, has come to light.

He subscribed always for the *Courier*, of Charleston, and had it filed away in the attic by months. "If a single copy was missing, that was sure to be the one he wanted." He was a great reader of the newspapers, and was a patron of DeBow's *Review*. What books were in his library cannot be determined now. He referred to Ure and Montgomery on the cotton manufacture, and constantly made use of the *Encyclopædia Britannica*. But in general he was a student of people and things rather than of the printed page. When Mrs. Gregg moved from Kalmia to Charleston, after his death, his library was sold off.[17]

Gregg's up-to-dateness, and his thoroughness in making improvements, were evident in his installation of illuminating gas in the Kalmia house. General Hammond was building a residence in Columbia, and Gregg wrote to him in February, 1857: "I have the gas fitters now at work . . . and expect to be lighted up this week. Come up if you can next week and see how it operates. The pipes are all between the weather-boarding, floors and plastering, as yours will have to be, and you will see at once the importance and economy of placing them in your house before the floors are laid or the plastering put on. It will be the same case with regard to your lead pipes and water works, now introduced into all good houses at the North and every where except at the South, where we are certainly behind the age with regard to the comforts and conveniences of life." Expert bell hangers should be obtained, from Charleston if necessary, to run the bell wires in small brass tubes so that if a break occurred, new wire could be passed through any distance. "If properly done, you will be rid of trouble for all time to come; if botched you will be annoyed always."[18]

At Kalmia there were five or six servants, and their children. These were the only slaves Gregg ever owned. They were all of one family, purchased from Mrs. Gregg's grandmother Jones' estate.[19] Gregg was always notably considerate of these servants.

At Kalmia, Gregg planted the first extensive peach orchard in the upcountry of South Carolina, the trees coming from New Jersey. He first set out 2,000 trees in front of the house, and before the Civil War 6,000 more to the rear. He was thus an agriculturist as well as manufacturer; the peach orchard was a manifestation of the same interest which prompted his regular attendance on the meetings of the Beach Island Farmers' Club. He was always vitally concerned to see Southern farm productivity increased, and used his peaches as demonstration of what could be done. In the fifties he began shipping the fruit to the North. At this time insect enemies of the peach had not shown themselves in that district, there was no spraying of the trees, and all the fruit was perfect. At packing time all about the house turned in to help, with occasionally some assistance from the village people. The fruit was carefully prepared for market, each peach being individually wrapped. The crates were taken from the packing shed down the hill to the Kalmia Station on the South Carolina Railroad, whence they went by night train to Charleston, and so by steamer to New York, where they arrived in fine condition, only three days removed from the tree.

Kalmia house burned down a few years ago, long since having passed out of the Gregg family.[20] The old road that wound over the hills to Graniteville, which was taken so regularly by William Gregg in the buggy drawn by "Jim," has now, after being closed for forty years in favor of another route through the valley, been reopened and clayed. Thus the traveler today may skirt the same fields and round the same bends that the founder of Graniteville knew so well.

CHAPTER VI

MIXED COUNSELS

The second annual stockholders' meeting, 1848, gave formal thanks to Gregg for his conspicuous service. It was resolved unanimously "That the thanks of the Corporation be tendered to the President, Mr. Gregg, for his untiring zeal and generous devotion to the interests of the Company. Resolved, likewise, That if (as we confidently expect) the enterprise should be crowned with success it is attributable, in no inconsiderable degree, to the intelligence, assiduity and consummate judgment which Mr. Gregg has exhibited in the management of the affairs of the Company, and which they will always fully appreciate." There was no break in this cordial admiration of Gregg until 1859, and then the disaffection, which will be described later, was among directors and not the body of the stockholders.

The minutes state only that Gregg submitted a verbal report of the progress of the work, and an estimate of the probable cost of the establishment when completed, together with a comparison of the cost of similar establishments then in operation. From another source, however, it is known that he reported the buildings as being in readiness to receive the machinery, which would arrive in a week or two. There were to be 9,240 spindles and 300 looms; when in full operation the mill would make from 13,000 to 14,000 yards of cloth daily. The

91

water power was competent to turn 20,000 spindles, "and it is contemplated ultimately to run this number by the erection of other buildings." The present factory would give employment to 400 operatives and 200 other laborers. Expenditures to this time were not quite 40 per cent of the entire capital; it would not cost more than $250,000 to put the factory in successful operation.[2]

The directors were authorized to fix the salaries of the treasurer, superintendent, "and other officers and agents of the Company. . . ." Omission of the president was deliberate, since Gregg was known to be asking no pay.

Resignation of the treasurer, A. R. Taft, was responsible for a special meeting of the stockholders in October of this year. Since Taft did not retire as director, C. K. Huger withdrew from the board so that James H. Taylor, who had experience in the Charleston Mill, might be elected director and treasurer.[3] Taylor served as treasurer about eighteen months, living and carrying on his business in Charleston.[4] The mill now having been completed, George Kelly was elected the first superintendent, but he, too, served only a short time. Kelly was a New England man, and brought four or five skilled operatives with him from that section to assist in starting the new factory with native labor.[5]

Gregg urged on the third annual meeting that the capital of the company be further increased by $300,000. The committee appointed to examine the report expressed confidence in the management and recommended that application be made to the legislature for permission to carry out the president's proposal. In anticipation of such amendment of the charter it was resolved that 120 shares ($60,000) be sold. The stockholders at the time of this meeting were to be given first opportunity to subscribe (in proportion to their prior holdings), and if any shares remained untaken by June they might be purchased without reference to the size of original investment. Only if still unbought were they to be offered to the general public. The new shares were to be paid for in equal quarterly installments, beginning with January, 1850.[6]

As it turned out, the company's charter was not this year amended by the legislature to allow of the new stock being issued, so that when the stockholders met again it was deemed inexpedient to declare a dividend upon it. Instead, the president was authorized to issue notes for such amounts as had been paid in, these to receive 7 per cent interest. Apparently Mr. Taylor had retired as treasurer by the time of this meeting. The stockholders placed the election of secretary and treasurer in the hands of the directors, changing the by-laws to allow of this.[7] Gregg did not see Taylor withdraw without trying to retain him and, moreover, to have him live at Graniteville, which would allow him to take over many duties which Gregg had been performing. A later statement of Gregg says: "We offered him $2,500 per annum to take the office and live at Graniteville. He asked us $3,000, and had he accepted our offer and applied himself wholly to our business, I have no doubt but he would before this time have asked for a much higher

93

salary. After his refusal to accept $2,500 we went the rounds, offering $2,500 and $2,000 to different individuals. . . ."[8]

This was a troublesome period for Gregg. Instead of a relaxing of his work, he shouldered new responsibilities in the growing business. The superintendent chosen to succeed Mr. Kelly, though a good man and recommended by some of the best manufacturers of Rhode Island, "proved to be . . . entirely inadequate to the charge." the company sunk from twenty to thirty thousand dollars by the change, and Gregg was "compelled to be president, engineer and general manager of the factory for more than a year."[9]

In 1851 the situation was partially relieved by the election of James H. Montgomery, "a good manufacturer," as superintendent. Merely to comply with the by-laws, Mr. Montgomery was also named treasurer, but "he was not conversant with book-keeping and had quite as much as he could attend to in the management of the internal operations of the mill."[10] The treasurer would normally have done much more, of course, than is implied in the title, but Montgomery did not even have the safekeeping of the company's funds. "The great duty of financeering and acting as general agent fell entirely on my shoulders," Gregg said afterwards; "indeed I had received very little aid from Mr. Taylor; having his residence in Charleston precluded the possibility of his taking such charge as to give me relief."[11] It would be a mistake to think Gregg's account of this period egotistical. It is probably less than the fact. ". . . you will perceive that I was not merely President but on hand at all times to fill any situation that happened to be vacated. If a dam broke, I had to be there in the mud, as no one about could do the work so cheaply and accurately as myself. If a wheel broke down and I happened to be away on business, an express or telegraph came after me."[12] It is true that Howland & Taft, and afterwards A. R. Taft, of Charleston, "relieved very much the treasury department by managing the sales."[13]

A notable neglect on the part of the stockholders in the scrutiny of the company's accounts in the early years would indicate implicit confidence in Gregg's management, and also lack of practice in customs of corporate enterprise. To begin with, Gregg was not only generally responsible for the finances, but himself performed much of the work in both particular and routine matters. The incomplete assistance which he received from the first three treasurers—Taft, Taylor, and Montgomery—threw a special weight upon him.

He had made a point of the indifference of the stockholders of the Vaucluse Mill to that company's affairs during the first years of operation.[14] While by no means careless in the same degree, and while having the competent management of Gregg to rely upon, the Graniteville stockholders were far from meticulous in their oversight. At the annual meeting in 1849 a committee of three (K. Boyce, Lamb, McBride) had been appointed to examine the accounts of the company. The members of the committee were present at the 1850 meeting, but rendered the report that three ineffectual attempts had been made to get the committee together, and so nothing had been accomplished. Thereupon a committee of six was appointed for the purpose, any three of whom would be competent to act. A report was to be made to the directors within five weeks. Only two members of this committee were present in 1851 (Beach and Boyce), and they presented a report dated a couple of days previous to the annual meeting, signed by McCarter, the chairman, saying that he had been unable at any time in the year to assemble the committee, but that he personally had gone over the books with the treasurer and found all correct. Thereupon a new committee, of which Gregg was chairman, was instructed to examine the accounts for the past year and have them published. It was felt that this detail of management (as many others afterwards) should be drawn from Charleston to Graniteville; so it was provided that a committee of five be appointed to meet in the company's office on the day previous to the gathering of the stockholders, to examine the books.

The following year (1852) only five stockholders were present at the meeting, including Gregg and Jones; even Ker Boyce was absent. The old indifference to the accounts showed itself. "Mr. Wilkinson, the only member of the committee appointed at the last meeting to examine . . . the annual report of the treasurer, being called upon for a report, stated that he had forgotten his appointment, and that if he had attended according to the requirement of the resolution, no other member of the committee would have met him to discharge the duty."

A new committee was appointed for the ensuing year, and in 1853 rendered a report that showed some progress had been made in discovering that the accounts were not perfectly intelligible to the investors. The committee had discharged its duty "as well as the circumstances would allow. In consequence of an arrangement of the expenses of the establishment under different heads, your committee found it difficult to compare the vouchers supporting the various charges, as the same bills contained items that were properly carried under the different heads. They, however, are satisfied that all the charges are properly vouched for and the account correct." It was found that the treasurer had charged more than $4,000 for oil, starch, and other supplies to "sundry contingent expenses," whereas this should have been carried into the weekly statement of expense of manufacturing the goods.[15]

In 1854 the examining committee was satisfied after a not very minute scrutiny, the next year all in attendance save William Gregg examined the officers' reports, and in 1856 the only record is that the treasurer's report was adopted as read by the president.[16] And so it went until after Gregg's administration ended, when there was a new inventory of the company's assets, a new set of books was opened, periodic reports to the directors were ordered, and the employment of "a competent accountant" to assist the auditing committee was provided for.

97

The legislature (December 20, 1850) amended the Graniteville charter to allow of the increase of stock,[17] and the 1851 meeting of shareholders ordered that stock certificates be issued to cancel the company's interest-bearing notes. Anxiety to have the company known and understood by investors led to a resolution that the corrected charter and by-laws be published.

The minutes of this year for the first time contain a balance sheet, showing a profit and loss account of $1,014.31. The new $60,000 of stock had all been subscribed, bringing the total to $360,000. Real estate and machinery were valued at $320,199, and merchandise and materials at $87,946.03, which last would indicate a full operation of the plant.[18]

The directors were authorized, the following year, to enlarge the capital to $450,000, for the purpose of acquiring the machinery of the Charleston Cotton Factory. Two methods of doing this were proposed—the first by purchase of the machinery with proceeds of stock sold to present shareholders, the second through the acceptance of Graniteville stock by Ravenel & Company, owners of the Charleston Mill. The water power was to be fully tested to discover whether it was capable of turning the added machinery.[19]

The Charleston Mill had failed, but, from the fact that Graniteville's capital was not increased, it is certain that the project of taking over the equipment of the defunct factory was not carried through, in all probability due to the depressed state of industry.[20]

A very full treasurer's report for the calendar year 1851 in the hand of James Montgomery, with penciled amendments by Gregg, has been preserved. The hard times through which the company had passed are reflected in a loss on the year's business of $12,565.29, which left the commercial capital at $25,813.01. During the year 3,361 bales of cotton had been consumed, costing for the first six months an average of 11.17 cents per pound, but in the second six months easing down to 8.76 cents; the average cost during the year, including all expenses of transportation, was 10 cents. The loss by waste in the manufacturing process was 9.14 per cent. The principal product was 7/8 shirtings, 2,181,020 yards; the total output, with 4/4 sheetings and drillings, was 3,296,910 yards. The average total cost of manufacture per yard was 5.636 cents—1.561 for labor and 4.075 for stock. The average number of operatives was 270, and wages paid in the year amounted to $47,417.75, of which $731 was for repairs to outdoor property.

Foreign sales were through four commission firms—Thomas & Martin, Wyman, Appleton & Co., Marcus, Spring & Jeffers, and Cothran & Co. The commission charge of the last of these was 3 per cent, and of the others, with guarantee, 5 per cent. All the foreign sales amounted to $56,154.58; the total expenses on these sales ran all the way from 15.21 per cent down to 4.72 per cent. It is clear from the statement why Gregg, as will be seen later, was irked at the substantial amount

99

going to Howland & Taft, who had charge of the domestic sales. This firm sold directly 2,162,808 yards, which brought $136,984.68. On these sales the expenses were $7,321.17. In addition Howland & Taft received 1 per cent commission on the whole amount of the foreign sales, and ½ of 1 per cent on the net proceeds of foreign sales, which brought the total charge of this firm to $8,140.45, or 5.94 per cent on all sales.

The village in January, 1852, contained 881 persons —225 males over 12 years of age, 324 females over 12, 247 children under 12, and 85 "blacks and colored." There were 5 public buildings at this time—2 churches, a schoolhouse, hotel, and market house, the last three belonging to the company. The village had 13 stores, 6 of which were the company's. Of 107 dwellings, 83 belonged to the company, and their rent, with that of the stores, amounted to a trifle over 6 per cent on the investment. The school had an average of 106 scholars in attendance. With the exception of "common colds and such like complaints" the health of the village had been good. Deaths numbered 16—2 from old age and 4 in infancy. There had been 15 marriages and 15 births. All the property had been kept in first-rate repair, and it was declared that "the prospect now for doing a good business, so far as Graniteville is concerned, is much better than at the beginning of the past year."

The year 1852 marked the recovery of Graniteville from the unfavorable conditions of the previous two years. The company now made net earnings of 8 per cent.[21] The minutes of the stockholders covering this year contain nothing of interest save their signing by B. C. Hard, now appearing for the first time as secretary, and the resignation of C. K. Huger as director.[22]

Business continued to improve in 1853, net earnings this year being $30,596.48, or 11½ per cent.[23] The directors in 1854 were authorized to add 36 new looms and their complementary machinery, provided this could be got into the existing building and be purchased with a portion of the surplus capital. Gregg reported that he had entire confidence in the enterprise despite the high price of cotton and the necessity, for some years to come, of making heavy expenditures in the outdoor department, particularly for stone dams and waste-ways.

The first salary to be paid Gregg was provided for in 1854; he was to receive $1,500 per annum beginning with January of that year.[24] A salary was offered him only when the constant demands upon him requiring his presence at Graniteville determined him to sell his house in Charleston and retire from the lucrative jewelry business in that city, which paid him, as he said, five times what he had ever received from the manufacturing company.[25]

Fortunately, the full printed reports of president and treasurer for the year 1854 are available.[26] Gregg began by congratulating the company on the fact that, after the period of depression in which it commenced operations, it was now increasingly prosperous. In 1854 the net earnings amounted to a fraction over 18 per cent and would have exceeded 21 per cent had the stock of cloth on hand

101

been sold or valued at the price prevailing in the spring of 1855. No dividends had been paid out of the earnings of 1853, and $64,954.93 had been earned in 1854; out of this total of $95,551.41 two dividends were declared in 1854, amounting to $32,400, and another, $18,000, was declared in January of 1855. This left a dividable sum of roughly $45,000.[27] From this Gregg proposed to declare an extra dividend of 12 per cent, to be paid in stock. Supposing this division made, it was apparent that the company had paid within a fraction of 7 per cent on the entire capital from the time it was paid in, thus remunerating the stockholders for any loss of interest while the mill was being erected, and also for the depression years of 1850 and 1851.[28]

The property was in better condition than when the company began business. Wooden dams and waste-ways had gradually been replaced with masonry. Gregg thought it would cost $50,000 more than the original price to reproduce the plant, for in the intervening time there had been an increase in the expense of both labor and materials. In the year 1854, $8,000 had been paid out on machinery with a view to starting 36 more looms, which, with no other increase in charges except that for labor to operate it, would add one-eighth to the company's productive power. The new equipment would more than pay for itself within twelve months.

This brought forward the importance of extending the work to the full capacity of the water power, equivalent to 500 looms. Dams, canals, wheel-pits, and conducting pipes to carry water to three wheels were in readiness.

Why should the company hesitate to spend $100,000 when the income would be nearly doubled thereby? The picker house was large enough for 15,000 spindles; the only new factory building required for the expansion would be a one-story weave house to hold all the looms.

Something of the optimism that preceded the panic of 1857 is seen in Gregg's recommendation that new stock be issued to the amount of $240,000, which would raise the total capital to $600,000. This additional stock would complete the new works and give a needed cash capital. The company had $98,000 cash capital on January 1, 1855, but there was also an interest charge of $10,800 for the past year, which showed that the company was always a large borrower. Gregg explained why so much working capital was needed: "Our cotton is purchased for cash. We pay cash for all our labor, while, on an average, four months elapse from the time the cotton is purchased until the goods are in the market; these again are frequently four months more on hand and are then sold on a credit of eight months; so that you will perceive our outlay is always a year or more in advance of our returns."[29]

If the present stockholders were unable or unwilling to subscribe for the new shares, then outside capitalists should be welcomed, Gregg thought, for additional investment would increase the profits from present capital, by enabling the use of all the water power.

Gregg referred to "a prevailing notion in the public mind, that the success of the Graniteville Company is an accidental exception to the general rule; that its

103

eminent success is alone owing to my skill and industry, and that so soon as I am taken from you, your brilliant prospects will vanish, your affairs relapse, and the property become unproductive." This idea he branded as a vital error and one that should be corrected, since it tended to depreciate the value of the stock. "I am willing to take all the credit that is due me," he said, "for judiciously locating and building up the establishment, and for its present organization: that is the important item on which the success or failure of a manufacturing establishment depends." This accomplished, he could select from among the stockholders many men, preferably with mercantile training, who with a little practice in the business could conduct the factory with entire success.[30] To show how strongly he believed that, should he die or resign, his place could be filled by another, he was willing to take more than his proportion of the new stock, and put in $20,000 to $25,000 toward the new extension, as a sure and profitable investment for his children.[31]

Under the guise of addressing his own stockholders, Gregg in this report really spoke to the moneyed men of the South in trying to stimulate cotton manufactures in the section. He knew there were misgivings; there was fear that original projectors were doomed to fail, and that plants would be sold for a fraction of first cost. There had been instances seeming to justify such pessimism, but he believed he could analyze the cause of disasters and point the way to avoidance.

Southerners were too apt to think they could erect an establishment for half what it would cost in New England. This was a mistake. The South required first-rate plants. Advantages in cheap water power and building materials were offset by the North's facilities for making machinery and the saving in freight there. He clearly discerned the genuine elements of superiority in the South, which are the main forces in the present movement of Northern mills to this section. He believed that, granted a well built and organized factory, "our abundant supply of cheap labor, our mild climate, and above all, the raw material so cheap at our door, and a home market for our products, give us, with good management, certain and large profits, while the cotton manufacturers of no other country can more than make a living."

Aside from the want of good day-to-day management, there were, Gregg said, five principal causes of failure in cotton manufacturing, not only in the South, but in every country where the industry was introduced. Before naming these he pointed to the example of Lowell, Massachusetts, in embracing, in 1820, the corporate form of enterprise. This was the right method anywhere, and the necessary one in the South. The business, to succeed, must be on a large scale, and command the services of skilled directors, and this, only associated capital could guarantee. "This branch of industry must, therefore, be carried on by corporations; and I can only say to those who wish to form companies, follow our

105

example, examine our establishment, look into its organization, go to New-England where information may be obtained, and above all things avoid the errors that I am now about to point out."

The cardinal sins were: (1) an injudicious selection of machinery, and of the kind of goods to be made; (2) a lack of steady, efficient, and cheap motive power; (3) a poor location; (4) lack of religious and moral training of operatives; and (5) last and most important, to embark on such an enterprise without sufficient capital.[32]

In deciding upon the character of the product, it was a mistake to try to supply the home demand by making a little of everything. Nor should a large mill be erected to run on osnaburgs alone. Osnaburgs were already overdone at the South. There was not half a cent a pound difference in the cost of manufacturing osnaburgs and sheetings and shirtings, yet the latter, of Graniteville make, were selling for 23 to 24 cents a pound in Charleston, while the former brought 16 and 17. Only the South took osnaburgs, while the whole world took sheetings and shirtings. "The first thing to be learned by a southern manufacturer is, that he must ultimately, if not immediately, look to a wholesale market for his products; and this seems, hitherto, to have been almost entirely overlooked. . . . He should have no other aim, than to take the place of the importer in supplying the wholesale dealer. . . . In order to do this, every operation about the establishment should be simple and direct. The whole establishment, however large, should be built and arranged to make some one thing rapidly,

cheaply, and perfectly. Success would be certain anywhere at the South with such a factory. . . ."[33]

As to power, he thought that steam should be avoided
in all instances at the South, as too costly to be used in
any place suitable for the location of a cotton factory.
It was good economy to install only the best water wheels
and other power equipment, and he urged that more
power be provided than the technical treatises calculated
was necessary.

A cotton factory should not be located in a city; there
it would be impossible "to control the moral habits of
the operatives, and to keep up a steady, efficient, and
cheap working force." Country people coming to a city
would be frightened away by any appearance of
epidemic. Hands must be paid more in a city location.
He must have had Charleston in mind when he said many
labored under the erroneous impression "that a declining city may be resuscitated by the introduction of large
manufactories, giving employment to the poor people
and occupation to the untenanted houses." Machine
shops and handicraftsmen built up a town, but a large
cotton factory would bring in country people who, injured by city life, would add to the pauper population.
A city which sighed for industry would do best to follow
Boston's example, and invest its money in building up
manufacturing towns in the region round about.[34]

Companies had attributed their inability to procure
steady, efficient labor to unwillingness of the poor people
of the South to work. In refuting this error, Gregg spoke
from experience at Graniteville, and betrayed an in-

107

sight on which, consciously or not, the industry in the South has generally proceeded since. "There never was," he declared, "a greater mistake." These companies had not known that "to get a steady supply of workers, a population must be collected that will regard themselves as a community, and that two essential elements are necessary to the building up, moral growth, and stability of such a collection of people, viz: a *church* and a *school-house*. There is not a better class on the face of the globe, from which to procure factory laborers, than the poor people of South-Carolina."[35]

There was not a single instance known to him of a cotton manufacturing enterprise, with the exception of Graniteville, where the capital had not been insufficient. Particularly with a corporation, lack of working capital created distrust which was apt to render its case desperate. Capitalists would soon come to shun it as they would a pestilence. And the auctioneer's hammer would end the first chapter in its history.

The stockholders' meeting requested Gregg to omit from his report specific references to establishments and individuals before it was published, but for some reason this was not attended to. He went on to instance the failure of the Saluda Factory, as he did at other times, and cited chapter and verse. Organized in 1832, this mill had stood for 23 years a warning beacon to the South.[36] Despite many drawbacks, the South had experienced no positive failures with the exception of the Saluda Company and the Charleston Factory, and few establishments had been embarrassed. There was no failure in Georgia during the pressure of 1850 and 1851, and most of the mills in that State were now doing well—those around Augusta were paying 20 to 30 per cent. The DeKalb Factory, near Camden, was making 15 per cent, and Vaucluse was earning money. Graniteville had, very naturally, experienced difficulty in training operatives at the start, for Gregg said "had our establishment been as well organized, and supplied with skilful hands as at present, we might have paid dividends even in 1850 and '51."

Graniteville, he said, was the first factory establishment in any of the Southern States to put systematic effort on the moral culture of operatives. The factories were looked upon as degraded and vicious, and he believed the poor people were right in refusing to put their children in them. At Graniteville, the new system had more than realized expectations. "We have always had a pressure upon us for situations, and could in a month stock another factory with hands, while the Augusta and Columbus Companies are always short of help, notwithstanding they pay much higher wages than we do."[37]

Mr. Montgomery, the superintendent and treasurer, who, after much experience in Scotland, had had charge of large mills in New England and New York, "thinks that for stability, controllability and productive power, they [the operatives] are not surpassed anywhere." A majority of the overseers were South Carolinians who learned the business at Graniteville. "The population of Graniteville is made up mainly from the poor of Edgefield, Barnwell, and Lexington Districts. From extreme poverty and want, they have become a thrifty, happy, and contented people." Graniteville might regard itself as the pioneer in developing the character of the poor of the State. When the people were first brought together, the seventy-nine out of a hundred grown girls who could neither read nor write were a by-word around the country, but that reproach had been removed. It is learned from this report that in addition to the week-day school and Sunday schools, Graniteville had a night school. "Singing-masters, music-teachers, writing-masters and itinerant lecturers all find patronage in Graniteville. . . ." The savings bank already had upwards of $9,000 on deposit, and Gregg believed that when the new stock was issued, operatives would be among the subscribers, despite the shares being $500.[38]

"A noble race of people!" he exclaimed, "reduced to a condition but little above the wild Indian . . . or the European gipsy, without education, and in many instances unable to procure the food necessary to develop the natural man." They had made no progress in the past hundred years, and would make none unless some employment be devised for them. They alone of South Carolinians seemed disinclined to emigrate. (Gregg was interested in improving the general level of life among the Poor Whites, but in addition to accomplishing this, Graniteville has had a number of natives of the place who rose to positions of measurable distinction—in business, the professions, and government service.)[39]

Planters looked to an El Dorado of the West, and men of means sent their capital to work in the North or elsewhere. Gregg, the patriot of Southern economic development, was deeply moved by this inveterate sapping of strength. The millions that had left Charleston alone, as he had said earlier in his *Domestic Industry*, would have drained the swamps, built railroads, and spun and woven the State's cotton. He brought his complaint home to the stockholders by instancing the heavy investments which, after the death of Ker Boyce, it was discovered he had made in New York and the far West.[40]

The treasurer's report showed that costs of labor and of cotton were lower than in 1851.[41] The output was larger than in 1851, standing this year at 3,854,059 yards, and the percentage of waste was now distinctly lower—7.81 as against 9.14 for 1851. The factory was making progress in efficiency. The heaviest single outlay was for cotton, $121,254.79, and the second largest was for wages to operatives, $46,834.13. Salaries amounted to only $5,100. About $3,500 had been spent in improving the company's outdoor property, most of it about the water. Curiously, though every other item is mentioned, the cost of the new water wheel itself is not given.[42]

The village had a population of 830; mortality among children was alarming—there were 43 births, and 28 deaths of children—though Mr. Montgomery made no comment. All had been peaceful, and the school had from 60 to 90 pupils.[43]

The meeting agreed to Gregg's proposal to increase the stock by $240,000 inclusive of a stock dividend of $42,000. As it turned out, no new stock was subscribed.

111

James P. Boyce, son of Ker Boyce, who was to play an important part in the affairs of the company, was elected to the directors on the resignation of General Jones.[44] Gregg's salary was increased to $2,500, and presents were to be given to officers and overseers.[45]

There are no records to augment the brief and uninformative minutes covering the years 1855-57.[46] At Graniteville as elsewhere all must have gone swimmingly. Gregg took pride, in 1857, in reading to the stockholders from a letter from Mr. H. Bartlett, "a large manufacturer at the North," paying high compliment to the Graniteville Company. It is easy to imagine the pleasure which Gregg had in returning courtesies he had received at the hands of New England cotton manufacturers, by entertaining visitors to the Horse Creek Valley.

Depression following panic had set in by the time of the meeting in April, 1858. Gregg in an oral report alluded to "the gloomy prospect of manufacturers, and the necessity of the company's advancing capital for commercial purposes, and suggested the propriety of issuing new stock."[47]

The lack of commercial banking facilities was a hindrance to all enterprise in the South; before and long after this period of special money stringency, Graniteville was a borrower from private individuals. For a year or eighteen months before and during the panic of 1857 the company had the use of $90,000 loaned by Gregg, paying probably 7 per cent. (This must have been capital which Gregg withdrew from the jewelry business

112

in Charleston). The company was paying from 8 to 10 per cent for bank loans, and had Gregg wished to take back his funds he might have bought commercial paper bringing 10 to 20 per cent interest. "At one time during the panic," he said later, "I could not get a dollar from any bank on the best mercantile paper, and I was forced to go into the streets of Augusta and purchase cotton with the Graniteville Company's note and my endorsement." The company had never had a dollar idle for more than ten days, waiting to be invested in cotton. "My correspondence with Mr. Taft [the sales agent] will give . . . abundant proof of the difficulties we have labored under for the want of cash means. As late as the 12th January, 1858, I advised him that it would be impossible to continue our operations at Graniteville under the eight months system of credits. To relieve that difficulty he adopted the plan of giving the purchaser the option of giving an eight months note or taking a discount of 5 per cent and give a four months note. It will thus be seen, that we have been giving at the rate of 15 per cent to obtain such short paper as would enable us to realize through banks."[48]

William Gregg, Jr., was elected treasurer, giving $20,000 bond with two sureties. Preparatory to an adjourned meeting, the treasurer's reports of previous years were to be condensed and printed. The stockholders assembled a month later[49] in Charleston, the exigency in the company's affairs helping to secure a large attendance. Gregg reported assets of manufactured goods on hand, cotton, business paper, and un-

113

closed sales amounting to $210,000, being about $55-000 in excess of the indebtedness on account of borrowed money. He proposed, in furtherance of his plan of issuing new stock which should be taken up quickly, that the legislature be applied to for permission to lower the shares from $500 to $50. In this Gregg had a double purpose—to allow the operatives, for their own advantage, to become stockholders, as he had seen them at the Merrimac Mill at Lowell; and to tap a new source of capital at a time when the company was hard pressed. The legislature granted this permission the same year.[50] By 1859, however, Graniteville was prosperous again. A 20 per cent stock dividend was declared and the previous decision to reduce the shares to $50 each was rescinded.[51]

Apparently Gregg called the directors together immediately on the adjournment of this meeting in April, 1859, and at this time the first misunderstanding in the Graniteville official family occurred. It led on to a defining of Gregg's whole service to the company, and was undoubtedly an advantage in the end. It is not unlikely that reaction from the strain of the panic and depression was partly responsible for the frank expression that was given to differences. That directors lived in Charleston and had little practical knowledge of affairs at the factory entered also; beside, there may have been jealousy of Gregg which grew as he added one success to another. Robert Owen at New Lanark had found himself even worse beset by his investors. The whole episode sheds light upon William Gregg's unstinting contribution to the enterprise.

114

When William Gregg, Jr., came from college, his father persuaded him to go into a mercantile house for two years for business training. The young man was then brought home to Graniteville and placed in charge of the outdoor department, receiving no pay from the company but taking the place of a man who had received $50 a month. Gregg paid his son from his own pocket. The outdoor duties occupied only half his time; so William learned the office routine, bookkeeping, and the making up of complicated statements of manufacturing operations. At the end of two years of this service, his application to business and his thorough acquaintance with the details of management at Graniteville being remarked by everybody, his father recommended that William be elected treasurer at the nominal salary of $50 a month, he supplementing this from his own salary by $1,000. This was accordingly done, as has been seen, in 1858.[52]

When Gregg launched Graniteville he had retired from business with an ample fortune. As was noticed earlier, he meant to employ an engineer to construct the plant, equip it, and start it going. This he found it impossible to do; so he threw himself into the work intending, when the factory was complete, to procure a capable agent to manage it. But this second was as much a dream as the first. The treasurer either lived in Charleston or, if at Graniteville, was in only nominal performance of treasury duties. A superintendent from the North proved himself impracticable. There were next to no trained cotton manufacturing executives in the South. Gregg was toiling away without compensa-

115

tion, as president, engineer, general manager, treasurer; he was changing the whole economic habit of the local community, and was educating a wider Southern sentiment, which had been either apathetic or hostile to manufacturing corporations. Under these circumstances, he had to look to his own family for assistants.

"I have long cherished the hope," he explained, "that my sons as they grew up, would become manufacturers, and in that way I would have security that my large property in the concern would be taken care of, and I would be gradually relieved from arduous labors that seemed to be fastened on me." William had entered on this program; Gregg's second son, James, on finishing college spent two years in the Graniteville machine shop, then went to New England for some months and to Europe for a year to study the industry, afterwards taking charge of Vaucluse. Still another son was at this time working in the machine shop.[53]

When Gregg called the directors together, he told them that his son William would not continue to serve for $50, and that he (Gregg, Sr.) was not disposed to supplement this with $1,000 from his own pocket any longer. He proposed, consequently, that the company pay William $2,000, and that the president's salary be left at $2,500, as fixed four years earlier. The prospect of increasing expenses by $1,400 "startled the board," and they would have liked to throw responsibility on the stockholders. After long and futile deliberation, which was necessarily embarrassing to Gregg, the directors adjourned to meet in Charleston. "My son,"

Gregg said, "insisted on resigning immediately, and I regret very much that I overruled him, by a promise of an additional $500 from my salary, and assurance that the board of directors could not be so ignorant of our affairs as to throw him off." The directors met on the matter again May 11, "when we talked the whole evening away without deciding," and agreed to meet the next night. William resigned, and previous to the meeting Gregg communicated this to the directors, offering as a solution that he himself serve in both capacities of president and treasurer at a salary of $5,000. In conversation with Mr. Beach, one of the directors, Gregg suggested as an alternative that the board give him $4,500 or $5,000 to be expended in the salary of president and treasurer, and he would stand between them and the stockholders in whatever he did.

"Had either of these propositions been acceded to," Gregg told the stockholders, "I should have tried to obtain the services of my son; failing to do that, should have looked for a treasurer in some other man." But the directors had been made parsimonious by prosperity. They looked only at the instant shilling and not at the remoter pound. Gregg's anxiety to get his sons into the business was natural and wise; his only impropriety was in not regarding a prejudice which, however unreasonable, was emphatic. "My verbal proposition," he continued, "was not delivered, the written one rejected on the ground, that the directors did not feel authorized to make an arrangement so materially increasing the expense of the Company for this *department* of its *manage-*

ment."[54] Further, they doubted their authority under the by-laws; they urged that Gregg call a meeting of the stockholders, then urged that he should not. Injured and indignant, he of course did call the stockholders together and laid the whole matter before them.

The meeting was held at the Charleston Hotel, June 22, 1859. It is probable that those large old rooms have witnessed few gatherings of more interest in the economic history of South Carolina. Of the 631 shares present, Blackwood represented 108; J. M. Perry, acting for the estate of Joel Smith, 100; Boyce, 100; E. Tweedy for the estate of McBride, 40, and Gregg himself, 79. Gregg explained why he was laying his case before the stockholders, and read them a long statement (from which some quotation has been made above) besides having the secretary read letters that passed between Gregg and Taft, Beach, and Allen. Gregg's statement is of intense interest, not only for the light which it throws upon his personality, but because it developed his whole policy as a manufacturer who was breaking new ground. His designs, particularly with respect to internal management and the sale of the product, were up to the best standards of today, when the South has had seventy-five years more of industrial experience.

Gregg declared that he could not remain under the imputation of having asked from the company more than he and his son were worth; rather than that, he would abandon his interest in the factory. "The action of the board has deprived me of the services of the most efficient agent I have ever had. . . ."[55] This is the first retrograde step that we have ever made, and places me

118

in a situation to meet embarrassments at every point. It cuts up by the root many plans which we had in view and others in progress which were to diversify our products." He then unfolded his purpose of accomplishing two objects which bulk large in the program of cotton manufacturing in the South today—the finishing of goods at the plant (or at any rate near by), and the direct sale of products. "We were making arrangements," he explained, "to put up a dyeing establishment, with a view to make stripes and denims. [This scheme of Gregg's was delayed just 65 years; Graniteville now has a model dyeing plant for heavy goods named for William Gregg.] My son William was posted up in these matters and was to superintend getting up the works and was to assist in their management when complete."

The directors had acted in ignorance of the responsibilities of a resident treasurer, "and of the talent, practicability and industry that is requisite. They were wholly ignorant of our affairs and how could it be otherwise? They were never about Graniteville and were of necessity uninformed as to the toil and trouble of managing a capital of nearly a half million of dollars and a thousand uneducated people. To call the directors together at Graniteville cost each of them the expense of $15 and the loss of three days; nothing but special emergencies could justify that. To carry them figures and statements to look over in Charleston gave them little or no light on the subject."

Business men in the South up to this time were merchants, not manufacturers. Gregg, in his dealings with his directors, was confronting a Charleston mercantile tradition with novel upcountry industrial problems. This difference came out acutely in Gregg's plans for marketing the goods from the factory rather than through a Charleston sales agent, and very likely this was the true apple of discord in the whole matter. It will be remembered that the Graniteville goods had been disposed of through A. R. Taft in Charleston, a director of the company. Referring to the directors' notion that the treasurer's complicated duties at Graniteville were subordinate to the sales agency, Gregg reminded the stockholders that "one of the gentlemen who compose your board and who acted in this matter, received from us last year in commissions and interest on commissions over $5,500, exclusive of drayage, postage, insurance and other incidental expenses. I do not name this to bring that gentleman in an unfavorable light before the company. He has been a faithful agent and has acted with great prudence and discretion, and worked for charges, as low probably as any responsible agent of equal ability would have done."

He was not quarreling with the man, but with the system. ". . . the agency labor ought to be done at Graniteville, and would be if we had the right man at the treasury desk. We were looking forward to the consummation of that object and had commenced by taking charge of the sales west of the Savannah,[56] and although not ready now, I did confidently look forward to the day, when with a good treasurer we would be able to dispense with our valuable agent in Charleston, and sell all our goods at the factory." William had shown acuteness, as merchant and manufacturer, in these plans. Their joint labors, Gregg believed, would have resulted in increased profits, in saving the company many thousands in expenses "and in placing us on as good or a better footing than any similar establishment in the country." They had meant to visit early in May New Orleans and St. Louis to procure orders "for all the goods we could spare from the Charleston market, without the help of agencies in the West. By working to order we could have saved to the company the expenses of the Augusta, Nashville, Knoxville and St. Louis agencies"—between $3,000 and $5,000 per annum. "The great field of operation must of necessity be at Graniteville, where you require intelligent, active, enterprising and practical men. No agency can compare in importance with the treasury department, and to get your work well done you will find it necesary to pay for it."

With a good business man under him at Graniteville, Gregg could have imitated the English system of selling at the factory, he thought, and frequently on order. "The manufacturers of this country are beginning to realize that the English have a wonderful advantage over them in their cash system and absence of commission agencies. The interest and expenses they save, and that we do not, is equivalent to a fine profit. . . ." In his farewell report, the year of his death, as will be seen later, Gregg dealt at greater length with the evils of entanglement with commission houses which extend credit and are represented on the board of directors of the

121

manufactory, evils which the South has known in abundant measure. Even as early as 1859 he is found observing that sales from the factory "would give . . . a direct control over prices which are now governed by the commission merchants of our cities and . . . who frequently rule down prices of goods without a seeming cause and generally without any reference to the cost of production." And again: "It is the policy of our company to keep out of the hands of commission merchants, and never to take advances on their [the company's] goods. It has led to the ruin of many a corporation, and sacrificed many enterprising individuals."[57] Graniteville's goods now had a wide reputation, were sought for by the best merchants from New York to New Orleans, and were "known to almost every Southern consumer. It is doubtful whether there is any establishment in the whole country that could so easily adopt the system of selling goods at home."

The remainder of Gregg's statement to the stockholders, in appealing from the ruling of the directors, was chiefly concerned with two points—the charge that he was showing favoritism to his three sons, and that he himself was engaged in projects which distracted his interest from the success of Graniteville. He broached both of these questions bluntly. "Some dissatisfied stockholders have openly accused me," he said, "of a desire to make sinecures for my sons, at the expense of the Graniteville Company. There never was a more unjust accusation, for if there is anything in my whole adminis-

tration for which I ought to have credit, it is, that I have
never allowed any one to eat idle bread."[58]

The objection raised against Gregg himself grew out
of his interest in the Vaucluse Mill, and his participation
in politics. It is a comment on the industrial inexperience of even the best business men in the South of the
day that they did not understand that the development
of other cotton mills near Graniteville, particularly if
they were in the Gregg family, would be of advantage
to the initial enterprise. They thought of the crowding
of a local market, while Gregg looked at the resulting
increased efficiency, through a supply of trained executives and operatives, which would contribute to a coun-
try-wide business. The whole process of localization of
industries in America gives the lie to their fears.

Gregg put the case squarely: "Some hints were thrown
out that I have become a politician, and was engaged
in a work at Vaucluse [this factory must have been idle
for some years previous] that would absorb my attention and render me valueless to the Graniteville Company and therefore I ought not to ask the company for
a salary. This was brought to my view by a member of
the board. I was in hopes that our stockholders would
cherish the idea of my extending my investments in
manufacturing in the immediate vicinity of Graniteville
even to the extent of my entire fortune, as being a sure
means of enlisting the entire and undivided energies of
myself, and sons, in that branch of business, and I felt
a confident hope that they would look far enough ahead

123

to see that the education of my sons to be manufacturers would in all probability result in a great security for the successful management of our Graniteville property after I am gone. Vaucluse is not in competition with Graniteville." There was an unworthy selfishness in some of the directors who objected to seeing Gregg enter into the improvement of Vaucluse, when he had been entirely the property of the Graniteville Company before. And maybe there was the contradictory feeling that, if he were interested elsewhere, Graniteville was strong enough to get along without him.

But whatever the animus of directors, Gregg pointed the lesson to the stockholders. "It is more than likely," Gregg assured them, "that the new investments I am now making in that way will settle and fasten down in Horse Creek Valley all my sons, and although they may not be disposed to take office in the service of the Graniteville Company, they will be large owners of the stock, manufacturers by profession and I trust good business men. Is it not obvious to you all," he asked, "that such a state of things would be of infinite advantage to your establishment? It is that class of men that we now need among us to guard against mismanagement and secure success." Gregg was justified in telling the stockholders that, viewing the matter in this light, he could not save his "astonishment and mortification" to see the directors refuse to give $4,500 for the joint services of his son and himself; and it was proper, too, to remind them that the Augusta Company, "composed of the most intelligent gentlemen of that city," after using every effort they

124

could to procure his services, had employed an untried man at a salary of $5,000 to perform duties not nearly so complicated as those at Graniteville.

James Gregg was now in immediate charge of Vaucluse; his father had been giving much time to the construction of a stone dam there, but this would soon be completed, and he would be needed only to give his son good advice about the conduct of the enterprise.[59]

As to the charge that he had been distracted by political activities, Gregg said that he was elected to the legislature in 1856 with a minimum of time given to campaigning, and that he would not involve himself again in such a fight as attended his second campaign.

Gregg drew for the stockholders a lively picture of the manifold duties of the resident agent and treasurer, and adverted to the disastrous experience of neighboring companies which had put faith in poor managers. This part of his statement must have disposed those who heard it to leave the filling of the position to Gregg's choice. The entire responsibility—fiscal, industrial, and moral—for the enterprise, with upwards of 900 people and $400,000 of capital, must fall to the agent. He must be manufacturer, merchant, cotton buyer, and judge of men. He must manage 10,000 acres of company land, and give intimate oversight to the village of workers. He must not be led away by plausible notions. A company in Georgia had failed utterly, with just such machinery as that at Graniteville. The company which took over the plant was persuaded by a new overseer to throw out the traveler spindles

125

("I think the best spindle in existence," Gregg said) and substitute cap spindles, such as Gregg was discarding in the modernizing of Vaucluse. The contractor who did the work in the Georgia mill had almost persuaded some of those at Graniteville to employ him there also, and it was clear that Gregg had scotched this danger. Gregg had advised the owner of the Saluda Factory not to permit a new agent to make changes in the machinery, he being "a notionate fellow." This advice was disregarded, the owner lost $30,000, and the agent was out of a situation.

He could not resist the opportunity of contrasting the control of Graniteville with that of similar establishments at the South, "when they have gone by the board by scores, for the want of proper management." The Augusta Factory, precisely similar to their own, and started simultaneously, had sunk its entire capital and was now in new hands. The paper company in Horse Creek Valley "passed through a period of unprecedented prosperity in that line of business, and is now tottering on the very verge of bankruptcy."[60] Could it be, that after he had toiled for the company thirteen years, and made such a reputation for the factory that a shingle stuck out anywhere with "Graniteville Shirtings and Sheetings" would bring unsolicited customers, the corporation would continue to pay commissions and freights to sell goods, and yet "stickle at the idea of advancing the pay of important officers and faithful agents a few hundred dollars?" Seeing how he had worked through life and brought up his sons to work, should not

126

the thought of his creating sinecures for them be dispelled from every man's mind? That Gregg had told the directors the company could not well do without him had produced "unpleasant feelings of dependence," and given uneasiness to stockholders. "It would probably have been better that I should not have dropped such an expression, but the stockholders must look at the facts as they exist, and it must stare all right in the face, that such is the case; but they should bear in mind that if it be a calamity, it falls on me more heavily than any of you. We are common copartners. . . . I am to be the greatest loser among you from bad management at Graniteville. By the very nature of things, you will always be in the power of somebody."

In 1855 Gregg had told the stockholders that since he had given the factory its organization and impetus, any one of several available business men could carry on the enterprise should he drop out. Now he was talking differently. Perhaps he was speaking a little for effect in the first instance, and probably added experience had taught him the reverse by 1859. Anyhow, his closing remarks were not needed to bring the stockholders to decision between Gregg and the directors. There was not much danger of their walking through the door which he flung wide to them: "Whenever you are tired of me, Gentlemen, I am ready to quit your service. There is no other corporation in existence I would hire my time to. You may get a talented agent, but rest assured if he be a lazy man, he will permit your property to go to dilapidation, and your village people

127

to relapse into dissipation, vice and idleness. If he be a visionary man, he will waste your profits and your capital in alterations and improvements that are not needed. There is just this difference in management: on the one hand you may have your property kept in splendid order and clear $50,000 per annum; on the other hand, you may not realize any profit, and by gradual degrees, permit your property to go into dilapidation."

It would seem that Gregg's opponents were not wholly silent. J. P. Allen, one of the directors, "addressed the meeting at some length, defining his position," and H. R. Banks brought it to the notice of the stockholders that the minutes of the stockholders and those of the directors were not on hand. Things were beginning to take an unpleasant turn, but "at this stage of the proceeding" Dr. Boyce proposed that a committee consider the condition of the company and report to an adjourned meeting that afternoon. This committee (consisting of Boyce, Perrin, Kerrison, Springs, and Huger) brought in a set of resolutions which, unanimously adopted, scored a complete victory for Gregg over the fearsome directors. The wording (after an opening statement that they had heard with pain and regret of a misunderstanding between the president and directors) deserves quotation; it was resolved: "(1) *That we have unbounded confidence in* both president and directors, and believe both have acted from upright motives; (2) That we have learned with unfeigned regret that we are to lose the services of Mr. William Gregg, Jr., and that this company will look forward with a lively hope that time may bring about such a change of circumstances, as to give us an opportunity to avail ourselves of his services again; (3) That we view with satisfaction the reopening of the Vaucluse Factory by Mr. Gregg and his son, as we regard it as an additional security to our interests at Graniteville. . . ." The fifth and last section provided that William Gregg, Sr., be appointed to the double office of president and treasurer at a salary of $5,000, until a suitable man could be found to fill the treasurership, when Gregg would retire from that office with a salary of $2,500 as president.[61]

A complication in the whole situation as between Gregg and the directors, and an episode which has historical significance for the Southern textile industry, had been William Gregg, Jr.'s, activity as proprietor of a store in Graniteville while he was serving as treasurer of the company. As his father said, "in addition to the labors which I put on him for the Company, he had various little speculations of his own going on, among other things an interest in a store for supplying the people of Graniteville with necessaries." When it was expected that his salary as treasurer would be raised, he promised to give up the store. The store property was probably one which Gregg, Sr., and Ker Boyce had purchased from the company in the beginning. Mr. Springs (unable to secure an expression on the point from the stockholders, as it would seem) brought up the question in a motion which would abolish one bad practice and substitute another hardly better, if at all. He

129

moved that "... inasmuch as it will require no increase
of capital, ... the president and directors may establish
a store at Graniteville for the purpose of supplying our
people and the country around, and with a view to barter
for cotton, ... but we deem it inadvisable that any of
the officers of the company should have any interest in
any store or calling at Graniteville outside of his special
employment." The meeting struck out all after the word
"cotton," but Gregg was glad, so far as he was concerned, to go along with the whole reform; he said
it was desirable that the company get back all the land
formerly sold, so that Graniteville could never be taxed
as a village, and he and the estate of Ker Boyce were
willing to sell back to the company the three store lots
and the buildings on them for the price originally paid
for the land alone. This was arranged then and there.
The company town with the company store did not then
appear to be objectionable. Plantations with their com-
missaries presented a parallel in agriculture. The village
was in the deep country, and the company was looked
to for every facility of life. The abuses which afterwards entered into company ownership of towns and
particularly of stores (too great paternalism, over-
charging, and avoidance of cash payment of wages)
were never farther from becoming dangers than in
Graniteville at this time.

So ended this meeting of William Gregg with his
stockholders, one of the most interesting of which we
have record. It was important because it marked the arrival of full unity of corporate action, and confirmed

Gregg in his policy of constructive leadership. He had impressed the lesson that every corporation is in the hands of somebody; the care should be to discover a wise and energetic general manager.

At the next regular meeting, April, 1860, Gregg said that some of the machinery wearing out, he had ordered new from England; and he "alluded to his intention of commencing preparations to make dyed goods." It is known from a later statement[62] that the company "projected large additions to their works, in which they included dyeing, bleaching and making canton flannel." The treasurer's report showed all in prosperous condition. There was no hint of the coming storm of war. William Gregg, Jr., was made a director, which was honorable amend for the row that had been kicked up over him earlier.[63]

CHAPTER VII

THE DECLARED PROTECTIONIST

Leaving the Graniteville story for a time, we may become acquainted in the next chapters with some of Gregg's other activities of this period—particularly his interest in the question of the State Bank, his desire to encourage industry through the South Carolina Institute, his advocacy of plank roads, and his adventures in politics.

Gregg supported James Henry Hammond in his opposition to the Bank of the State of South Carolina and to State subsidies to railroads. Hammond's antipathy for banks was older than Gregg's. Commencing with a dislike of them as early as 1834, he devoted much of his first governor's message to the legislature to an attack on the institution mentioned, and in 1847, under the name of "Anti-Debt," published a series of detailed articles with similar intent.[1] Though seven years Hammond's senior, Gregg did not turn his attention to public questions so early; he was accumulating a competence in his private business, and not until the middle of the decade of the forties, when he had enjoyed some leisure, did he express views on matters of State policy.

Hammond's articles in the *Mercury* were the occasion of a widespread controversy in the State.[2] Gregg had shown his imperfect sympathy with banks in his pamphlets on *Domestic Industry* and *Charters of Incorpora-*

tion two years before. Miss Merritt, the biographer of
Hammond, thinks the two met first in 1845 in connection
with Gregg's work before the legislature in securing the
charter for Graniteville, and says both "thought that the
Bank directors individually and collectively hampered
Gregg's cotton mill at every possible turn."[3] Gregg had
evidently been following Hammond's articles with keen
interest, for he wrote him from Charleston, November
15, 1847, on the appearance of the thirteenth number.
"You strike with a sledge hammer, each stroke will leave
an impression. The article is the street talk of the day."
He went on to explain, in the manner of one in Hammond's secrets, that he had taken occasion to draw
Elmore and Gadsden out on the writings of Anti-Debt
and No-Alarmist. They both seemed to know that it was
Hammond who wrote against the railroads, but they
were going right ahead with plans for an elaborate extension of railway lines, which to Gregg seemed pre-
posterous.[4]

Two days later Gregg wrote again, citing further circumstances unfavorable to the South Carolina Railroad,[5]
and a fortnight afterwards was still on the theme. He
had just read Hammond's articles in pamphlet form
and liked them better even than when he read them separately. None spoke against them except Elmore and
Gadsden. "Good will certainly grow out of them. The
ammunition of your opponents is expended. . . ."[6]

A year later, in the midst of the financial stringency
of 1848, Gregg wrote to Hammond urging that then was
the time to give the Bank the *coup de grace*. "We are

133

now suffering under one of the severest money pressures," he said, "that I have witnessed in Charleston, and I am satisfied that the Rail Road Bank and the Bank of the State are only allowed to exist by an indisposition on the part of banks and individuals to make a move against them. Both enjoy the unenviable reputation of making a living by kiting, that is, selling time bills on promise to pay in New York sixty days hence, at heavy discounts for ready money. Hutchison [Hutchinson] is here making money for his stockholders and makes no bones of . . . bragging of some of his operations." Elmore had been frantic in his attempts at refutation of Anti-Debt's charges. "My impressions are," Gregg ended, "that there never was nor probably will be a time when well directed blows would tell better, or have more effect than at the present time, and I think that you had better strike while you hold your strong position. . . ." The banks would find needy friends in the winter (among others railroad men unable to pay their contractors); so Hammond had better go for them now.[7]

At this point in the correspondence Abbott H. Brisbane enters and is a foil to throw Gregg's opinions on economic reorganization into bolder relief. Brisbane, a military engineer, was born in South Carolina; he graduated from the United States Military Academy in 1825, and served on topographical duty in the City of Washington and on the South Atlantic Coast until the end of 1827, when he resigned his commission. He served in the Florida war against the Seminole Indians in 1835-6 as colonel of South Carolina volunteers, and

134

afterwards turned his attention, as engineer, to the project of a railroad from Charleston to Cincinnati (the Blue Ridge Railroad), "having especially intrusted to him the examination of the mountain passes through which it was to run." He received the appointment of contracting engineer of the projected road, which place he held from 1836 until 1840. From this scheme he went into the building of the Ocmulgee and Flint Railroad in Georgia (1840-4), which was financed on a shoestring, and to which reference is made below. He held the chair of belles lettres and ethics in the South Carolina Military Academy from 1848-53, when he retired to his plantation near Charleston.[8]

Brisbane having asked Hammond to act as patron for a society which was to stimulate South Carolina's interest in manufactures, Hammond wrote to Gregg inquiring who his correspondent was. Gregg's reply shows that the writer was no utopian, and believed that even with practice to point his preachment, industrial development in the South would be the work, not of meetings and declarations, but of patient years. Gregg wrote: "Why, don't you know that Gen. Brisbane once built a rail road one hundred miles long without a dollar to do it with, and but for the fact that the iron masters took it into their heads that they must have money in hand for their indispensable material, there would have been a rail road in . . . Georgia without the expenditure of money. The General now seems to entertain the impression that he has conceived a plan by which he will be able to revolutionize public sentiment throughout the Southern

States and change our industrial pursuits as it were by magic."

He was sorry he did not know much about the plan, but he believed that the mechanics of Charleston had been called together a few months before to form themselves into an association; some twenty attended, and were addressed by Brisbane. Gregg was one of those appointed on a committee to make further plans, but the committee did nothing until Gregg's return to town, when Brisbane called on him with the result that "four of us met and the General read a report, &c., and stated that he had three men in view to head the grand movement in contemplation, that is, Langdon Cheves, McDuffie and yourself." Cheves and McDuffie were open opponents of industrial development, and while Hammond, probably largely at Gregg's urging, served the industrial gospel with words,[9] he was primarily planter, politician, and secessionist.

"I believe his [Brisbane's] notion is," Gregg continued, "that it is only necessary for the mechanics of this State to form themselves into a body and make choice of some distinguished statesman as leader, to form a front which would at once invite the formation of similar associations in other Southern States, forming together a body which would be irresistible politically, upturn all our slothful and anti-economical habits and make us, as it were by magic, a great manufacturing people.

"You are fully aware that all such bubbles must end in wind, that to carry out such a revolution in our cus-

toms and habits and the application of labor as you and
I are aiming to effect, will be the work of an age, and
that neither of us need expect to live to see the work
carried out." Gregg thought of Hammond's service as
being chiefly in agriculture—the introduction of fer-
tilizers and the diversification of crops—for he continued: "I am satisfied, however, that we are on' the
right track. The result of your labors will be the cultivation of that portion of our State hitherto neglected, but
which will render her one of the most productive in
the Union. The day, I trust, is not distant when the
ditches and dykes which once made a garden spot of our
low country will again be brought into use and the thousands of acres of land now not worth a dollar be found
to be superior to those of the far West now selling for
$20 to $30."

When on such subjects, he rarely forgot to stress the
mutual benefits which would flow between factories and
Poor Whites: "And with this I trust we will learn how to
appreciate the labor of the thousands of poor idle people
in our States, more in number than would suffice to spin
and weave our entire cotton crop, putting [it] into a
shape to be consumable by us and exportable at three
times the worth of the raw material."[10]

From a letter of Brisbane's to Hammond, a year later,
it is learned that his agitation had taken form in the
launching of the South Carolina Institute, with which
Gregg had to do as a member and an exhibitor at its
fairs. Brisbane had apparently asked Gregg to settle
a date with Hammond when the latter would make the

first address of the Institute. It was finally decided that this should be November 20, 1849.[11] Gregg's influence was evident in Hammond's address. There was a subduing of his jealousy for agriculture; indeed, he became a little sarcastic about the way in which the planting interest chose to look down upon the manufacturing arts.[12] The Graniteville Factory had been started in active operation, and Hammond probably saw Gregg at intervals through the summer in which he was composing the oration. It is likely that Gregg supplied him with books on the cotton manufacture from which he quoted, as it is certain that many helpful object lessons from Graniteville's experience were at his service. "The agriculturist," Hammond declared, "has converted seed into cotton of little value as it passes from his hands. The mechanic converts it into cloth, fit for immediate and indispensable use; but first he has converted wood and iron into machinery, that can perform the labor of a thousand men; he has turned water into steam, to give it life, and has spun from the produce of a single seed, a thread more than a hundred and sixty miles in length. Which is the most wonderful work? Which requires the most comprehensive genius? Which is the nearest approach to the creative power?"[13]

He pointed out that while Leonard gave 5.26 cents as the cost of producing No. 14 wide sheeting at Northern factories when cotton was 6 cents a pound, the Graniteville Factory in South Carolina had not been in operation nine months before it turned out the same cloth for 4.84 cents per yard with cotton at 7 cents.

"And these very goods, made at this establishment, at this rate, have recently taken the *first premium* at the exhibition in Philadelphia."[14] In contrast to his address before the State Agricultural Society in 1841, when he believed slave labor would be used in cotton factories, Hammond now urged that operatives be drawn from the 50,000 Poor Whites in South Carolina.[15] Gregg had gone through this same transition of opinion; the Graniteville experiment clinched the decision in favor of white labor. He undoubtedly coached Hammond in this particular.

The Institute address was a great success, and no one could have appreciated it more than William Gregg. To have a leading politician and planter come out so emphatically with the advocacy of cotton manufacturing must have seemed to him a notable justification and forwarding of his own purposes. Yet it was all by way of talk. A few spindles started turning were worth the winning over of many publicists and many congratulatory dinners tendered by the Charleston Chamber of Commerce.

William Gregg himself made the address before the South Carolina Institute at its third meeting, in 1851. He had made progress in his thought and expression since the publication of the *Domestic Industry* six years earlier. Now he had the success of Graniteville back of him. He dealt only with essentials and was even more direct in his criticisms of South Carolina and compelling in his recommendations for her improvement than before.[16] The Address, in its fervor for mechanical development, reminds one of Hamilton's *Report on Manu-*

factures, and in its grasp of the true elements of a community's wealth repeats the lessons of List's *National System of Political Economy*. Gregg, no less than these men, saw clearly the destructive effects of dependence of an agricultural country upon industrial neighbors.

"Industry," he began, "is the foundation of all human happiness—without it, we can be neither good nor great." He was willing to make his bow to agriculture, but quickly passed beyond it: "No one can doubt for a moment that agriculture is the foundation of all human thrift, a natural and blessed pursuit. . . . but to stop at the mere feeding the animal, is but one step in advance of the savage. . . . and no community can expect long periods of prosperity, which becomes so engrossed in a single pursuit, that the various orders of talent may not be put to profitable use. . . . Diversity of pursuits I then hold to be indispensable. Its tendency is to vivify the intellect of the people, and render them, as a body, energetic, active and powerful." The slothful operation of hand labor was now repudiated by all nations; even Russia was turning to machinery, and he asked, "shall we in South Carolina content ourselves to stand in the same relation to the Northern States, and the balance of the manufacturing world, that Ireland, poor Ireland, does to England—hewers of wood, and drawers of water?" He had a quick apprehension of the potential power of the common people of the South. "Who can doubt the fact, that hundreds of the sons of South Carolina have lived and died in ignorance, who with proper opportunities would have been great in their day and generation? . . . that we have living boys now amongst us

with natural talents to fit them for any profession? . . .
How many persons have we in South Carolina who
really believe that great changes in our industrial pursuits are not necessary? . . . Who is it amongst us that
believes that we have not the energy and all the
requisites to success?"

He summed up the current arguments against industry
in the South, and answered them in a fashion to do
credit to a thinker thoroughly trained in economic
science. "Many objections," he said, "have been urged
against the introduction of manufactures among us.
Some say they have a demoralizing tendency; others ap-
prehend the dissemination of Abolition principles;
others again flatter themselves, that notwithstanding out-
ward appearances are against us, we are wealthier, more
prosperous, and in a better condition . . . than any of the
Eastern States. Let us not blind ourselves with such false
notions, but make the inquiry—What is national wealth?
It does not consist in money, which can take wings and
fly away. . . . It consists in the mental and physical improvement of the people [what List called 'economic
power']; the draining of swamps and bringing of waste
lands into cultivation; resuscitating worn-out soil; increasing population; the construction of railroads, turn-
pikes, fine bridges, and all the facilities for internal
communication; the increase and improvement of our
cities, rearing new villages, and durable and comfortable country dwelling-houses."[17]

He doubted that manufacturing had made England
worse off because of attendant pauperism. In the time
of Charles I wages were lower and commodities were

as high as in 1846—paupers constituted one-fifth of the population. "Are we to entertain the exploded doctrine that we can hold our position among the nations of the earth by the exclusive pursuit of agriculture?" Ireland, the size of South Carolina and having 9,000,000 people, sent to England annually $50,000,000 worth of agricultural products, "and what does she receive in return? The, to her, costly products of England's workshops! The product of the labor of ten able-bodied Irishmen is produced by a child in England! South Carolina claims to be strictly agricultural. She produces three to five bales of cotton with an able-bodied hand. It is sent to a foreign market and returned in a manufactured state, its value increased from three to ten-fold by the labor principally of women and children. . . ."[18]

However, Gregg was not willing in 1851 to urge, or perhaps to accept, the full force of his own arguments. Eight years later, whether because he attended less to policy or because he had developed in his own thinking, he espoused the principle of a protective tariff for a varied Southern industry. Now he limited his doctrine to cotton. "The reasons in favor of this species of manufacturing will not . . . apply with the same force to other pursuits—it is not desirable that Carolina should go generally into manufacturing, particularly where governmental protection will be necessary to sustain a competition with other countries. Let her husband her own resources, and the articles which will incidentally follow the manufacture of cotton will be quite sufficient for us."[19]

Gregg declared that slavery would be a foremost as-
sistant to industrial development in the States of the
South Atlantic seaboard; "it is the means of giving to
capital a positive control over labor, and of that kind
of labor which nature seems to have adapted to agricultural pursuits. . . . In all . . . manufacturing States,
labor and capital are assuming an antagonistical position. Here it cannot be the case; capital will be able to
control labor, even in manufactures with whites, for
blacks can always be resorted to in case of need." This
seems a Bourbon attitude in Gregg. Several facts, however, must be held in mind in judging him. In the first
place, trade unionism as we have known it since, was
taking form; the socialistic and agrarian projects which
took the workers' attention in the idle years following
the crisis of 1837 were giving way to practical demands
in the matters of hours, wages, and union recognition;
strikes were soon to become abundant. Gregg was one of
the few large industrial capitalists and employers in
the Southern States, and by percussion and repercussion
of reports from the North and West may easily have got
an exaggerated notion of the gathering conflict. And
thirdly, he was anxious to present industry to a slave
community in the most feasible light. There were few
at that time, anywhere in the country, who in point of
practice maintained such a generous attitude toward
workers.

In the South there need be no fear of overcrowding
in manufacturing towns, with attendant lapse of morals.
Some manufacturing towns should actually be founded

before the people became alarmed. "Our population will certainly bear doubling before we are elbowed out of the country." And industrial self-sufficiency would not mean diminished commerce, but increased trade with other parts; of this, New England was a clear example. Southerners took a vast alarm at the proposal of cotton manufactures. But an overthrow of the agricultural interest was not implied, and scattered factories would be the rule instead of great industrial centers.[20]

In contrast to the general view, Gregg thought that manufacturing labor was a more befitting employment for Southern than Northern peasantry—that any one who had spent a summer as an operative in the shade of a cotton mill would not return to the broiling sun of the cotton field. One million spindles (three-fourths of the factories making yarn and one-fourth cloth) would cost some $22,000,000, which it would not be difficult to secure over a period of twenty years. The unemployed or unproductive white people in the State numbered 125,000, and a fifth of these could operate the million spindles.[21]

The educational fund in South Carolina was a failure; nothing at that stage could induce many Poor Whites to send their children to school even were there good ones. This was because the Poor Whites were neglected by men whose enterprise went into directing slave labor. "These people must be brought into daily contact with the rich and intelligent," Gregg said, "—they must be stimulated to mental action, and taught to appreciate education and the comforts of civilized life; and this we believe may be effected only by the introduction of manufactures, for there seems to be no other employment so well calculated to induce them to habits of industry." His experience at Graniteville had convinced him of this. "Our company are determined to spare no means which will be necessary to school the children at Graniteville. We have collected at that place about 800 people, and as likely a looking set of country girls as may be found . . . but deplorably ignorant, three-fourths of the adults not being able to read or write their names." The company furnished everything for the school, "and notwithstanding our rule that no one can be permitted to occupy our houses who does not send all his children to school that are between the ages of 6 and 12, it was with some difficulty, at first, that we could make up even a small school." After some time had elapsed, only 60 out of 100 children were got into the school.

He would welcome practical workers to South Carolina, who could set up all sorts of manufacturing establishments. He spoke prophetically when he said of such enterprisers that "your example and your facts will do more in a generation than politicians, statesmen and philosophers would work out in centuries." The South is rapidly being persuaded, sixty years after Gregg's death, that the only progress—mental, spiritual, physical—lies in economic activity.

Gregg praised the men who had erected a small steam cotton mill in Charleston, and went on to brand a ubiquitous Southern proposal which has not to this day lost its

145

ability to pop up with a new life. "It is perfectly idle for us to talk about combinations to shorten the production of cotton. Our only hope for successful efforts lies in making available the magnificent sources of wealth which nature has scattered around us." South Carolina's prosperity would be in full tide "when we shall hear of large factories putting up at the East to be filled with thousands of power looms to weave up our Southern yarn"; when swamps were cultivated, hills covered with sheep, railroads and pikes ran to every part of the State, and lumbermen were getting out planks to build South Carolina towns. "We shall then no longer be under the necessity of looking for relief through limited production; we shall have ceased to be under the fluctuations of the Liverpool market. . . . Our tub will stand on its own bottom."[22]

Hammond's defiant valedictory of South to North was delivered in the United States Senate on March 4, 1858 —the speech in which he declared the slave class formed "the very mud-sill of society and political government," and asked "What would happen if no cotton was furnished for three years? . . . No, you dare not make war on cotton. No power on earth dares to make war upon it. Cotton *is* King." The biographer of Gregg could wish, for the sake of consistency, that he had stood out against secession through thick and thin, after the manner of James L. Petigru. Certainly, as an honest servant of the South's true interest, he had more right to do an unpopular thing than those who showed their loyalty by declarations and the inflaming of resentments. However, it makes him more human that he came, at the last, to share in the prevalent Southern distrust of the North. If he had influenced Hammond earlier, so now did Hammond influence him. Graniteville and all it stood for in constructive economic pursuit within the Union must prove subordinate to the supposed interest of the plantation, of which Hammond's "Redcliffe" was the type. The long brave contest of Gregg to turn the tide of Southern opinion was to end in failure. The old drift of thought and habit was too strong for even his wisdom, ingenuity, and perseverance.

At the end of the month Gregg wrote to Hammond: "I have stood back in silence until the wave of public laudation . . . of your speech has passed over, and now say, well done good and faithful servant. You hit the nail on the head, and drove it deep, and I think it is clinched on the other side, not to be drawn by Seward, Hamlin and all the great and small fry of Yankeedom put together." There is nothing here to prove that Gregg ever came to the point of inviting a severance of the South from the North. He may have thought that the South would never be attacked and that honor was justified in going the length of stating a position declaratively; he may, indeed, have deplored the war in every point of view, even when it broke. But if his mood was anything like that of Hammond at the time the March speech was made, he had become a Confederate.[23]

Early in 1857 Hammond had declined to run for the seat in Congress made vacant by the death of Preston Brooks, who had represented the district in which Hammond's plantation of Redcliffe and Gregg's Graniteville lay.[24] He wrote Gregg of his feeling, and Gregg, with no high opinion of political office, replied characteristically: "I think you are about right with regard to a seat in Congress, a place occupied largely with inferior men. Just look at the batch of candidates now before us. It does seem to me that we ought to do better, though they may be a fair exponent of the intelligence of our people at large."[25] Two years later, however, Gregg was running for the State Senate. Hammond had become United States Senator and was recognized as a principal spokesman for the South. Gregg wrote[26] thanking him for some government reports. "This token of your friendship," he went on, "is particularly gratifying in as much as it places me on the list of your friends, no small matter just now, when it is likely that the patronage of Uncle Sam's government is to come into your hands, and I being a candidate for office. Now, my dear Sir, let me apprise you that I am out for any office from the Minister at St. James to receiver of the customs at Charleston . . . —excepting one only, that of *Minister* to *Russia*. You will of course remember me when you get into the White House."

He changed this banter to a more serious topic. Hammond in his speech at Barnwell Court House, October, 1858, had declared the Union subordinate to the rights and interests of the slaveholding South, and had pleaded, "let us develop and consolidate all our resources, and devote ourselves manfully and hopefully to the accom-

148

plishment of the magnificant future that is within our
reach." This speech, Gregg thought, might in reality
place the presidential mantle on Hammond's shoulders.
But he quarreled with Hammond's attack on the protective tariff, and in justifying his position gave his most
extended statement on this subject. It is deserving of
quotation because it is an early instance of that support
of the protective principle by a Southern cotton manufacturer which, from the time of Tompkins a generation later, has occupied increasing prominence in the
economic and political life of the section. Hammond
probably took no notice when Henry C. Carey wrote him
urging his conversion to protectionism, but that Gregg,
a dozen miles from his own plantation, should make
the same argument must have given him cause for
thought.

Said Gregg: "I approve of everything in that speech
except your remarks about the Tariff; I think that might
have been left out, for it is a subject that is destined to
give us a great deal of unnecessary trouble. What is a
tariff but a bounty held out for capital to embark in
competition with foreign producers, to such an extent,
as to so over produce, at home, as to make cheaper
articles of common consumption than they may be imported for, from any other country. The whole history
of protection tariffs, and their results, prove this to be
the case, and I have no doubt that the South has been
paid back, tenfold, for what she suffered from 1828
to 40—all kinds of cotton goods except the finest are

THE DECLARED PROTECTIONIST

produced here, cheaper than in any other country, and this includes a large portion of our articles of prime necessity.

"How is [*sic*] our iron and coal mines to be brought into use, except by a protective tariff?—our mountains from Maine to Alabama abound in iron ore, which will sleep until a thousand years shall exhaust the English mines, before they will be worked unless some stimulant be offered. A protective tariff on iron would in a few years set our mountain country in a blaze, millions of capital would be sunk in overproduction, and we would find our railroads in all quarters supplied with rails made of material twice as durable as the *pot metal* rails, usually brought from England.

"It was protection that gave an impetus to the cotton manufacture in this country and a home consumption for 750,000 bales of cotton. It is from that source that our Southern mills sprang, and although much capital has been sunk in cotton spinning, who can doubt the advantages we have obtained by that branch of industry."[27]

A decade earlier Henry C. Carey in *The Plough, the Loom and the Anvil*, had declared as much very flatly. A Southern correspondent had boasted that his section was turning to diversity of pursuits and instanced the prosperity of Graniteville. "Here is your problem," he said, "working itself out naturally to a . . . successful issue, *without* the tariff of 1842." Carey rejoined: "We also point to 'Graniteville' as evidence of what might, and would long since have been done . . . but for the total failure of the free-trade system which preceded and led to the adoption of the tariff of 1842. To that tariff [carrying a duty of 30 per cent on cottons] is the existence of that village due. . . ." Carey rightly contended that Gregg and other builders of cotton mills in the South drew comfort from the tariff of 1846, which, though by its backers called a revenue measure, was genuinely protective. "Abolish the duty tomorrow, and establish free trade with Europe, and the factory would disappear. . . ."[28]

CHAPTER VIII

PLANKS VERSUS RAILS

Gregg was not likely to be led off after a fad, nor was he apt to espouse old-fashioned rather than mechanical methods of accomplishing work. The notable exception to this rule is his advocacy of plank roads as against steam railroads. He opposed internal improvements when these depended upon State subsidy, thought the country had been oversupplied with railways, and fought the Blue Ridge Railroad with special vigor. This dislike may have been due to his partiality for manufacturing establishments. It irked him to see money freely poured into transportation projects which, he thought, neglected the country districts to benefit the cities, when economic rejuvenation, to his mind, would come only through building up a variety of industries which would employ local workers in local communities.

However this may be, Gregg became a principal proponent in the plank roads movement which figured prominently in the decade 1846-56. The country's first plank road was built in New York in 1846, and five years later this state had over 2,000 miles similarly constructed. In other districts, from New England to the West, there were other thousands of miles of these roads. Pennsylvania incorporated 300 companies to build plank roads, and Michigan in one administration saw the chartering of 50 companies. The roads, for

which so much was claimed on the score of cheapness
and efficiency, were soon shown to be failures—they
were expensive to maintain and could not compete with
railroads.[1]

Gregg was moved to his *Essay on Plank Roads*[2] by
the circumstance that "A company of gentlemen of Edgefield District, with a few individuals of Charleston, propose to build a plank road from this city [Charleston]
to the mountains." Here he was following his custom
of backing his projects by pamphlet advocacy, as he had
done previously with his *Domestic Industry* and *Charters of Incorporation*. This practice, besides its excellence from a promoter's point of view, shows that he
studied carefully the undertakings into which he went.
This plank road was to be commenced at Charleston and
proceed to the vicinity of Abbeville Court House, taking
the direction of the South Carolina Railroad, crossing
the Edisto River between Branchville and Orangeburg;
then it was to strike the dividing ridge between the two
Edistoes and so continue, without crossing water, to the
ridge separating the Savannah and Saluda. "There is
probably no location in the United States," Gregg said,
"which will afford easier average grades—they may
certainly be reduced to 1 in 50 both ways as far as
Abbeville, and beyond that 1 in 30."[3]

Good common roads, Gregg argued, tend to change
the condition of the farmer wherever extended, and the
plank road gave a thoroughfare superior to any other,
being peculiarly adapted to the wants of a people who
necessarily maintained a large number of horses which

were fed and kept in idleness at the season when crops were sent to market.[4] If introduced they would "annihilate one of the greatest evils known to our country—the mud and mire through which our bulky and valuable products are yearly dragged to market."[5] Plank roads penetrating forests would find their material at hand, and, as they were constructed, would be the means of taking timber to parts of the State where the woods had been exhausted. The plank road was the road of the people, open to all.[6]

He thought the plank road originated in Russia and was introduced into Canada a dozen years before the first of them was built in New York; since then they had spread to North Carolina, Georgia, and other Southern States.[7] In some instances plank roads had maintained successful competition with railroads, paying 10 to 15 per cent interest and carrying passengers at 2 cents a mile. A mule might draw twice as great a load on a plank road as on a macadamized road. "While we see other States progressing in this practical way," he continued, "we in South-Carolina are in the midst of a rail-road mania. We seem to have passed by, unnoticed, the fact that, notwithstanding 18 years have elapsed since the S. Carolina R.R. to Hamburg was put in operation, the country through which it passes remains a comparative wilderness, with its hundreds and thousands of acres of heavy timber untouched. . . . A plank-road would have long since carried this timber to market, and converted the present wild lands into cultivated fields."[8] The feverish excitement over internal im-

154

provements in the State in 1820 caused the expenditure of millions on works for which the country was not prepared; particularly, the money put into useless canals would have built macadamized roads to every section. These would now serve as a base for the plank road, "so admirably adapted to our country," Gregg said, "and which, in my opinion, is destined to supersede all other modes of transit."[9]

Gregg was appalled at the overhead expense of a railroad, and in this he saw the pith of the argument in favor of plank roads instead. Outlays for complicated machinery, workshops to keep it in repair, "the necessity for high salaried officers, such as a President, Treasurer, Auditor, Agent of Transportation, Civil Engineer, and foreman of workshops" were heavy items. The mere working of the South Carolina Railroad cost $1,200 per day. Gregg's own Graniteville had a daily operating cost just about equal to this, but he evidently was not struck by any analogy between an industrial plant and a railroad.[10] The history of railroads in America, particularly in the West, has borne out his contention that "they are only fitted for locations where they can obtain the patronage of an extensive mercantile or manufacturing population."

On the other hand, he pointed out, the permanent cost of a plank road ceased with its construction; with the same original expenditure, it would accommodate a thousand or a million tons of transportation, while a railroad required large investments in machinery for any additional influx of trade. "The plank-road is ca-

155

pable of meeting all the wants of our country, and superior to the rail-road in every particular but that of indulging our fancy in rapidly passing from one point to another; it is so simple and cheap in its construction and management, that there is scarcely a village or an agricultural section of our country that cannot afford to build and maintain one."[11] In Great Britain or the Eastern States, which were industrially developed, mechanical power was undoubtedly superior to animal power, but in South Carolina steam locomotives could not lessen the number of mules to be maintained; because of the great amount of power necessary to the growth of a cotton crop, there must be a mule to every $1\frac{1}{2}$ tons of this staple, but 1 mule answered for raising 15 tons of wheat and 40 tons of hay.[12]

He had gone carefully into the calculations as to possible loads on a plank road. Assuming that the resistance from friction to wheels in motion on a wooden plane was 1 in 60, then on the road which was proposed to be built, 4 mules could draw 53 bales of cotton 2 miles an hour in places where the incline was 1 in 50, and faster on the rest of the road.[13] The total cost of construction, he believed, would not be more than $1,800 a mile. If any thought a plank road could not thrive in the vicinity of a railroad, he would remind them that 5,000 wagons now passed the Six Mile House, coming to Charleston, some of them from sixty and even ninety miles distant. He figured that tolls on wagons alone would amount to $76,000 a year on the plank road; "the effect on Charleston would be, to bring back, with a ten-fold increase, that important wagon trade, which once gave value to King Street. . . ."[14] He thought that paving the streets of Charleston with stone was the only means of ridding the city of yellow fever, but he considered that a plank road from the depot to the wharves would save one-half of the then high drayage cost.[15]

Gregg's preference for private as opposed to government investment was responsible for his concluding suggestion that South Carolina would do well to discontinue keeping up the State road, and give it to a company to construct a plank surface upon it. Charleston investors would be sowing the seeds of prosperity for the city by putting a half million dollars into such a work.[16]

Not enough became interested in his plank road scheme, however, to make it more than a scheme. The episode is significant as showing Gregg's concern for the economic betterment of the whole area of the State as distinct from the advantage of the single port of Charleston.

Internal communication and industrial development were two of the topics which drew Gregg into the series of commercial conventions held in the South between the years 1837 and 1859, and which form one of the most illuminating incidents in the history of the section. Economic improvement was the moving force in the first meetings, but even here was the strong flavor of sectionalism in the dominant desire to be independent of the North in trade, finance, and industry. As time passed, the conventions drifted more and more into political assertiveness and the nourishing of Southern interest in

157

slavery. It all went to illustrate how incompatible slavery was with economic progress. The South sighed for transcontinental railroads, for direct trade with Europe, and factories to make up its great staple at home, but these things were impossible so long as the main loyalty of influential men was given to protection of the slave system—the South could not have its cake and eat it too. Few who spoke of industrial upbuilding understood what the task involved in time, talent, and effort. The South was cursed with orating politicians, and these were not long in turning the conventions into their noisy forums. There was talk, talk, talk, but precious little action. Until 1857 there was at least an ostensible interest in material development in new directions, but from this date the reopening of the slave trade and secession from the Union were the engrossing purposes.[17]

Gregg was invited to be present at the Southern and Western Railroad Convention in New Orleans in January, 1852, and make an address on the development of manufactures and the influence these would exert on the system of internal communication, but the request came too late for him to accept it. He sent a letter, however, setting forth views which the delegates would have done well to heed. "In order to keep pace with the advance making everywhere in this utilitarian age," he said, "we must give up our notions of exclusive agriculture in the planting states, and turn more of our attention to those branches of industry, which will so diversify occupation, as to give a field for the development of the powers of every mind." Industries would bring out "the whole physical and productive force of our country. . . ." Factories and railroads would react to the advantage of the cities which furnished the capital, and he was not timid about giving them Boston as an example. The motto of the South should be "the Plow, and Anvil, and the Loom." Whites would never be efficient field laborers, "but when the now unemployed or unproductive white people of our country are looked on in a proper light by our great capitalists, they shall soon be brought to employ themselves in the arts. . . ."[18]

Gregg was present at the convention in Memphis in 1853. Here the sectional spirit made further progress. Domestic economy was less attended to than schemes for introducing slavery into near-by countries of Latin America; free navigation of the Amazon and passage of the Isthmus of Tehuantepec, a railroad from the Mississippi to the Pacific, and Southern school books by Southern writers vied with each other in impracticability. However, Gregg was appointed a member of a committee of five which was to prepare a comprehensive report on the facilities offered by the South for cotton manufacturing, and this was to be distributed in the industrial districts of Europe and America.[19] Gregg was likewise present at the Charleston convention in 1854, the largest and most spectacular of the meetings. Declamation was the order of the day. The tariff was a principal subject discussed, especially with reference to remission of duties on railroad iron. Gregg wanted the

159

resolution, which finally called for a reduction rather than a remission of duties, to include locomotives and other machinery, but his amendment was not accepted.[20]

William Gregg kept a diary regularly, but unluckily only one year of it has survived, that for 1856. His daily jottings were very brief, never more than two or three lines, on blank pages bound in with *Miller's Almanac*. Even so, they throw light on his habit and on his daily doings, reflecting his domestic life more than his business activity. During this year, at least, he was a systematic observer of the weather, never noting the temperature less than twice a day, and often three and four times—at sunrise, noon, nightfall, and bedtime. This was a singularly hard winter in that region of South Carolina, the ground being frozen from December the 26th to February 1st—36 days in succession—"a circumstance almost unprecedented in the recollection of the oldest person."[21] He made interesting allusions to the cold; thus on January 30: "Sap saw logs in the saw-mill cut as hard as lightwood from being frozen." All of the ponds at Graniteville and Vaucluse were sheeted entirely with ice. Gregg was plainly vexed over so much frosty weather, and kept eagerly on the alert for signs of the early Carolina spring.

From an occasional entry of "did not go to Graniteville today" it is clear that ordinarily nothing detained him from attendance at the factory. His noon observations of the mercury would indicate that he drove home always to dinner. He went to Vaucluse about every week, rather less frequently he visited Augusta with Mrs.

Gregg or his daughters (he probably to buy cotton or
attend to other business, and they to shop), and there
were comings and goings between Kalmia and Charleston. As in all Southern country homes, there were longish visits from relatives and friends. On the day of the
annual meetings of the Graniteville stockholders, the
gentlemen seem to have taken a meal at Kalmia.

The diary affords many evidences of his interest in
orcharding and gardening. On February 29 he had to
record that vegetation was late, "not a peach or a wild
plum bloom yet out." In this backward season he occupied himself out of doors with work on the old Bridge
Creek dam, wharfing and raising it. On March 5, a sum-
mery day, he planted Macartney roses on the breast of
this dam, and set out arbor vitae hedges at Kalmia. By
the 8th he was delighted to be making a large grape
arbor and, besides, he bedded yams, planted water-
melons, and grafted Chinese peaches. "The first apricot
bloom opened today, but no peach blooms still."[21]
Gregg's visits to Governor Hammond at Redcliffe a
dozen miles away must have developed conversation on
many topics and projects in which they were mutually
interested, farming not the least of them. He spent the
night of June 6 with Hammond and came home the
next day, but that evening attended the meeting of the
Beach Island Farmers' Club and went to Hammond's
again afterwards. Late in June he noted that his Tillot-
son peaches were soft on one side and he gathered the
first of the season. By July 4 he was picking peaches in
quantities; he went to Charleston by the night train to

161

forward 27 boxes, and four days later he was sending an increased quantity to New York, and baskets to Charleston besides.[22] By the end of the year he had planted a new peach orchard with 8,500 trees. This was a large and, for that day, a very enterprising operation in South Carolina, and is to be reckoned among his most useful accomplishments.[23]

Mishaps to the dams received prominent notice. On July 6, while he was absent in Charleston looking after shipment of his peaches, the Bridge Creek dam broke, though the dams below resisted the rush of water. This was the time when he borrowed wheelbarrows and railroad hands to repair the damage. On August 11 he went to the North with members of his family,[24] and when he returned on September 3 found that a freshet had carried away 600 feet of the canal bank, so that it was necessary to stop the factory for eight and a half days. Probably because he was so busy about this work, he made no entries in the diary for a fortnight.

There are entries of James returning from the University in April, and of William commencing with the Graniteville Company on May 9. He recorded spending various days in working the roads; but was interested in less routine engineering matters also, for he went to Augusta "to meet Capt. Bigelow and see water experiments" (doubtless some tests of the hydraulic power), and a little later was sending a theodolite to Philadelphia, probably to have it repaired in anticipation of surveying, which he later did in the Hampton Hollow. He would go to Graniteville in the evening to hear a lecture, or to Augusta to buy a pair of horses, or to get the buggy which figures so vividly in the recollection of old Graniteville inhabitants.

The diary has numerous references to his attendance at political campaign meetings and the sessions of the legislature, which will introduce the topic of the next chapter.

CHAPTER IX

A REALIST IN THE LEGISLATURE

Gregg told his stockholders in 1859, in reply to criticism of his taking time for politics, that when he was nominated for the legislature in 1856 he replied to his friends that he had neither time nor inclination to make the usual campaign, and that without going from home more than five days he was elected.[1] His diary shows that in the summer and fall of 1856 he attended (and probably spoke at) a number of political meetings in Edgefield District—apparently more than he remembered when he made the above statement. Any civic occasion which brought the men together was turned to political account. Gregg seems to have started the rounds in July by attending "Lamar's barbecue" on the 26th. During most of August he was on a trip to the North, and when he returned home, as already mentioned, found the canal bank carried away for 600 feet by a freshet, but was too busy at the factory to give a thought to anything else. On the 19th and 20th of September he attended a cavalry review at Hamburg, on the 22d and 23d was at Richardson's for muster drill, on the 26th was at "Bunson's parade," and put in the next day at a general muster. He frequently did not return to Kalmia between these engagements, but spent the night with friends. In October he went to a muster on the 4th, and on the

164

13th went to Hamburg for the election, that apparently being a critical point in the district for Gregg.

Pasted in the front of the diary is a newspaper clipping giving the election results for Edgefield District. Of thirteen contestants for the South Carolina House of Representatives, six were to be elected. Gregg ran fourth, receiving 1,345 votes (Z. W. Carwile received 1,412, James Blackwell 1,408, and M. C. M. Hammond 1,376). The others elected were Robert Meriwether and Abram Jones. W. C. Moragne and Geo. W. Landrum were unsuccessful candidates for reëlection. Graniteville cast 230 votes, of which 193 were for Gregg—44 more than the village gave to any other candidate. Gregg received the second highest number of votes at Hamburg, but was low man at Edgefield Court House.[2]

Gregg's first experience in the legislature was in the special session of November 3-5, 1856, called to choose South Carolina's electors for president and vice president of the United States.[3] The only incident of the session approaching a contest was over a resolution of Mr. Bryan "That in appointing Electors . . . the General Assembly feels no obligation to sustain the nominees of any 'National Convention,' or of any other irresponsible or self-appointed body whatever, but reserves to itself the constitutional right of selecting, as heretofore, such citizens for the office of President and Vice President as may be deemed worthy of the confidence . . . of South Carolina." After debate it was declared by both houses,

165

however, that in the appointment of electors "no reference to the opinions of the candidates of the National
Nominating Conventions is held by the Legislature."[4]

Gregg was present in Columbia for the opening of
the regular session on November 4th.[5] He must have
chafed under Governor J. H. Adams' message, which
was a plea for the reopening of the slave trade. Gregg
regularly pleaded for the immigration of white mechanics from the North. The governor wished the slave trade
had never been closed. "If we cannot supply the demand
for slave labor," he said, "then we must expect to be
supplied with a species of labor we do not want, and
which is, from the very nature of things, antagonistic to
our institutions. It is much better that our drays should
be driven by slaves—that our factories should be
worked by slaves—that our locomotives should be
manned by slaves,—than that we should be exposed to
the introduction, from any quarter, of a population alien
to us by birth, training, and education. . . ."[6]

It was pointed out in debate that if the reopening of
the slave trade was to be viewed as a practical proposal,
it meant South Carolina's secession from the Union.
Gregg voted with the majority in opposing the reference
of the governor's recommendation to the Committee on
Colored Population, and preferred giving it to the Committee on Federal Relations. In the end a special committee was appointed, and this recommended laying the
whole matter on the table.[7]

Gregg's first remarks in the House were apparently on
the proposal to reduce the tax on banks chartered in

166

South Carolina on the ground that the taxes then collected (40 cents on the $100) unduly increased the representation of Charleston in the legislature. In the absence of evidence on his stand, it may be safely conjectured that he was opposed to any lessening of the banks' burdens.[8]

Gregg's speech on the Blue Ridge Railroad, made at this session, was in some respects his finest public pronouncement. It showed his personal courage because he attacked the subterfuge and incompetence of men who were his friends. It evidenced his patriotism in trying to save the State from uncalculating subsidy of an impracticable and selfish scheme. It was informed throughout with the wisdom of developing all the latent energies of South Carolina rather than seeking to achieve a miracle by drawing upon riches across the mountains. Here was Gregg standing at full stature—possessed, informed, illuminating in his strictures, weighty in his simplicity.

One of the ruling influences in the antebellum period was Charleston's design to get a connection with the Ohio valley. Meetings held in Buncombe County and in Asheville, North Carolina, in 1832, looking to a railroad across the mountains, are believed to have been inspired by Charlestonians.[9] At the completion of the Charleston and Hamburg Railroad in 1833 its president, Elias Horry, sought to reinforce this transmontane project. When, after a lapse of two years, it was given new impetus in Cincinnati, Charleston immediately took hold again, drew in the State of South Carolina, and through

167

it North Carolina, Tennessee, and Kentucky. The Knoxville Convention of July, 1836, saw the Louisville, Cincinnati, and Charleston Railroad Company fairly launched.[10]

This abortive undertaking, as it developed, led to the same kind of manipulation which Gregg condemned in the succeeding enterprise of the Blue Ridge Railroad. The Southwestern Railroad Bank was provided for as ancillary to the railroad to encourage subscriptions for its construction; the Charleston and Hamburg Railroad was absorbed for the prime purpose of increasing assets of the company to bring them up to the point where the bank could begin operation; the State endorsed the company's bonds for $2,000,000. This project, in spite of Hayne's exuberance and every device to bolster it, collapsed, so far as concerned the ambition to get over the mountains, in 1840.[11]

The Blue Ridge Railroad, the affairs of which occasioned Gregg's speech, was, as Professor Phillips has pointed out, a "recrudescence of the Louisville, Cincinnati, and Charleston project in a modified form."[12] The route, instead of following the French Broad, starting at Anderson, South Carolina, was to lie through Rabun Gap, follow the Little Tennessee River, and go northward to Knoxville, a total distance of about 195 miles. South Carolina, North Carolina, Georgia, and Tennessee all granted charters, 1851-2, to as many companies, with different names but the same object.[13] South Carolina in 1854, withdrawing promise of aid in another form, agreed to issue bonds and subscribe for stock of the

168

South Carolina company when individuals or corporations had subscribed for $1,000,000, and to make an additional subscription of like amount when $500,000 more had been added from other sources, one-fifth of the total capital to be subscribed by responsible persons and private corporations; the State of South Carolina further agreed to guarantee the company's bonds to the amount of $1,000,000 to be secured by the whole road.

The first contractors were to receive payment monthly, one-half in cash, one-fourth in stock, and one-fourth in the company's unguaranteed bonds.[14] This firm, after a disruption and reorganization, was dismissed from the work, April 1, 1856, and the new contracts let the next month required payment in cash, thus making it impossible to use expenditures in stock to meet requirements for the second State subscription. None of the many tunnels and bridges had been constructed, and expensive grading must deteriorate until these were ready. "The problem of the directors now centered in the 5,800-foot tunnel through the Stump House Mountain on the one hand and in the South Carolina legislature on the other. . . . Throughout 1857 and 1858 the chief engineer, Walter Gwynn, bent all his resources upon the tunnels, bridges, and heavy grading; while the president, Edward Frost, labored with the legislature and the public to get more funds."[15]

William Gregg came into the controversy at the commencement of this combination of feverish construction and solicitation, in December, 1856. The immediate occasion of his speech in the legislature was an amend-

169

ment offered to the Act of 1854, striking out the requirement that directors of the Blue Ridge Railroad should
each in his own right hold $5,000 of stock of the com-
pany. As a member of the Committee on Internal Improvements, it was Gregg's duty to give special attention to the railroad bill.[16] The friends of the Blue Ridge
project had been abundantly assisted by the *Courier*,
which had published an appendix giving reports of the
president and directors, and of the chief engineer, "designed to furnish information unreserved and conclusive
on all points and incidents involved in the great enterprise. . . ."[17]

The night session on December 12 was devoted entirely to the amendment to strike out Section 9 of the Act.
The members looked jaded, but they had refused to plan
for an early adjournment. Judge Edward Frost, president of the Blue Ridge Railroad, was invited by the
House to appear before it, and spoke two and a half
hours, as the *Courier* said, "in behalf of the great enterprise of scaling the mountain barrier, which yet
frowns between us and an enriching western trade. His
special object was to induce the House to pass a Bill,
repealing the clause of the existing law, which makes
the payment of the further subscription by the State,
conditional on a given amount of individual subscription. Judge Frost's exposition was able, clear and convincing to all not prejudiced against the undertaking."[18]

Opponents of this measure were present in strength,
while many of its friends, having heard a similar speech
from Frost shortly before, were absent. When the speech

was over, the opposition, according to the *Courier,* taking advantage of the situation, tried to kill the bill then and there, but by desperate use of parliamentary tactics the majority finally succeeded in making the bill the special order for December 18th; the understanding reached was that no final vote would be taken even then, in effect postponing the matter until the next session of the legislature, since the Senate had fixed that date for adjournment.[19] The next year fresh matters pressed for consideration of the legislature, and this phase of the Blue Ridge project was dropped.

Gregg began his speech and continued it with bluntness: "I believe . . . that every dollar the State puts into the Blue Ridge Railroad will be lost, for I have not the slightest idea that she will respond to the calls that will, necessarily, be made upon her before this work will be so far completed as to become available." His friendly advice to the president of the road would be to stop the work until the people of all four States came forward with means to furnish the construction in their respective territories. As a citizen of Charleston he had vigorously opposed the council's subscription for two reasons, first because the work could not but end in disaster if commenced with so little capital, and second, because Charleston's resources ought to be used to develop South Carolina internally.[20] His arguments directed at Charleston emphasized his old thesis, that "her destiny was fixed and indissoluble with the State of South Carolina, and that mainly her great investment in Internal Improvements should be made with a view to developing

171

the resources of the immediate country around her. . . . the dormant wealth of Charleston might be so directed as to be felt in the remotest parts of the State, in stimulating agriculture, draining our great swamps and putting into renewed culture our worn-out and waste lands; diversifying industry, stimulating the mechanic arts, and increasing the population and wealth of the State." Charleston was rich, but she would not invest in the building up of South Carolina.

Individual subscriptions had not been procured in this instance. A flourish of trumpets which reminded of "the long since exploded Cincinnati scheme," led on from the rash to the disingenuous. He did not like the way in which, after getting the City of Charleston in for a large investment, and without drawing upon their own means, "a certain set of Charleston gentlemen came up here, [to Columbia] with all the influence that men can sometimes bring to bear, and besieged the legislature. . . . I have been watching the movements of the parties engaged in this work from the commencement, and I must say that when I saw gentlemen from Charleston, on this floor, asking State aid, wealthy gentlemen, some of whom have ships floating in every sea; I say when I saw such gentlemen here, asking State aid to build a road which is to be purely commercial in its character, for the accommodation of the shipping interests of that city, a work which can do the State at large so little good, and those gentlemen not willing to take stock themselves, I could not divest myself of the apprehension that all was not right." Gregg's belief in the superiority of private enterprise to public subsidy prompted him to go further with a remark that must have spread consternation in the House: "The gentlemen who have been most prominent in this work have no pecuniary interest in it, except such paltry sums as were necessary to qualify a Director, and enable him to participate in expending the State's money."[21]

Only $52,000 had been raised by private subscription when preliminary contracts were let for a road which was to go through mountainous country with 13 tunnels, one a mile and a tenth long, and 32 bridges, some as long as 600 feet and some as high as 90 feet. Before embarking upon any construction at Graniteville, Gregg took the greatest pains to acquaint himself with all similar work that had been done elsewhere. He blamed the directors of the Blue Ridge Railroad for rushing into the undertaking with inexperienced engineers and dishonest contractors. His solicitude for internal improvements came out in his lament that the legislature stood ready to grant such abundant support to this over-ambitious project reaching far beyond State boundaries, when a loan of $100,000 had been refused the Greenville Railroad.[22]

Gregg calculated that the work, including a line from Anderson to Charleston, would cost more than $13,500,000, of which, leaving out the State of South Carolina, less than $1,500,000 had been subscribed. He burst out with a question which was a comment on the expansionist flights into which Charleston was trying to thrust the legislature: "In the name of common sense, Mr.

173

Speaker, let me ask you where is all this immense sum to come from?" Not only, however, was the plan of financing lacking, but the basic scheme of construction was incomplete. Gregg wanted to know "where this great trade is to find a channel of communication with Charleston if the work is to stop at Anderson?" And he went on to sketch, with a deftness and a spirited sarcasm not so bad in an unpretending man of sheetings, the brilliant picture which railroad advocates were constantly splashing before the people. Spokesmen of the enterprise had "eloquently set forth the immense commerce which is to be set in motion; the State is to be flooded with cheap western products; the seas are to be whitened with the commerce that it is to give to Charleston; the wilderness swamps in the vicinity of Branchville and down to Charleston, that have slept under the sound of the engine's whistle for twenty years, are to be waked up; the body politic is to be exhilarated, and South Carolina is to wipe off the reproach of Rip-Van-Winkle sloth by a hearty coöperation in this work."[23]

It was absurd to contend that the Greenville road could bring such a vast amount of Western produce away from Anderson.[24] And supposing the freight got to Columbia, the South Carolina Railroad could not add to "its present enormous business the trade which will be necessary to support a $9,000,000 road" penetrating the mountains. A double track to make such traffic possible would simply insure domination of the Blue Ridge company by the South Carolina road, upon which it would be dependent. Gregg had explained earlier that though he was a stockholder in the South Carolina Railroad, and its officers were his friends, he would speak frankly of it to reinforce his point. He referred to it now as "That great Company which monopolizes everything. . . . If the South Carolina Railroad Company does not kill the goose for the golden egg, she will at least put it on short allowance." Besides his general dislike of the policies of the State's chief road, Gregg had particular reason to complain against it. In this instance he cited the fact that if "Our Graniteville cloth, the product of South Carolina industry, goes to Charleston, it pays 25 per cent more than similar goods from Georgia, although we are ten miles nearer." The Graniteville Company was charged 15 cents a hundred pounds for the ten-mile haul to Augusta, which was the price of freight from Charleston to New York and a third of the rate from Charleston to Liverpool. He had sympathy with the Columbia people in trying to reach Charleston by boat rather than use the railroad, and with those who chose the "back track up the Charlotte Road" rather than patronize the South Carolina company; he emphasized his sympathy in advocating plank roads as against railroads generally.

The South Carolina Railroad would not seek to develop the country along its line until forced to look for business at home, or until the people found some other means of getting to market. Well timbered lands right at the tracks and within forty miles of Charleston sold for a few cents an acre, and Gregg had bought the Graniteville tract at about a dollar an acre. While the road carried for the West it would not encourage lumber mills along its route, and meantime it got ties and fuel at give-away prices. The South Carolina Railroad was a monopoly which the legislature, by withholding investment, ought to discourage.[25]

The other States which had chartered companies to coöperate in the building of the Blue Ridge Railroad —Georgia, North Carolina, and Tennessee—had subscribed entirely inadequate, even comically small sums toward the work. Almost the whole payment would fall to the lot of South Carolina, and this State did not take the precaution, as did Tennessee, of extending aid only after the road was graded and the superstructure in place, then taking a first mortgage on the entire property. If South Carolina were able to assume the burden, her contributions would become so reluctant as to render the work extremely costly. All of this was on the wrong principle. "I am not willing," he said, "to see the State . . . engage in any public work without having at least three-fifths of the stock subscribed by responsible individuals. Individual enterprise and capital ought to predominate in every great work."

It is frequently said that the South gave proof of her economic activity by building railroads in the antebellum period. Gregg put his finger on a difference between Southern and Northern roads which went far to diminish the credit claimed for the South, namely, that Northern works were more largely the result of private investment. "Did you ever know a State government to carry on a business right?" he asked. The wastefulness in the building of the South Carolina capitol and the ineffectiveness of the first three years of the construction of the Blue Ridge Railroad were cases in point. The Pennsylvania system of public works was notoriously badly managed. The Georgia State road, successful in the main, suffered its embarrassments through the failure of the State Bank at the wrong juncture.

The Erie Canal had been successful. Gregg approved of it on much the same grounds as he did of plank roads—every man might use his own conveyance, the State having no management, and simply collecting tolls. The success of railroading, on the contrary, depended upon the excellence of the operation; there was "no business which requires such comprehensive liberality connected with driving enterprise, and minute detailed economy."[26]

Independent of other experiences, South Carolina had had evidence of the State's embarking upon engineering works. Gregg referred to the $2,300,000 the State had lost between 1820 and 1824 in internal improvements. He then entered into a running account of the previous project of connecting Charleston with the Ohio country —the Louisville, Cincinnati, and Charleston Railroad, chartered by South Carolina in 1835. He referred to the opposition from Kentucky until won over by Colonel Abraham Blanding by the promise that the road should connect with Louisville; "one of our most talented young men, now a member of this House, was sent, at an expense of $5,000, on a special mission to Frankfort . . . to make an appeal to the Legislature of that State. His

177

eloquence was triumphant. . . . Kentucky . . . purchased the finest horse in the State and sent our minister home upon him. Cincinnati was illuminated on that occasion; transparencies were hung up in the windows, representing passenger trains of cars departing for Charleston. . . ." Two years after this, Gregg said, he traveled in a private conveyance (on his way to Kansas, it was) near the line on which the engineers were at work in the mountains. He came to the conclusion that the road would not be completed in his day, but could find none in Cincinnati to believe him. After the bubble burst in 1840, and the company was contracted to intra-State objectives, Gregg labored for a decade, he said, to save himself from serious loss, and his experience taught him the dangers a State ran in participation in such ventures.[27]

He condemned the purchase by the Louisville, Cincinnati, and Charleston of the Charleston and Hamburg Railroad in order to secure State aid. The bargain soon cost the new company heavily in repairs to the old road, and it threw out of the board of directors the original experienced Charleston business men, in favor of "conspicuous gentlemen and politicians, scattered from the seaboard in South Carolina to the banks of the Ohio River. Nothing short of a general or a leading politician was thought to be in keeping with this gigantic enterprise. . . ."[28] Likewise, he called up the error of building the line from Branchville to Columbia the long way by the expensive Congaree River route rather than the short way (which men using their own money must have chosen), direct from Blackville over firm ground. The opening of the Camden branch, which was contemplated in the plan of reaching Columbia by the eastward course, must have angered Gregg particularly, since it delayed elimination of the troublesome inclined plane at Aiken and was responsible for poor maintenance of the whole line which served Graniteville.[29]

Gregg declared that he lost his seat in the boards of directors of the Southwestern Railway Bank and of the South Carolina Railroad Company "by efforts to bring matters into something like a business shape. . . ." This was not accomplished until the State was eliminated as a partner. He determined then to have nothing further to do with public works in the management of which the State had a voice.[30]

He was perfectly alive to the incalculable advantages of railroads, where properly located and managed with spirit. Boston, through railroads, had reinforced her prosperity.[31] But private investors in Charleston were not moving to make commercial outlets for the city. This was due to the "bungling legislation" which had shut her out from the back country by granting (acts of 1827 and 1828) to the South Carolina Railroad and Canal Company exclusive rights of operation for 36 years between Charleston, Columbia, Camden, and Hamburg; intermeddling of politicians in this road had kept out individuals with money. "Charleston is asleep and slothful," Gregg told the legislature, "because you have made her so; and she helped you to do it." Private subscriptions in Charleston had been negligible in the case

179

of the present project, and he drove this point home mercilessly. For example, "out of the four daily papers that made so much dust in getting up the breeze for the Blue Ridge road, only two have subscribed one share each." Wealthy merchants had shaken off solicitors with agreement to take $100 of stock only. "Why, the chimney sweeps and shoe blacks of Boston would do better than that if in earnest." And the Baltimore and Ohio was launched with a full complement of private backers.[32]

Gregg had witnessed to good purpose "the last onset for the Blue Ridge Railroad in 1854," when Charleston interests had marshaled the influence of the Bank of the State and of every branch road to fight for legislative assistance. He denounced the mania that plunged the State into "this ruinous subscription," with all Hammond's effectiveness and with more brevity. The expedient of bonds was too lightly resorted to. If the State House were to burn, a temporary one would be erected not from taxation but with 6 per cent bonds. "Such has become the reliance of all projectors of public works on State and corporation subscriptions, that *private capitalists*, our only security for good management, are not regarded to be at all essential." And the amendment under debate would rob the State of such guarantee as she did have by permitting men with no financial interest in the Blue Ridge Railroad to become directors.[33] Private capital had no confidence in the Blue Ridge scheme partly because the men at the head of it "had just completed a very wasteful expenditure of about a mil-

lion of dollars for the South Carolina Railroad. . . ."[34]
Better undertakings found ready assistance from
Charleston, which had twice as much banking capital
as the city required. Graniteville's stock had been subscribed without difficulty. Gregg had been of a group
which proposed to build a railroad from Charleston to
Macon, and all the capital necessary was promised when
the plan was balked by the refusal of a charter by the
South Carolina legislature on the ground that any encouragement of a new line would be an act of bad faith
toward the South Carolina Railroad, which had been
granted exclusive rights.[35]

In a decade of experience at Graniteville Gregg had
learned that the construction of a work must be followed by painstaking, clever operation of it to achieve
success. He made a profound comment upon the uncalculating zeal of early railroad projectors when he
pointed out that "The trade of the great West will not be
so easily turned to Charleston as some persons imagine,
the matter cannot be determined by an arithmetical calculation of distance. In railroad operations, the outfit
may be so much more complete and the management so
much better on one establishment than another, that it
will carry commodities double the distance in the same
time and for a less cost."[36]

Gregg was an inveterate realist. In the first ten years
after the building of the line from Charleston to Hamburg the population of the former city, instead of increasing, actually retrograded. Charleston, by extravagant promises of commerce to come to her from the

181

Mississippi, had subscribed half a million dollars to the stock of a railroad from Nashville to Chattanooga;[37] Gregg doubted whether a single bushel of corn had reached Charleston by this means, though the line had been in operation three years. Instead, Charleston had lost valuable trade of the Chattanooga country, which was now supplied by New Orleans through Nashville.[38]

This whole speech, as with so much else that William Gregg said and did, went to show the importance, in his mind, of the rigidly economic motive as applied to the problems of the South's betterment. Advancement must come through material interest and not through sentimentality and excitement, which would accomplish only a bogus progress.

At the end of the session Gregg appeared in another debate, this time on the completion of the State House, a matter which frequently aroused his comment. That his brother-in-law, General James Jones, was commissioner for the capitol[39] did not modify his strictures on the conduct of the construction. When the bill to authorize the issue of bonds to continue the work on the building was taken up for a second reading, Gregg offered an amendment providing that the bonds should bear 6 per cent instead of 7 per cent interest, and requiring the Bank of the State to act as agent for the sale of these. The Bank, he said, should advance the funds and, as the bonds were sold, place the amount to the Bank's credit. He had heard of two directors of the Bank who had borrowed $250,000 each, and if this was so, he did not know why the State should not draw as much on account. "It had been said by some that the officers of that bank would not obey the wishes of the Legislature. If this were true, they should be turned out, and others put in their places. He meant no disrespect to the present Board; they were as good a Board as we perhaps could have . . . ."

To this Mr. Seymour rejoined that the zeal of the gentleman from Edgefield had led him astray. "He would ask him when was it that any two men drew $500-000 from that bank? He doubted . . . whether the gentleman himself could draw the half of that amount. This amendment was a side blow at the bank, and he would not vote for it unless it be amended so as to allow the bonds to be sold at their market value, instead of at par as now." Mr. Memminger said he had been one of those who desired to see the bank wound up, but since the State had decided otherwise, he wanted to do it justice. He did not wish to see the bank burdened with the construction of the capitol; the State should assume part of it. Gregg's amendment was a correct one; the bank should be the agent for the sale of the bonds, and they should be 6 per cents. The 7 per cent bonds could not be sold. But he would amend the amendment by permitting the bonds to be sold at their market instead of their par value. In this form Gregg's amendment was agreed to, and the bill was ordered to the Senate.[40]

Gregg was undoubtedly glad when the legislature adjourned. Sessions had been held daily from 11 o'clock in the morning until 4 in the afternoon, and again from 7 until 10 o'clock at night, the evening sessions being particularly trying. Many members had got leave of absence to go home, but Gregg seems to have left Columbia only once, when he returned to Graniteville in the middle of the session over Sunday.[41]

By the time he went to the legislature for his second regular session in November, 1857, the depression was the dominant economic fact before the country. The discovery of gold in California and the land grants to railroads had encouraged speculation, with heavy investment in productive enterprise. In August, 1857, the Ohio Life Insurance and Trust Company failed, and a general liquidation followed. In the South no such precautions had been taken against the excesses of State banks as were represented in the Suffolk Banking System in Massachusetts and the New York Act for the deposit of securities against note issue. Most, but not all, of the South Carolina banks suspended specie payments. The farmers had fairly heavy crops of cotton and rice to be moved. When the legislature met, the question was whether the attitude toward the suspended banks should be lenient or rigid—specifically, whether the law of 1840 placing a tax of 5 per cent per annum on the note issues of suspended banks, and the requirements against usury, should be enforced.[42]

Gregg appeared in the legislature on the second day of the session, November 24, and immediately introduced a series of resolutions on the bank question.[43] They were: (1) The distressed state of the country and the derangement of monetary affairs made it incumbent on the legislature to amend the bank charters so as

184

to restrain the issue of paper money in future; (2) However, the money pressure and want of confidence made it desirable at present to remove all unnecessary restrictions upon the banks, so that they might be able to give a forward movement to produce waiting to be sent to market; (3) There was confidence in the solvency of the South Carolina banks and in their disposition to resume specie payments as soon as possible; (4) A committee should be appointed to study the whole subject of banking in the State and report a bill.

The next day C. G. Memminger of Charleston, chairman of the ways and means committee of the House, introduced resolutions in the main opposed to Gregg's.[44] He wanted the banks penalized for suspension. They were given the note issue privilege on the implied condition that they would redeem with coin; the failure to perform this condition justly forfeited the privilege and should operate to deprive the banks of the profit arising from note issue. Banks not suspended themselves, but paying out notes of suspended banks, were issuing depreciated currency, and should be prosecuted by the attorney general. Banks should deposit public stocks as security for note issues, and issues should be so limited as not to cause inflation. Restrictions on interest and discount charged by the banks should be repealed, but their dividends should be limited. Denominations of notes ought to be reduced.

The next move was notice given by Gregg on November 26 that the following day he would ask leave to introduce a bill to amend the bank charters of the State.[45]

185

Four days later Memminger introduced his bill to regulate and limit the issue of bank notes.[46] The *Mercury*, without mentioning names, in an editorial opposed the pound-of-flesh attitude of Memminger and espoused the policy of Gregg.[47] South Carolina banks had not suspended specie payments because they were insolvent; not a dollar of their capital was at any risk. In a panic such as that which arose in New York, banks ought to suspend. To force collection would but spread a wider ruin.[48]

Debate between Gregg and Memminger began on December 1. Memminger spoke first. Members of the House, knowing many bank directors, would be tempted to avoid the issue, but the situation demanded frankness and courage. He reiterated his catalogue of ills worked by suspension and called for the penalty in collection of the tax. His speech was a long one, but was listened to with deep interest.[49] The *Mercury*[50] thought, however, that he did not entirely convince his hearers. Gregg then spoke to his resolutions. Being "a gentleman of experience and practical judgment," it was reported that his sentiments were received by the House with much respect and attention.[51] Gregg had not finished his speech at the hour of adjournment, and concluded it the next day.[52]

In public matters as in problems arising in his own business, Gregg generally had a policy which he believed it advisable to keep steadily in view, but he was no doctrinaire. The long-time program should be modified by a lively sense of expediency. This characteristic of his mind is apparent in his *Speech on the Bank Question.*

Supporting his resolutions, Gregg declared that the law of 1840 imposing a 5 per cent tax on the issues of suspended banks should be repealed. There was no point in chastising the banks when every blow inflicted a wound upon the people. Every warehouse in the interior was full of cotton, and the banks would not relieve this stagnation by lending at 6 per cent, when they must pay the State 5 per cent.[53] If the banks were left free of prying, so that one did not know what the other was doing, they would expand, cotton would be purchased, and all would be able to pay their debts. In 1840, when the banks suspended, he was a bank director in Charleston. His institution had $600,000 circulation and only $30-000 specie; though all the banks knew this and were afraid of it, his bank expanded further, to $800,000 on cotton drafts, with the result that its mercantile customers were soon able to pay back, so that this weak bank shortly resumed specie payments and led others into doing so.[54]

He was surprised to see gentlemen still clinging to the idea that stocks and State securities formed a fit basis for a bank circulation. Gregg probably had in mind here the early unfavorable history of the New York State banking system. "We had better come to the reality at once," he said, "and provide for a contracted paper currency, with a strong specie basis." He was opposed also to restriction of banks to 7 per cent dividends—this would simply make for high salaries and extravagant

187

bank buildings. What was needed was a reduction in the number of banks and less capital devoted to banking.[55] He was opposed to inflicting any punishment on the banks at this time. The plan of the Suffolk Bank in Massachusetts of refusing to accept the notes of non-specie-paying banks, could not have seemed to him wise for the South. It would not be fair to hurt prudent banks with the reckless, which he thought would result from such a scheme, since a general run would pull down the strong institutions for the very reason that they were favorites for collections and deposits. The State had been instrumental in bringing about the elements of suspension, and, while it should incorporate in bank charters restrictions that would prevent recurrence of the difficulty, the rod should be spared for the present.[56]

A general resumption, which was the thing hoped for, could not be brought about except by an expansion of bank issues. Sudden contraction would put the whole community further in the toils. If the State called for the forfeiture from the banks, it would be a case of the pot calling the kettle black. The State was in a condition of suspension herself. Her own bank was the first to suspend. She was unable to pass her bonds at par; she was paying the interest on the public debt in her own irredeemable bank bills, and her laborers on the State capitol were paid in the same way. Moreover, she had invited the present embarrassment by creating new banks when and where they were not needed.[57]

Nothing could be done suddenly to relieve a calamity that was brought on by a series of years of neglect; the only hope was to prevent it in future.[58] All restrictions had failed. The banks of the State, with a million of capital, might issue three millions in bills, and not have ten thousand dollars of specie in their vaults. The New York plan had proved fallacious—the banks suspended and stocks deposited against paper issues brought little in hard money.[59]

He gave, from his own experience, a little review of the waves of prosperity and depression. In 1817 it was his lot to commence early in life to provide for himself. The five years after that were dull (this would be, fortunately for him, the period of his apprenticeship only), and the closest economy was necessary to the successful development of any enterprise. About 1823, signs of prosperity appeared, and things continued to improve up to 1833, "when a period of bank inflation and speculation commenced, which in a few years run the people of our country mad." His account shows how he preserved his own sense of proportion. "Negro fellows went up, in a short time, from $350 to $1,500 and $1,800. . . . Every man expected to be a *millionaire*, and there was scarcely a successful merchant in the country that was not preparing to branch his concern, and spread his business to the winds. Soap and candle-men had become *wholesale* merchants, and looked forward to the day when they would be ranked among the Rothschilds. . . . The banks and speculators, who later embraced half the people of the country, had so bloated up their affairs, that an explosion *had* to take place."[60] In the recent period of excitement, the wild spirit of land speculation, which had ruined so many in 1818 and again in 1837, had developed a third time "and more land has been entered and paid for by speculators, than can be settled by increase of population in fifty years." We are not surprised to find him deploring the lack of attention to upbuilding of industry, though, as a matter of fact, the fairly prompt recovery from the panic of 1857 was partly due to the preponderance of this sort of investment over more insubstantial speculations. "Indeed every thing has been taken hold of with avidity," he lamented, "except such investments as were necessary to develop the industrial resources of the country. They have been thrown in the shade. . . ."[61]

Gregg proposed the following program for preventing suspension in future: (1) Repeal of usury laws; (2) All banks should be required to keep one dollar in specie for every three in circulation; (3) No bank note was to be under the denomination of $20; (4) Passage of an act to raise the limit of interest of bank discounts to 8 per cent on notes or bills of exchange; (5) No bank in South Carolina to be permitted to purchase notes of individuals; (6) Nor was any bank to lend capital on call to persons outside of the State; (7) Banks which suspended to be required to issue new bills from new plates, and must pay 10 per cent damages for the act of suspension to holders of old bills, and 8 per cent on the bills during the continuance of suspension; and (8) The cashier must monthly take oath that his bank had not violated its charter. Such provisions, he felt, would put the currency on a sound basis and guarantee against superabundance of banking capital in future.[62]

It was a mistake to suppose that the banks consulted the general benefit. "The country at large is interested in a sound, and, as nearly as possible, a hard money currency. The banks are interested . . . to drive out of circulation every hard dollar, and put in its place three of paper money." He held excessive bank issues responsible for raising the rate of interest and consequently for crisis and ensuing reaction. The best shield that could be thrown around the people to protect them against exorbitant rates of interest would be proper restrictions on the issue of paper money; this would reach indirectly an object which usury laws would utterly fail of accomplishing.[63] He appealed to his own experience at Graniteville as illustrative of his doctrine. In 1845-6, (when the Graniteville factory was projected) when the bank circulation was low, agricultural and industrial enterprises in South Carolina and Georgia went steadily ahead. "No man, who could raise money, thought of giving over 7 per cent. As President of the Graniteville Company, I borrowed large sums of money . . . at 5 per cent, and that, from some of the best financiers of the country. As paper money became more abundant, speculation commenced with it, so that in 1848 I had to raise my rate of interest to 6 per cent and in 1850 to 7 per cent. After 1850, I was floating on the open sea, and when the Company required temporary loans, the interest ranged from 8 to 10 per cent."[64]

191

Touching his proposal to require the deposit of one dollar in hard money against every three dollars of paper issued, he observed that people little understood the use of bank bills. "Banks can add nothing to the wealth of a community by the issue of paper money, but may frequently, if improperly located, do more harm than good. . . ." Banks should be confined to mercantile cities, he thought. (It is interesting that he believed "legitimate banking" could not "be extended much beyond facilitating the export of the produce . . . from the country, and then to aid merchants to import into the country. . . ." The supplying of bank loans to industrialists was not common in the South at this time, and Gregg probably got most of the money he needed to borrow for the operation of Graniteville from individual capitalists. This was due in part to the undeveloped state of manufacturing in the South, but was also due to the view that an enterpriser bore his own risk). What did a planter or mechanic want with paper money that he should clamor for banks? The prices of the products of industry and agriculture had not gone up with the cost of equipment for carrying these on. And he quoted Liverpool cotton prices to prove his point.[65]

He did not wish to bring the Bank of South Carolina into discredit. He knew personally every bank president in the State and most of the directors. He did not believe there was a better managed set of institutions anywhere, but there were too many banks. The new banks, chartered since 1850, had drawn the older institutions, which had given a high character to South Carolina bank bills, into bad practices. "Their competition has nearly uprooted all our old modes of doing business, so that to sit down and do nothing more than the legitimate *business* of the country, is downright fogyism."[66] Too many railroads had been built in the United States, and the Blue Ridge Railroad and the too handsome State House were unwarranted speculations for South Carolina. A succession of short crops had maintained agricultural prices, thus blinding the South to the effects of inflation. Inflated currency, however, had "cast a withering blight upon all manufacturing industry at the South."[67] Depression would call for the curtailment of the paper circulation to half its present amount. The banks need not suppose that it was a special imposition upon them that they must reform their methods. "The banks may look for hard times, and so may all indebted men."

Six months after Gregg made this bank speech in the House of Representatives he defended it in an open letter to Thornton Coleman. He was now running for the State Senate and made this letter a campaign document to give his views on other questions besides that of the currency—notably State extravagance in public works. The letter, as it lights up the episode of the bank speech, shows that William Gregg was not a deft politician by any means. Though his object had been to sustain the public welfare, and particularly that of cotton growers, he was accused of being a partisan of the banks. His honesty and considered moderation were fatal to his chances of election at a time when candidates

193

courted success by joining in the popular clamor, however unthinking it might be. Blasts against the banks won votes, though these might redound to the hurt of the people; it was a thankless task to seek to protect the State's credit, for heavy compensating taxation, however it might loom for the future, was held in check by self-serving officeholders.

Gregg complained in his open letter that many had been led to believe that because he voted to legalize suspension, he was a large bank stockholder and favored the banks against the people. "That is a radical mistake," he explained. "Everybody, that carefully reads my bank speech, will see that I am strictly an anti-bank man." He had not been, for some years past, he said, a large bank investor, having now but a small amount of stock, and that in one bank only. "For every dollar of bank stock, held by me, I have at least forty dollars, invested in great branches of productive industry. My business sympathizes with every branch of industry in the country, and not with banks and money brokers."[68]

He had voted against contraction because, under the existing circumstances of over-trading, a sudden checking of the currency would bring disaster to the whole country. He told how he reasoned when the question came before the legislature. His analysis was penetrating and just. The banks had loaned to the people their entire capital, $17,000,000 and also $17,100,000 in bank bills. News came that the banks in New York were about to suspend, and the State was being drained of its hard money. The banks called for the repayment of

194

even a small part of the people's debt to them. The debtors answered that they could not pay unless the banks loaned to merchants so that the cotton crop might go to market. The merchants urged the banks to suspend. Old England, New England, and every cotton-consuming country had led the way. The legislature would never penalize such an act. Cotton had sunk from 16 to 10 cents. "Under a pressure of specie, and a clamor for loans, the banks suspended; and, just as things began to grow easier, down comes the Comptroller on the banks, for the monthly rate of 5 per cent per annum, on their outstanding circulation, which the people owed them. The people now say to the banks, you have dishonored and brought a stain upon the credit of the State, by a suspension of specie payments, and, although your bills are willingly taken for anything we have to sell, . . . yet, for the sake of consistency, you ought to be required to pay the penalty affixed by law for suspension."[69]

To this the banks responded that if the people demanded that the letter of the law be adhered to, the banks could escape the penalty by resuming specie payments—to the dire distress of their creditors. Gregg was convinced that, rather than be liable for what would amount to a tax of 16 2-3 per cent on the $3,000,000 extra notes which they were asked to issue, they would have carried out this obvious threat. "The banks could have been soon replenished with specie at some sacrifice; but they would have forced every dollar that could have been collected from the country. With a pressure on every man who owed money, and the absence of means to

195

purchase the produce of the country, what would have been our condition? There would have been a harvest for shavers and lawyers, but ruin to every other interest." The banks in South Carolina had not been responsible for the suspension of 1857; it was a world convulsion, and currency debates in a cotton State only served to depress the price of the staple.[70] Gregg's wisdom in refusing to coerce the banks to resumption was shown, as a matter of fact, by their return to specie payments soon afterwards, half a year before the date set by law.[71]

To return now to the proceedings in Columbia, following Gregg's speech the debate continued in both branches of the legislature. Meantime, the New York banks resumed specie payments. On Gregg's side in the controversy were DeSaussure, Mitchell, Yeadon, Mc-Carter, Boylston, and Thompson of Abbeville.[72] Gregg seems not to have made any other speech, though on December 11th he said a few words regarding the private banks.[73] Test votes indicated that in the House the decision would be close. After amendments to both House and Senate bills and further changes in conference, a bill was carried, December 19th,[74] which represented Gregg's wishes with the exception that the commission of inquiry was dropped out.

When, the next year, Gregg was nominated for the State senatorship from Edgefield, he consented to run if he were not expected to make a campaign, and for a while it was thought that he would have no opposition. As soon as a candidate came out against him (Judge

Carroll) Gregg used his best endeavors to decline making a contest. He wrote to Hammond from Kalmia that people in his neighborhood were beginning to talk about local elections, the senatorial in particular, "and I begin to wish myself out of the scrape. It would suit me much better to remain at my own quiet fireside than to go to Columbia where I can see no comfort, and gain no laurels that can add to my fame."[75] "But the party who nominated would not listen" to his withdrawing. "I was therefore pressed into the field and had a hot contest such as I never expect to involve myself in again."[76] Gregg had no idea that his bank speech in the legislature the year before would be used against him and he was even more surprised and hurt to discover that even his Graniteville enterprise was being seized upon by his opponents, who claimed that he was overworking and underpaying the people of the village.[77]

Tompkins has told of an incident in the campaign of Gregg against Chancellor Carroll for the place of State Senator, in words which may be quoted: "It was the habit of candidates to appear together and speak to the people from the same platform, and at the same meetings. On one of these occasions, Mr. Gregg spoke first. He stated that he solicited votes on the ground that he had built a factory, which gave work to poor white people. It enhanced the value of cotton by manufacturing it. He had planted peach orchards to develop new avenues of profit and advantage to the people. . . . whereas, Chancellor Carroll had never made two blades of grass grow where only one grew before.

197

"Mr. Carroll followed Mr. Gregg. He was an accomplished orator, and praised in eloquent terms, Mr. Gregg's enterprise in building a factory. He eulogized his plans for fruit culture. He admitted, with humility, all the delinquencies Mr. Gregg charged against him excepting only one: 'He says I never made two blades of grass grow where only one grew before. Having faith in Mr. Gregg's plans and advice about orchards, I planted one, and if anybody is disposed to believe I never made grass grow, I simply invite them to go look at that orchard. It is literally run away with grass.' The crowd laughed, voted for Mr. Carroll and the cause of slavery went forward while Mr. Gregg staid [*sic*] at home and the cause of civilization languished."[78]

There is an interesting picture of the Graniteville villagers in 1858 in a campaign document of Gregg's, to which reference has been made.[79] He had thought the Graniteville enterprise would commend him to every one, but busybodies were circulating reports that he was exploiting the employes. He hastened at the outset of his defense to reply to these charges. Any one who would take the pains to come and see for himself, would find the population of Graniteville thrifty, he contended, "and possibly one of the happiest on earth. It has been the work of twenty years of my life," he said, "to promote the welfare and better the condition of the class of people, who are settled at Graniteville. The widow and orphan there find a home and protection; the laboring man, too, finds employment, and his children are educated free of charge, and brought up to habits of morality and systematic industry." As badly off as some would have the mill people to be, they had about $12-000 in the savings bank. One is reminded of the stories of the farmers' daughters at Lowell a generation earlier, in the statement that a hundred young women, weavers, earned from seventy-five cents to a dollar a day, and many of them accumulated enough to buy homes for their partners when they married. "Will you believe me, when I tell you that pianos have been purchased, and music lessons paid for, in the same way. Negroes also have been bought, and the Company is about to sub-divide the shares of stock . . . that the operatives may become stockholders." Graniteville, distributing a thou-sand dollars a day for labor and the produce of the country, furnished a ready cash market for everything raised within twenty miles of the village.

Since Gregg's time there have been defenses and eulogies by employers of their mill villages, extolling in-dustry and good morals. If there is some cant in the modern picture, there was none in the older. In the general admission and in the eager testimony of the surviving inhabitants of the place who knew him, Gregg was right when he declared: "Graniteville will be a monument to the memory of its projectors, when time shall have swept away the present generation. The chil-dren, now growing up and receiving education at Gran-iteville, will recollect us, and what we have done for them, when the active men of this day shall have all passed away."

The peace and order here described were not brought about without watchfulness on the part of the Granite-ville officials. A decade later, when the poverty ensuing

199

on the Civil War gave the Poor Whites of the district a special incentive to seek a refuge and employment in the manufacturing village, Gregg reminded his stockholders that living at a distance and coming only now and then to look on a pretty picture, they could have no idea of the difficulty of keeping up a working force of the right kind of people. "If bad people get into our community, and vicious habits begin to prevail, the better class of people who are the most valuable to us, will gradually leave the place. There is a pressure on us all the time for places—many good people and many bad ones want to come, so that a vacant house and an opening for employment bring a dozen competitors for the favor. . . . We are annoyed all the time by wagon loads of people sent here by neighborhood contributions to get clear of them."[80]

Something of William Gregg's requirement of strict discipline in the working force may be seen in an old set of *Rules and Regulations of the Graniteville Manufacturing Company*. These are signed by his son, James J. Gregg, as superintendent, and may have been promulgated subsequent to the father's death, but in any event these customs would keep to his tradition. The first seven rules relate to overseers and second hands, enjoining promptness, attention to the efficiency of machinery, and a close supervision of operatives. The next five rules pertain to the workers. "All the operatives will be *required* to be *promptly* at their stations for work at *the last tap of the bell*. They must be respectful both in language and deportment to their . . . overseers . . . and observe

200

every rule of the room in which they are employed. They must be *particularly* attentive to the *cleaning* and *oiling* of the machinery on which they are engaged, and neatness in their own person and habits is enjoined." To protect operatives against being caught in the machinery it was a rule that "No Hats, Caps, Coats, Bonnets, or Shawls must be worn during work hours." Intemperance and profanity are given with other offenses, as cause for dismissal. Any willful damage to machinery or other property of the company would be charged double the cost of repairs and the offender dismissed. "The drinking of intoxicating liquors in or about the Mill, will not be allowed." Two weeks' notice was required of operatives leaving the company's employ, or they must forfeit the wages due them. "Each overseer is required, by precept and example, to enforce a steady compliance to the foregoing Rules; should he violate them, or in any manner undervalue or disparage them . . . he will be disqualified for the important post he occupies and need not complain if he is dismissed."

CHAPTER X

GRANITEVILLE MOBILIZES FOR WAR

There is little to indicate William Gregg's attitude toward secession and the Civil War. At the time he was writing his pamphlets, fifteen years before the conflict broke out, he disapproved of all the incitements that might lead to an appeal to arms. Certainly everything that he argued for—the planting of manufactures and economic improvement generally—would thrive best upon peace and union. The practical lesson of industrial progress which he preached at Graniteville led away from the political dogmatism of the ruling school of South Carolina spokesmen.

As the conflict came to appear inevitable, Gregg was moved to throw in his loyalty with his State. Gregg's contacts with the Northern industry, his friendships with Boston enterprisers, and his own national position in the cotton manufacture, quite aside from his broad wisdom as an economist, predisposed him against the war. On the other hand, as the master of Graniteville he had a special duty to his seceding State and soon to the Confederacy. A principal cotton mill was second in importance only to munitions works. He was for long years a Charleston man, after his removal to Graniteville was constantly back there, and necessarily felt the indignation which had its fountain head in that city. Hammond—nullifier, disciple of Cal-

202

houn, exclaimer of "Cotton is King!"—was his friend
and near neighbor at Graniteville. Had there been a
more numerous class of manufacturers in the South at
this time, Gregg might have led in an opposing sentiment, but he was surrounded by men of the landed and
slaveholding interest, or merchants and bankers closely
associated with agriculture.

At any rate, we find Gregg one of the delegates elected
from Edgefield to the convention of the people of South
Carolina to consider the relations of the commonwealth
"with the Northern States and the government of the
United States." He was one of that grave assemblage
which met in the First Baptist Church in Columbia on
December 17, 1860, and he went with the rest, on account of smallpox in the capital city, to resume the convention the next day in Charleston. He must have
marched into Institute Hall arm in arm with Judge
Carroll, who had been his political foe in Edgefield,
for the signing of the Ordinance of Secession. Gregg's
fine, bold signature appears on the document immediately under that of Carroll.

It is not surprising to find in the minutes of the
Graniteville stockholders, under date of June 5, 1861,
that "Owing to the political state of the country the Annual Meeting which should have been held on the 18th
April was postponed until today." Most of those interested in Graniteville were residents of Charleston,
with large investments there and important men in the
turmoil of the times. Major Anderson, starved and bom-
barded into submission, had surrendered Sumter on

203

Saturday, April 13, and on Sunday had marched out of the fort. The week that followed was too crowded with portent and high excitement to permit any one to think of the affairs of a little mill in the interior. Lincoln issued his proclamation calling for 75,000 volunteers on Monday. Tuesday the Massachusetts militia began to muster, Wednesday the Sixth Regiment started for Washington, and Virginia joined in secession. Thursday (the regular day for the meeting of the Graniteville stockholders) the Federals abandoned Harpers Ferry and burned the arsenal. The next day brought the first bloodshed of the Civil War when the Massachusetts troops were assaulted by a mob in the streets of Baltimore, and the same day Lincoln proclaimed the Atlantic coast from South Carolina to Florida blockaded. The week was brought to a ringing end when Lee resigned his commission in the United States army on Saturday.

By the time of the Graniteville meeting, the Confederate government had been organized with a permanent constitution, an army was rapidly forming, and the Congress, which was soon to move to Richmond, had authorized a loan of $50,000,000. Gregg had foreseen years earlier and had declared in his *Essays on Domestic Industry*, that if the South went to war with the North, she would not have industries to supply her wants as a belligerent.

On the eve of the Civil War Gregg was burning to turn sectional patriotism to account in furthering his lifelong design of building up Southern manufactures.

204

He published a long series of articles in DeBow's *Review* in 1860, pleading with Southerners to put themselves in an economic posture for defense. He had ardently cherished the Union, but he was forced to believe separation inevitable. The North had become fanatical. Southern industry must be patronized and not, as in the past, suspected. Southern cities must be developed as distributing centers. "Wild Africans" were not needed in the South—rather, the poor native whites should be welcomed into factory and shop, and then, if more labor was needed, Europeans should be invited to immigrate. The failures which has occurred in Southern industry were owing largely to home neglect and need not be repeated. The arguments of his *Domestic Industry* reappeared, but now were sharpened by impending crisis. But in complete disregard of such warnings, the South thought only of provocations to war, and not at all of necessary supplies for war. The section had no powder works, little machinery for making small arms, few foundries, opened few iron mines, and possessed only here and there a nucleus of needful manufactures.[1] As one devoted to the study of material resources, and the head of a young industry which would be called upon to play a leading rôle in the coming struggle, Gregg must have been struck with consternation at the prospect before him when he met his stockholders at Graniteville that day in June.

Enlargement of the factory was set about immediately. It was decided to increase the capital to $550-000, the proceeds to be invested in new machinery. In order to stimulate the taking up of the new shares, a dividend of 10 per cent was to be declared, payment being in stock rather than in earnings in hand, the earnings being reserved for the purchase of equipment. In this summer buildings were erected for finishing goods, and estimates were received from an English machinist to furnish the additional machinery, together with new equipment to refit the old mill. Some of the machinery, evidently that ordered in the spring of 1860, had been received before the blockade, and some ran the hazard of the Federal fleet. It must have been a peculiar relief to Gregg at this juncture that his second son, James, was elected treasurer. Since 1859, when William Gregg, Jr., withdrew from the treasurer's post, the father had been doing double duty, so that his work at the factory itself had forced him to give up some of his plans for extending Western sales.[2]

The spring of 1862 found Graniteville reflecting war stringencies. The period just preceding the stockholders' meeting on April 24 had been a trying one for the Confederacy. Fort Henry and Fort Donelson fell, the Monitor destroyed the Merrimac, and North Carolina ports were occupied by the enemy. The Congress suspended the writ of habeas corpus, declared martial law in Richmond and some other cities, and passed, April 16, the first conscription act. Gregg reported "the serious disadvantages under which the mill labored for the past year": the "military draft upon the operatives" had reduced the production, and, taken with the "immense increase" in the price of supplies, had greatly run up the cost of

206

the goods. The draft was not the conscription of eight days before, because thirty days were allowed for the men between the ages of 18 and 35 to respond, and besides, on April 21 workers in cotton factories had been specifically exempted from service. Those who went from Graniteville were volunteers numbered in the 19,000 calculated[3] to have gone from South Carolina by the end of 1861. The gold premium had jumped from 30 per cent in March to 50 per cent in April, and was on the climb which carried it to 6,000 per cent four years later.[4]

The meeting discussed methods of controlling sales of the Graniteville goods "in order to put down the unjust speculation which was going on throughout the country. . . ." Apparently the stockholders felt that the speculators depreciated the currency, rather than that the redundancy of currency invited the speculation.[5] The conclusion in these circumstances was dictated as much by a desire to capture the advancing prices for the advantage of the company, as by patriotic virtue. At the commencement of the war there had been a let-down in all business in the South, and Graniteville was particularly affected by the trade inactivity in Charleston.[6] Gregg said later: "The price of Southern domestics did not advance for four months after the blockade of our ports, and not until our manufacturers began to be alarmed at the prospect of a short supply of oil, card-clothing and many other scarce and indispensable articles. When it became apparent that the supply on hand was being rapidly exhausted and had to be re-

207

newed by running the blockade, everything of the kind advanced to such a degree that manufacturers were under the necessity of raising the price of cloth long before cotton or any other agricultural product (except bacon) had risen at all."[7]

In the face of the brisk and accelerating demand for the products of the factory, it was decided that when present orders had been filled, the president should proceed to hold weekly "trade sales" (i.e., for brokers and merchants) of all goods produced at Graniteville; due notice was to be given to the public when the first sale would take place, and the way was left open for the unexpected by providing that the company might change the place or the mode of disposing of the product.

Holders of the company scrip were to be allowed to pay a sufficient amount in cash to convert it into capital, and a 5 per cent dividend was declared.[8]

The old conflict as between sales through a Charleston agent and sales direct came to a new crisis through the policy of auctions. The stockholders were called to Graniteville for a special meeting July 15, 1862. Gregg in his report explained that there was much dissatisfaction among the Charleston merchants who had sent orders under date of February 17, to be put on file and filled in turn, the company appropriating half of the product of the factory for that purpose. With many of these orders still unfilled, the officers had some doubts about carrying out directions to commence sales at auction, "and were exceedingly perplexed, after the Augusta Mill commenced the auction system, to know what we should set as the current value of our goods." Gregg watched the results of the experiment at Augusta. The first sale marked an advance in prices, but not beyond what every merchant was willing to pay. Besides commitments to Charleston buyers, there was a growing public antagonism to give Gregg pause. Reviewing this period later, he said: "By the time 4-4 sheetings, drills and osnaburgs had advanced to twelve and thirteen cents—a price quite reasonable, and such as English competition will allow us even without a tariff—we had the whole community down on us, berating us through the newspapers, at public meetings and even in the pulpit, as a set of heartless *extortioners,* worse than Yankee vandals. And before our goods had reached twenty-five cents, the public mind had become so exasperated that many thought our mills were in danger of violent destruction from the *mob.* These prejudices spread far and wide, and evidently influenced the action of Congress and our State Legislatures in their many unjustifiable exactions."[9]

To the next large Augusta auction Gregg sent a few bales of Graniteville goods, similar to those sold at the first auction, and they went off at sharply advanced prices—32 cents for drills, 31 cents for 4-4, 26¼ for 7-8, 22⅞ for 3-4. This sale was considered a fair test of the current value of the goods; Gregg advised his correspondents of this and gave them the privilege of countermanding their orders if they wished. Taft & Company were asked to explain the situation to Graniteville's Charleston customers, making it clear that their orders would be supplied at the last auction price, or they might cancel their orders. Taft & Company replied that all orders through them were to be considered countermanded.

So matters stood until a large Charleston house advised Gregg that a group of merchants in the city intended to claim the goods at first auction prices or sue for damages, since they had not received notice of the factory's policy, had not authorized the countermanding of their orders, considered themselves badly treated, and would never purchase Graniteville goods again if they could avoid it. Gregg, not conscious of having done anything to incur the displeasure of the Charleston trade, had decided to lay the matter before the stockholders. Though a man of forbearance, he was by no means lacking in discernment and could speak plainly. In this particular instance his old inconveniences from Graniteville's dependence upon Charleston pricked him on. "I think much of the discontent," he told the stockholders, (and it must be remembered that some of the Charleston merchants in question were present at the meeting) "resulted from an indisposition on the part of the merchants to order ahead of their immediate supplies. While other merchants more secure from the dangers of war were anxious purchasers and ordered freely, Charleston orders were held back, until there was a general advance in our goods far ahead of our asking rates and it had become a matter of speculation to obtain our goods, and it was then and only then, when we discovered a desire to obtain our goods for Charleston trade. It became urgent for the reason that every bale which was received under former prices previous to the auction sales yielded them a profit over former prices of from $60 to $80 a bale."

Due to the war demand, coming on the top of years of progress, Graniteville had become more than an appendix of the trade of one city. Charleston merchants, Gregg said, should not expect to get goods at prices lower than large and respectable dealers in other cities were ready to give. "They must all be fully aware that our Company have never had the slightest disposition to cramp them in their supplies, or to do them (our former and great customers) the slightest injustice," and he believed they would recognize this.

Mr. Gilliland spoke for the Charleston merchants but did not make out a case, for it was concluded that all merchants who had declined taking the residue of their goods at auction prices had no further claims on the company. However, there was some question as to whether the policy of auction sales should not be dropped for the future. Mr. Yeadon offered a motion that "The attempt of this Company to fix the price of their fabrics by sales at auction, has proved a failure and subjected the Company to the odious charge of extortion and that the same be . . . abandoned." But Gregg's policy was sustained, the motion being tabled.

The net earnings of the company for the six months previous were $225,788.09, of course in currency. It was proposed to divide 10 per cent in anticipation of

211

the next January. Gregg believed that to do more than this would be imprudent, that it would be more advisable to make a special extra dividend at some other time. His reason for this counsel shows him the thorough manufacturer. Few were as alive as Gregg to the uncorrected wear and tear which must be set over against extraordinary war gains. "When the war came on," he explained, "we were importing from England to replace gradually out of our extra earnings, machinery that had become worn and not exactly such as would keep us up with the age. The war of course cut off those supplies and has interfered materially with keeping our machinery in working condition, so that we are now compelled to run at high speed, without the necessary additions and repairs." He was constantly thinking of the long-time result, which he knew was conditioned by the quality of the Graniteville product. "The consequence is," he continued, "that much of our machinery is so worn that we will not be able after the war to make such goods as we at first made and such as will give us the command of the markets of the country, which I think is all important for us to do. This dreadful wear and tear will in my estimation require an outlay for new machinery and repairs of $80,000 to $100,000."

For some time, as Graniteville succeeded, he had been growing away from the early fear of diversification. Also, since the outbreak of the war, Graniteville was relieved of any competition from fine goods mills in the North and in England. With such an overhauling as he proposed, Gregg said the mill could "be put in such a plight as will enable us to make better goods than we have ever done, with the ability to change to a variety of styles of goods, such as would have enabled us in the last 12 months to have realized more than double what we have made." He recommended that a large surplus be held toward the purchase of a 225 horse-power engine and a third more machinery; at the proper time there should be such an increase in stock as would furnish a money capital to render the company in some degree independent financially. Gregg was able to report that he had on hand 4,218 bales of cotton invoiced at 9 cents per pound.[10]

Before the meeting closed, $2,500 was appropriated to the equipment of the Edgefield Rangers, and $500 more was put in the hands of Lieutenant Gregg "for any exigencies of individuals of said Company." This was probably James Gregg. John Gregg was the first of the sons to go into the war; he was first lieutenant in Company F of the Seventh Regiment of South Carolina Volunteers, which was composed entirely of Graniteville boys, and served throughout the war in Kershaw's Brigade. Lieutenant Gregg died of pneumonia the opening winter of the war, at Charlottesville, December 1, 1861. From this organization Pinckney and Tillman Faulkner were detailed by the War Department to return from the field to work in the mill at Graniteville.[11] It was told me by one of the old members of Company F that three captains of the organization were killed. The military company spoken of in these minutes of 1862 had doubtless been enrolled under the first conscription law. Earlier, in April, troops enlisted from Graniteville had shown an indisposition of volunteers, common enough in the Confederacy, to serve outside the boundaries of their own State. The Nineteenth Regiment of South Carolina Volunteers reached Augusta on April 12 on their way to the West. On coming to the Georgia Railway depot more than a hundred of the men refused to go further, saying they had enlisted to serve their own State only, and had not been consulted by their officers before the move was made. "The officers urged in vain the stigma that would rest upon them for refusing to go where their country most needed their services, and the reproach they would bring upon the State of South-Carolina, which had been foremost in the work of resistance. Their appeals were unavailing, and the malcontents returned to the Carolina depot. . . . About thirty of the mutinists belonged to the command of Capt. Gregg, Graniteville. He was proceeding to execute the order of Gen. Gist [to arrest the men as deserters of the worst character], when many of his men and others that refused to go on in the morning took the evening train which conveyed the Tenth regiment, Col. Manigault."[12]

In these years Graniteville was looked upon as a principal recourse by the countryside, and William Gregg's charities expanded beyond the limits of his own village. "During the war everybody about the office was over worked," Gregg said later. "Sometimes as many as two hundred letters were received in a day, and I had to answer the Government requisitions and all the beggars that came in person or by letter. . . . Soldiers' aid societies, sewing societies, stocking knitters, soldiers' wives, indeed, every class of applicants had to be answered and conciliated. If we refused to grant their demands, however unreasonable they might be, the pulpit and the press denounced us in unmeasured terms of abuse.[13]

Gregg had hard time enough feeding the people of Graniteville. Thus we find him writing to Hammond in June, 1864: "I find so much trouble in procuring corn in small quantities, having to haul it when I do purchase, that I now regret I did not take a part of that which you said you were going to sell at $8.50 when I was at your house. I will take 4,000 or 5,000 bushels for the Company . . . The Government is taking the corn up and down the railroads and when we purchase a lot it is impressed immediately, but has always been released when we demanded it to feed our people now working almost entirely for the Government."[14] It is not certain whether this lot of corn reached Graniteville, for it may have been impressed despite Gregg's exemption.[15]

The demands of the government upon a factory like Graniteville not only were felt by anxious executives, but entailed extra exertion on the part of the operatives, who were already working twelve hours a day exclusive of mealtimes. It would have been difficult to add to the force of hands—men were needed for the army, and women and children, if they were moved to the village, would have to be accommodated in new houses built for the purpose. Shortage of operatives was responsible for the fact that the mill was not run in two shifts through the 24 hours.

Overtime was the only answer, and Gregg consequently issued over his signature the following "Appeal
to the People of Graniteville," which was probably distributed to the homes.[16] The mill at this time was making large profits; yet the note of patriotism was undoubtedly sincere. The appeal read:

"The Graniteville Company wish to run the Mill two
extra hours at night, for which they will pay double
wages, thus allowing each individual a third of a day's
work. The Government is pressing us for more cloth,
charitable societies and the people are pressing us—
the whole country is suffering. Our fathers, brothers,
sons and husbands in the army want clothes, and the
quantity made is not sufficient. The patriotic women of
our land, rich and poor, are working day and night
for our suffering army. The girls of tender age, as well
as older maidens and matrons are working by candle
and torch light in the relief of our soldiers, and shall
we, at Graniteville, hesitate to do our part? In two hours
at night we can make five thousand yards of cloth, a
day's work for six thousand women—enough to make
a shirt apiece for a thousand men, and shall we shrink
from this additional labor? We hope not. The spark of
patriotism is kindled in every Southern bosom, even to
the little children who cannot go to the war to fight, but
will be found willing to toil and suffer for their country's
good." This meant that the Graniteville operatives must
work 14 hours a day.

There was an overwhelming demand for the output
of the factory, as Gregg said, and profits shot up. Gregg
had a difference with the directors as to what should be

GRANITEVILLE FACTORY

done with the surplus funds, he wishing, to judge from a more serious crisis which arose the following year, to invest heavily in cotton. He called the stockholders together in December, 1862, to settle the matter. Boyce and Taylor, the latter a member of the directors, were for using the money for increase of plant. They proposed: (1) That $234,750 be set apart for increasing the manufacturing powers of the mill "to the extent of the new building" (that is, to equip the finishing plant); (2) That $115,250 be appropriated to replace old machinery with new; (3) That $50,000 be appropriated for cash capital. What disposition was made of these proposals is not noted in the minutes, and in the absence of a record of what the earnings were it is impossible to say whether a part or all of this program was carried through by a motion unanimously adopted; this motion provided that a stock dividend of 50 per cent and a cash dividend of 25 per cent be declared and paid on the 20th of the month.

Choice between would-be buyers of the Graniteville goods remained a puzzling matter; Gregg must have sought to get the backing of the stockholders in a plan as to which he had encountered opposition from the directors, but the meeting, very properly, threw the problem back upon the officers of the company. It was decided that the distribution of all goods on sale be left to the president and directors. Three proposals were received as suggestions: (1) That all orders by the Confederate and State governments, all orders of soldiers' aid societies or by South Carolinians in behalf of indigent soldiers or their families, should have preference in order of time and amount; (2) "That merchants in the regular trade shall be supplied in the order as they present themselves, the limit in amount to be determined by the president and directors"; (3) That stockholders be placed on the same footing with other individuals. This last suggestion was perhaps aimed particularly at A. R. Taft, a director and Charleston agent for the mill's goods; at any rate, Mr. Taft resigned from the board. James P. Boyce was elected in his stead.[17]

Harmony prevailed at the next meeting of stockholders, April 23, 1863. A resolution of cordial approval of the administration of the president and directors was passed. The company regretted losing the services of James Montgomery, the superintendent; the resignation of Montgomery must have been a blow to Gregg in the midst of the war period, but the place was well supplied by H. H. Hickman. The company had now gone into the store business; here goods from the mill were bartered for corn, peas, bacon, lard, sugar, molasses, and other supplies, which were in turn sold to the operatives. The store was now a great source of revenue to the company. In all probability operatives were paid partly in kind, which gave them more for a day's work than they could get with depreciating currency, and this plan also made the adjustment of wages simpler for the mill. The prosperity of the company was reflected in new improvements in the village; Gregg sold 110 bales of goods for the benefit of the school and churches, particularly for building an Episcopal church.[18]

In the long year that followed,[19] crowded with problems of war-time operation, a conflict of policy between Gregg and the directors, which had been hinted at before, came to a head. There were on hand surplus profits of $1,099,976.16 (currency) and 6,512 bales of cotton inventoried at 40 cents, its average cost (again currency). Shortly after the capital had been increased with a view to extending the works, Gregg invested the surplus capital ($342,000) in cotton, and for many months had about 6,000 bales laid aside to preserve that capital, which, due to the blockade, could not be spent for equipment then. His intention was to hold this cotton and purchase other cotton as it should be needed to run the mill.

Boyce represented the opposite view. He addressed the meeting at some length. He did not like the policy of investing the surplus capital in cotton, for holding such a large supply at this time was inadvisable. (He may have been afraid of its destruction by Federal troops, though nothing of this was spoken outright. Gregg at one time during the war did store cotton in temporary shelters in a field a little removed from the mill.) Boyce may have been influenced by changes in the price; the price had more than doubled early in the year, had risen further in March, April, and May—to 17 times its 1860 price, in currency. There were fluctuations in June and July, and he may have foreseen the drop that ensued in August and September—a fall of one-fourth—and calculated upon taking the profit. He was in favor of selling the greater portion immediately and purchasing for

219

the mill as it might be required. An animated discussion followed. Taylor, who had usually stood with Gregg, offered a resolution, "chiefly to test the sense of the meeting," that for the purpose of changing the investment, so much of the cotton as represented the surplus capital should be sold. There were few present at the meeting, but the Greggs, Boyce, and Taylor held many proxies. The motion was lost, 486½ shares for and 579½ against, only William Gregg and his son being in opposition. There was a pause, in which Gregg was told that he had voted against the wishes of some of the largest stockholders. He then, after some consideration, asked permission to change his vote, which left only his son voting in the negative, and the motion was carried. Boyce now secured assent to a motion that all of the cotton which could not be brought to Graniteville and kept in the warehuses there should be sold, enough of the proceeds to cover the cash capital to be "invested safely" and the balance to be divided.[20]

Thus directed, Gregg proceeded to sell cotton and purchase English exchange. But, as he said later in excusing a want of cash capital, directors "were anxious to hold as little property as possible, and to divide everything that could be divided among the stockholders, in currency, during the war. Our stockholders were also clamorous for sales of cotton and distribution of the proceeds." The directors met at Graniteville in October and were convinced by a letter from Boyce "protesting against the investment of money in sterling exchange, and asking the board to consider the making

a cash dividend of one hundred per cent."[21] Here was
an end of the tilt. Gregg looked to the continuing health
and prosperity of the manufacturing enterprise. He saw
beyond war years. He had tried against odds to keep the
plant up to par, wanting to emerge from the struggle
with as nearly as possible normal facilities in cash and
equipment. If cotton was not a suitable security for the
surplus funds, he had no such dislike for England's
policy toward the South as would forbid investment in
sterling exchange. But others had a shorter view. They
did not realize, as Gregg did, that wear and tear of plant
must soon be made up for. They wanted the immediate
gain.

How did manufacturers in the South regard Confederate war policy? Much is to be learned from an address made by Gregg before the Manufacturers' Association of the Confederate States, at Augusta, Georgia, in
May, 1864.[22] It was a complaint that the government
had discouraged industry where it ought to have enabled
it. A coöperative policy would have been wisdom from
the standpoint of the prosecution of the war, but also
Gregg was disappointed that the permanent stimulus to
manufactures which the conflict might have imparted,
had been lost through obstructionist tactics. It is apparent here as elsewhere that Gregg was thinking in
terms of public economy, that he had in mind the long-
time advantage of the people. He began his address by
lauding the power of association. "We may collectively
bring an influence to bear on our Government," he said,
"that would be irresistible in obtaining permission to

221

take out cotton and bring in supplies. . . ." Steamships might be purchased for the purpose. If the war was to be drawn out longer, it must be recognized that shiploads of machinery and tools to make it would become as important as arms and munitions—the government might be obliged to offer bounties for the extension of manufactures, "instead of the clogs heretofore put upon them." In spite of fabulous prices paid for goods, profits had been withheld from manufacturers and transferred to traders and speculators, and "contrary to all expectations at the commencement of the war, manufacturing production has not been increased, but retrograded; many mills have been destroyed by the enemy, and some by accident, while none have been built, and no new machinery has been put into operation."

To explain this sad state of things, he recalled something of his own efforts in industry. ". . . I have spent a better portion of my life in assiduous efforts with my pen, and by my working example," he said, "to establish the manufacture of cotton on a permanent basis in the South." After a struggle to obtain a charter, Graniteville was started, and simultaneously a number of other large factories were erected. "Many of the companies failed from bad management and other various causes, but principally from the want of proper support and patronage by our own people; some of them sinking the entire capital invested. Such was the indifference of the Southern people to the success of these useful and interesting establishments, that thousands of bales of our fine, honestly made domestics were shipped an-

222

nually to New York, Philadelphia and Baltimore, to find Northern and foreign customers, while our people were contented to be supplied with an inferior Northern made article, composed of material not much better than the waste we discard from our mills." Gregg had at least hoped that if he could raise manufactures in the South there would be a home market for the product, but he had not counted the force of an ingrained habit of dependence on the North. "In many instances," he continued, "these goods, after paying freight, storage, commissions, interest on advances and other expenses which were ruinous, were sacrified in Northern markets and sent back to compete with the break-down Southern prices, where domestic goods were invariably sold at rates so low that an English manufacturer could not come in competition with us, even if he were allowed to bring his goods in free of duty."

From 1848 to 1861 manufacturing in the South dragged. The best managed mills barely paid interest on capital, without laying up a fund for renewing worn equipment. This revived and confirmed the old antagonism toward industry. "The impression was becoming general that our Southern States were not the atmosphere for manufacturing, and the great body of the people seemed quite reconciled to the idea that Southern manufactures would be entirely abandoned. Indeed, many had become inimical to such enterprises, and regarded them as nothing less than hot bed attempts to rear up a branch of industry antagonistic to free trade and exclusive agriculture if not nurseries of

223

Abolitionism." Then the war brought a shortage of supplies, these advanced in price and put up the price of goods in turn, so that cotton manufacturers were branded as extortioners. The government was influenced by this outcry in making what Gregg called its exactions.

Congress passed an act, March 26, 1863, to regulate impressments. The president appointed a commissioner in each State where property was taken for public use, and the governor appointed another commissioner, the two constituting a board to publish at intervals schedules of prices to be paid for impressed goods.[23] "Had it been the design of Congress," said Gregg, "to restrict the advance of manufacturing industry, and confine it to a limited and sickly existence, they could not have adopted a more certain means of reaching that object than they obtained by the Conscript Act, which undertook to regulate and limit the price of manufactured articles in the hands of the producer, while it left every one else to speculate on and sell such articles for all the market would afford." The unfairness of setting an arbitrarily low price was vigorously protested on all sides. The policy had the effect of raising prices in the open market, because producers tried to recoup themselves for losses to the government, and on account of the attempt to cover the risk of impressment. Also it diminished production, and this contributed to high prices.[24] The Act relaxed all of the economies of production, which was in itself enough to condemn the legislation in Gregg's eyes. "It limited producers to prices that were not remunerative, unless the cost of production was largely increased," he complained. "In this way, it opened the door for extravagant expenditure; indeed, it offered a *premium* for the most profligate outlays and enormously high wages in every branch of mechanical industry, and accelerated at a rapid pace an advance in the price of every article used in the factories."[25]

Gregg recognized the dangers of being deceived by the pathological economic conditions prevailing in war time, and he warned his hearers not to deal in distorted values. It was a common sentiment with politicians, he declared, that manufacturers should be compelled to disgorge their extortionate gains, that no exactions were too heavy for them to bear. That some manufacturers had realized large profits he did not question, "but, in the main, I do doubt very much whether, as a class, we have realized the substantial profits to which our business entitles us in times of peace." He was fully alive to the fact of inflation and its effects. He knew that redundancy of currency, and not greed nor business cunning, put up prices. Many had deceived themselves in thinking they were getting enormous profits from manufacturing—"they probably have not taken into account the amount made on the cotton purchased in advance of consumption, and that such has been the advancing tendency that nothing could be purchased and held sixty days without paying a large profit." Payments for foreign supplies and machinery brought in through the blockade told the tale. "As a class of men, we must of necessity reduce everything to a gold standard," he re-

225

minded, "so that a million of earnings counts no more than fifty thousand. . . . We can neither renew our machinery nor extend our works, except it be with gold, and it takes three dollars in gold now to purchase what one dollar would before the war." It was impossible, moreover, to insure mills at their current value, so that companies should make a heavy deduction since they had begun to take their own risks. And the great item of depreciation of machinery driven at high speed and without proper repairs was often not set off against profits which seemed to be realized. Graniteville in 1863, after turning over half its goods to the government at cost, and after paying taxes and making all proper allowances, made only 7 per cent on the investment—no better than in some former years before 1860.

In answer to the objection that manufacturers should not make profit at all while others joined the army and risked their lives without price, Gregg replied that the country could not be supplied with "clothing from home-made cloth" unless encouragement were given to investment. He resented the acclaim given the blockade runner, while execration visited the home manufacturer. We must believe better of Gregg than to think he drew this distinction because of the competition which blockade goods offered to his own. Rather, he was the old enemy of dependence upon outsiders for manufactures. If profits, he said, were confined to even 25 or 30 per cent there would be no blockade running; and fifty to sixty millions of dollars had gone into this traffic, while scarcely a new dollar had gone into manufacturing. "There seems to be a general antipathy to manufacturing

226

profits, while every one seems willing to bestow honor on the individual who has been able to amass millions by the hazard of importing. The blockade runner exhausts the capital of our country by importing all kind of Yankee notions; he imports calicoes, too, worth where it [sic] is made no more than ten or fifteen cents, and sells it for seven and ten dollars a yard, and receives the commendation of everybody—while the manufacturer gives employment, comfortable homes, education, and an independent living to soldiers' wives and children, and from their labor produces an article quite as much needed, and sells it for two-fifty to three-fifty per yard, and is condemned by the public as a heartless extortioner."[26]

The war might have brought the realization of Gregg's dream of an industrially self-sufficient South, especially had the Confederacy won independence. There would have been a rush into manufacturing, with subsequent steady growth. But after thirty years of working toward this end, the great chance was slipping before his eyes. There was bitter disappointment under his words: "But for Government interference, and the odium attached to selling domestics from the first hands at market value, millions of dollars would have gone into manufacturing during the last three years, and we would now be supplying the country with stripes, prints and bleached goods, which though not as elegantly finished as those imported, would have served to render us independent."

Here was a belligerent virtually without home industry, and blockaded against foreign products, and yet enterprise in the building of new plants and even in

227

the expanding of old ones was amazingly lacking. Much is to be attributed to agricultural habit, something to the hope of an early end to the war, but the government policy of stifling enterprise was heavily to blame.[27] The project of equipping and operating the finishing works at Graniteville fell to the ground when it was apparent that the profits must be transferred to others. Textile plants might be run in the South, as elsewhere, at night; there were laborers enough, but the move had not been made because it would involve additional outlays of capital, which the anticipated profits, under war restrictions, did not justify.[28]

Gregg was glad of the repeal of the Conscript Law; manufacturing interests were placed now in the hands of the War Department, which exercised a dictatorship, with the right to require supplies for the government on such terms as were deemed expedient, and with the power to detail artisans taken in the draft to operate the works. Graniteville was fortunate in the agent sent to represent the War Department at the factory. A thorough man of business, Gregg believed he would, after further experience, modify the plan he at first adopted of requiring two-thirds of all the goods turned out at a price which Gregg considered less than cost. Manufacturers ought to protest, Gregg thought, against the new practice of requiring mills to furnish cloth and yarn at cost prices, to be exchanged by the government for agricultural products which farmers were unwilling to sell for currency. This policy paralyzed industry and would come to no good end.

228

The war pressed problems upon Southern industry which in the natural course of things would have come slowly over many years. The attempt at careful estimate of manufacturing cost was one of these. But the very exigency which made such a computation urgent rendered it especially difficult. It is noteworthy that Gregg had been at work on such an accounting system before the war. "To make an estimate of the cost of production for a large establishment," he said, "is the most difficult task I have ever undertaken, and I have never yet arrived at its truth. In all our particularity in making weekly statements of the cost, the balance sheet has invariably proven at the end of six months that we had fallen short of the reality." Many extraordinary charges, such as those caused by breakdowns and strikes, defied foresight. The cost-computing system adopted by the convention held by these Confederate manufacturers in 1862 had seemed to allow of a profit, but Gregg was now sure that in nine cases out of ten the calculation had been too low, and that any profits had been made on the advance in price of cotton rather than on manufacturing proper.

His parting words to his fellow manufacturers were characteristic of the practical economist he was. He never lost a chance to impress a large lesson in favor of manufactures for the South. He reminded his hearers that "there are people, though few in number, who understand how important you are as a class to the Confederate States, and let me exhort you to hold on and improve your talent for the prosecution of a business that is of immense importance to our country. The day will come when we are not at the bid and call of military authority, and when all men will see that to be independent we must of necessity make all our coarse fabrics at home. The manufacturers [*sic*] of iron and steel, of agricultural implements, wagons, carriages, leather, and shoes, coarse woolens and cottons, must be brought into existence, or we will not long remain an independent people. I do not expect to live to see the day when all we in the South will be compelled to admit that diversified industry in the Confederacy will be necessary to sustain our national existence. The day, however, will come and it is close at hand. It is not present profits but prospects ahead, that gives such value to our manufacturing property. Looking to such a future, it does not require much forecast to see that the mills now running, although it may be necessary to renew the machinery entire, are to reap the first harvests of manufacturing profits, and I think it may safely be predicted that those who are now actively engaged in manufacturing will be regarded as benefactors, and leaders in pushing forward enterprises that are to make us independent as a nation and happy as a people."

One would suppose that Federal commanders in the vicinity of Graniteville would have made the factory an object of attack. It has been stated that Sherman, in his march from Atlanta to Columbia, sent a detachment of troops under Kilpatrick, from Branchville, "with orders to destroy the mill," and that "they were met at Aiken by Gen. Joe Wheeler's men and turned about face."[29] I can find no warrant for including Graniteville in the designs of the Union forces in the action centering about Aiken on February 11, 1865. The reports of the fourteen commanders involved make no mention of the factory or village. General Kilpatrick came from Barnwell and Blackville rather than Branchville, and his troops never got west of the town of Aiken.[30] The Federal commands moving along the South Carolina Railroad between Blackville and Aiken did great damage to Graniteville, however, by destroying the line, burning the ties, and twisting the rails beyond further use.[31] This necessitated hauling the factory's product to Orangeburg, forty miles. The fodder which Gregg sought to buy from Hammond was for feeding seven six-mule teams which were kept on the road, leaving Graniteville on Monday and returning Friday.[32]

CHAPTER XI

THE LAST STAND

By the time the Graniteville investors came together again, April 20, 1865, Confederate hopes had flickered and gone out. Eleven days before, Lee had surrendered at Appomattox. It was a saddened little group that met at the factory to hear a report of amazingly inflated currency profits, and to salvage what was left of genuine value. In the treasurer's statement the plant was carried at its old valuation. Earnings for the year 1864 had been almost twice those for 1863—$3,585,533.92— but the depreciation in the currency had averaged two and a half times as much in the latter year as in the former. Dividends running from $155,000 to $357,000 had been declared on the first days of January, February, June, and December; $26,250 had been paid in interest on 4 per cent bonds of the company, issued probably to secure additional ready capital.

Making all deductions for current outlays (though including no allowance for the overwhelming depreciation in plant which had occurred), surplus profits on January 1, 1865, stood at $3,605,592.51. The mill had turned out 3,627,693 yards of goods, within 80,000 yards of the amount manufactured the year previous. More cotton had been consumed than in 1863—3,189 bales as against 3,146—probably accounted for by greater waste this year due to worn machinery, higher

232

speed, and new operatives; the waste of cotton is given as 21 per cent, about twice the normal. It will be remembered that Gregg had been directed by the stockholders to sell most of the cotton on hand in 1864. Accordingly, 1,294 bales were sold in Augusta; 336 bales were burned in Hamburg, and 34 more suffered the same fate in Columbia; these deductions, taken with the bales consumed in the factory, left on hand at the beginning of 1865, 2,577 bales.

It was not known what the victorious Federal authorities might design. In this crisis, it was decided that all of the quick assets of the company, excluding surplus capital and the evidences of this surplus in bonds and sterling exchange, should be divided forthwith. The treasurer was directed to have all unpaid dividends, bills, gold, and cloth packaged and marked with the names of the stockholders to whom they belonged, these bundles to be held at the order and risk of the investors, notice having already been given to that effect. The treasurer was to make such disposition of the books of the company as would best insure their safety.[1]

Earnings during the year 1865 were $288,125.09. The factory must have continued in full operation despite the collapse of the Confederacy, for it consumed 3,053 bales of cotton, making 3,239,039 yards of cloth —almost as much as in 1864. On January 1, 1866, there was a total surplus of $101,986.09, a large part of which was represented by cotton valued in gold at about 35 cents. The new year, however, brought a different story. Cotton, and consequently cloth, fell in price, so

233

that between January 1 and May 22, 1866, the company lost (as expressed in currency) $42,537.46. The internal revenue tax was a heavy burden—the company paid out, on this account, $14,500 in the first four months of the year—a sum equal to a dividend of 6 per cent on the capital right there. Gregg, in his report as of May 1, thought it right, in the face of the loss, to review the history of Graniteville as to dividends. In the sixteen years of the operation of the mill, 1850-1866, average annual dividends of 12.56 per cent had been paid, and in the last thirteen years of this period they had averaged 15.45 per cent.[2]

The current loss was really one in inventory value largely—that is, due to the drop in the price of cotton and goods in hand—though high wages and short production played their part, too. Gregg was nonetheless put out, and proceeded to flay again his own stockholders and the Confederate and State authorities for their war-time policies. "We would have been a rich company," he declared, "had not our stockholders been so anxious to receive large dividends during the war. . . . The dividends we paid in currency seemed to be excessive, and imbued the public mind with the idea that we were heartless extortioners." The exactions made upon the company and the restrictions on the price of the finished product forbade plant extensions for the increase of goods which were necessary to the success of the Confederate cause. Gregg must have been keenly envious of the Yankee manufacturers who were consistently and progressively assisted by high protective

234

tariffs during the conflict. This wise policy of the North, he pointed out, resulted in the erection of hundreds of woolen and flax mills in that section. "So determined did our Government seem to be to exact from us all that we could possibly bear, that we were forced after January 1865 to enter into a permanent arrangement to give one yard out [of] every three we made, for which we received no compensation, and the State of South Carolina levied a tax of five bales out of every hundred." The goods thus taken were worth 30 cents a yard in gold in any of the markets of the world; the Confederacy took 4,000 yards and South Carolina 600, making a combined value of $1,380 a day taken by the two governments.

But for the large store of cotton which Graniteville had to fall back upon, which saved purchasing raw material with currency that was paid out in dividends instead, it would have been apparent that the company was on the road to ruin. It was Gregg's opinion that the demands of the government would have closed all the factories had the war continued a year or so longer. As it was, Graniteville at the end of the war found its capital short $280,000. This was more than made up by the rise in cotton and goods in the remainder of that year, so that the company began the year 1866 with a surplus of $101,986.09. This surplus was more than lost, as has been seen, in the ensuing four months.

There must have been a strong temptation at this unhappy juncture, with the home market almost destroyed and a large sum of money suddenly lost, for

235

the company to take in sail and proceed close-hauled. But this was not Gregg's way. Rather, the dilapidated condition of the equipment (it had been impossible during the war to keep it in repair) forced upon his mind "the necessity of immediate activity in the way of procuring new machinery. For our goods were below standard value in the great markets 2½ cents per yard, causing us to lose the making of $300 on every day's work." Aside from defects in quality, there was an added heavy loss due to decrease in quantity of production. His decision showed rare character and wisdom. Though Gregg urged upon the directors as forcibly as he could the need of refitting the plant, they hesitated two months and then acted with reluctance.

Finally, on July 4, 1865, he left home to buy new machinery. He traveled over New England to find the most approved new mill making the kind of goods Graniteville contemplated, but after a month's work he discovered that none had been erected since the war commenced. Also, such was the demand for equipment once the war was ended, he found that no first-class machine shop would promise to deliver an order within twelve months. Determined as ever, he went to England and spent three months there looking for a model mill on coarse fabrics made from American cotton. Disappointment awaited him again. The mill owners had changed their machinery during the cotton famine to work Surats. Without seeing a factory of the type he sought in actual operation, he had to judge as best he could what machinery was adapted to Graniteville's purpose.

Though the company was down in plant and pocket, he wanted his little mill in the deep South to stand with the world's best. By the middle of November he had concluded contracts for $120,000 worth of new machinery; though not enough to make the mill complete, this was all he thought the company could afford.

After completing all his contracts, as he thought, he visited the Continent for about two months. He wrote a characteristic letter to a kinsman, dated "Rome in Italy," December 28, 1865, which gives an interesting picture of the impressions he was receiving and his reflections on the new world in which he found himself. He remained the solid bourgeois, abundantly capable of admiring the sights and yet reverting to economic aspects of what he saw. His party reached Rome just at the time of the Christmas religious celebrations. Gregg was rather sarcastic over the enormous dignity accorded the Pope. "The presence of that august *simi*, almighty man, the pope, was exposed to view in various churches, but as none could get near enough to get sight of him unless dressed in black with a dress coat and other accompaniments of the ball room," Gregg decided to wait until the next day for his view, get some sleep, and save the dress-coat money. Starting out next day after a leisurely breakfast, he found himself in great luck. He got an excellent view of the procession with "magnificent carriages, more elegant in finish than any thing I have ever seen in S. Carolina." The procession moved within twenty feet of his party, "and as the people were mostly good Catholics, they prostrated themselves and

237

gave us a full and fair view of the . . . cardinals, bishops and the Pope on a splendid, gilt chair, sitting on a platform carried on the shoulders of 8 gorgeously dressed men."

Gregg was struck with admiration by St. Peter's. He spoke of its occupying 350 years in the erection. "No living man can estimate its cost—our state capitol with all the money spent on it is not equal to one of its small wings. . . . We went the next day for a more general inspection, and of course went on top. When we got on the roof, about 150 feet from the ground, we found it paved with brick and cement and if it had a foot of soil it would make a good corn field. There were men, dogs and cats living there." All the pomp of the Pope's procession and churches that took five centuries to build only emphasized, in Gregg's thought, the decay of Rome. Once having 2,500,000 people "whose brilliant orators and great men sent forth light to the whole world, who were renowned for the knowledge of the arts and sciences and who were conquerors of the world, now moldering in the dust, and its population dwindled down to 150,000 people largely mixed with robbers and beggars, we are forced to the conclusion that there has been a retrograde going on since the commencement of the Christian era."

He found as much fault with the lack of mechanical improvements in Rome as in his own Charleston. "Everything is made here by hand work, no steam and no improvements except the rudest kind to apply water power for even grinding purposes. . . ." He admired, however, the assiduity with which every foot of ground, even on the mountain sides, was placed under cultivation. He remarked the working of women in brick yards, "behind a plow, and in some instances made to pull a plow in place of mules. . . ." He believed "the average of the female slaves of the South were far better off than the females of Germany and Italy." If he thought the women worked too hard, their husbands did not work hard enough. "The men of the country are soldiers, priests, monks, sculptors, painters, etc. Indeed [if] the labor . . . so employed [were] in productive pursuits, they would make the country rich. Fresco painting is a business here that employs thousands. You can scarcely enter a house in Italy, either private or public, that is not painted from basement to the top." Gregg was not prudish, but much of the Italian art struck him as strange, to say the least. "Instead of the papering we use, it is all fresco here. . . . Beautiful walls, and handsome human figures over head, in many instances naked people, male and female, that made our weaker ones blush when they first beheld them . . . we scarcely passed a day without seeing marble statuary representing men, all their parts exposed, just as you would see a man or woman standing face to face before you, perfectly naked without even an effort made to cover private parts." He gave a careful description of the construction of the Colosseum, not forgetting to mention its old purpose to contain bulls, tigers, and lions, and gladiators sometimes fighting in boats. The destruction which had taken place in Rome during the dark ages worried his economical,

239

if not his artistic sense, and he several times spoke of the burning of marble columns and statues to secure their lime—objects worth then only a few cents to a lime burner, which in the present day would bring thousands of dollars.

While on the Continent he came to an important decision to diversify the production of Graniteville. He made up his mind from information received from home of the company's prosperous condition, to make new contracts for the supplying of a complete new outfit "that would enable us to produce almost any variety of goods from the coarsest to the finest fabrics and of such superior quality as will enable us to meet the most skillful manufacturers and obtain the highest prices in all markets."[3]

He then spent three months in England again in "intense anxiety," for his new resolve meant that he was to plan an entirely changed system for Graniteville. The new purchase of machinery went far beyond the cash means of the company, and Gregg drew on his private funds for something over £5,000, and he remitted £2,000 more from New York. "I expect to charter a steamer," he wrote from Manchester in February 1866, "to carry our machinery to Charleston or Savannah, which will sail from Liverpool about the tenth March and we expect to follow about a month later." His son Joseph would probably accompany the machinery and they would all reach home about May 1.[5]

When he reached America again he was still possessed with the notion of acquiring more equipment, and bought from an approved New England machinery maker ten specimen looms at $110 each, "said to be superior to any English looms." After a year's experience with all of the new machinery, he reported that he found the English looms to be infinitely superior to the New England looms, and "so far ahead of our old looms, for speed, quantity and quality of light fine cloth, that our master weaver thinks it advisable, by all means, to procure 220 more English fast looms, otherwise we will be scarcely able to command the best weavers to work our former looms," and he advised that this be done as soon as the company was paying dividends again.[6] Gregg brought back with him four or five experienced English operatives to help install the new machinery and start it in operation.[7] This would require some months to accomplish, and also a considerable outlay of capital to support the working force during the weeks of suspension. However, the money so expended would have been lost were the mill in full operation in such a period of stagnation of the cloth market. On the return of prosperous times, he said, "we will be prepared to take advantage of it, and to go forward with a flood tide and fair wind, and be able to compete more satisfactorily than ever before with manufacturers from all quarters, and to realize large profits, if they can be made any where else."[8]

When Gregg returned from his exacting work in Europe, he was plunged into new exertions for the next year, for he found his beloved Graniteville in a disordered plight. His exposure to hot sun and wet weather made people wonder that, elderly as he was, he could endure it. His labors in rejuvenating the factory undoubtedly hastened his death. The new buildings were in an unfinished state, the old ones were to be refloored and reroofed, old machinery must be taken out and repacked, and new put in its place—and all of this with a scant supply of skilled labor, rehabilitation of the railroads of the South having absorbed many mechanics. A principal job was the putting in of a new water wheel and rearrangement of shafting. On May 1, 1866, Gregg employed an experienced hydraulic millwright at $15 a day, and another to help him, to accomplish this work. They remained at Graniteville five months, and as a result of their labor, what with the new turbine wheel which they installed, the mill gained an amount of power which Gregg thought would obviate the necessity of putting in a 200-horsepower auxiliary steam engine.[9]

The dams and canal banks were out of order and in a dangerous condition, and needed much labor to repair them. Besides, from 1860 until Gregg's return from Europe, the creek below the mill had not been cleaned and so had filled up with fallen trees, trash, and mud until its bed was raised fully four feet, thus lessening the factory's power by one-tenth.[10] No sign of the property being down at heel, in however small a particular, was insignificant to Gregg, but pained him. In his passion for having all shipshape and above everything else sober and industrious, he set about policing the village. To quote his words: "During the war, and while I was in Europe, our property dilapidated rapidly and our

242

people became demoralized and ungovernable. On my return I found four stills in operation near Graniteville —one within three-quarters of a mile of the place—and the products of stills were brought to this place from many miles off, and there were many places in and about Graniteville where spirits were retailed—mostly by women and negroes. The firing of pistols and guns and drunken rows were common occurrences in our streets; fences were being torn down, gates unhinged, and in one instance a house burned, in short, such a state of affairs as was entirely incompatible with successfully prosecuting our works." He broke up the stills, indicted many for retailing and for riotous conduct, "discharged men and women without reference to their skill as factory operatives, and brought the population back to order and steady work."[11]

We come now to the last phase of our story. At the meeting in May of 1866, Gregg had announced to the stockholders his intention of retiring from the presidency of Graniteville when another year's work, of refitting the mill and restoring the whole property, should have been accomplished.[12] He had expected to leave his post with the next annual meeting, which was to be July 18, 1867, but a special meeting having become necessary in April, in order to find commercial capital to continue the business, he decided to date his retirement from then. There is reason to feel that some among the stockholders welcomed the announcement.[13] The war had brought extraordinary stresses, with differences of policy. Gregg was pushing forward vigorously his program of enlargements, and this gave the more pause to cautious minds because it required the idleness of half the mill; further, the affairs of the company had come to a critical juncture where, to supply operating funds, the old conflict of opinion as between direct sales financed on money borrowed in the open market, and sales through agents who would be the company's heavy creditors, had to be resolved. Moreover, Gregg had been president twenty years, and in this time, particularly latterly, not a few of his original associates, who looked upon Gregg and Graniteville as synonomous, had died.

"I have been heavily tasked," he said, "with a merely nominal compensation, and feel greatly relieved to find that other Stockholders, more deeply interested than myself, are now willing to relieve me, and assume the responsibility of selecting in future suitable agents and of supervising the management of our affairs."

If there was opposition to him, the kindliness of his leave-taking, the affection, and generous wisdom of his words, rose superior to any dislike. He would consider the past score of years of his life badly spent if the enterprise could not now be carried on profitably without him. Though his resignation, as a matter of fact, was not accepted, he lived only five months afterwards, and this was in reality his farewell. An ancient in blessing his son, come of age and ready to fare forth into the world, could not have spoken with more love than Gregg in giving Graniteville into the hands of others.

His good-bye, which was the lesson of his life, deserves to be remembered by all who are glad to call themselves Southerners: "I trust that Graniteville will bloom out afresh with the new administration, and that our enterprise on Horse Creek, will stand out as one of the beacon lights, to encourage the investment at the South of many millions of capital in this useful branch of industry, so charitable in an industrial point of view, and so eminently profitable to the nation and people at large. Such establishments are centres around which agriculture and all the mechanical arts thrive. They are inexhaustible feeders to railroads, and the life springs of commerce. Without them I fear that our beloved South will be to the balance of the Union what Ireland has been and is to England. This establishment, while it assists in the education of the laborers' children, and encourages temperance, and well directed industry, is a mine of wealth within itself, if its reources be not thrown away, or its affairs be not lamentably misdirected."[14]

He trusted that the meeting would not open the way to partisan advocacy of candidates to succeed him, or to supply other places, and that "our future administration will avoid the tempting snare which awaits all such institutions—that of yielding to the wishes of personal favorites, and needy aspirants, who seek to fill offices, the duties of which, they may not be able to perform." That Gregg practiced what he preached is evident from an episode of two years before. When General Jones died in October 1865, leaving the place of treasurer vacant, a kinsman of Gregg's wrote him in Europe applying to be put in the position. Gregg answered: "It

245

would afford me infinite pleasure to have it in my power to promote the welfare of yourself, Sarah and any one of your family. The office of treasurer of the Graniteville Company wouldn't suit you at all. None but an experienced merchant will be able to fill the office when I give up the Presidency, which I intend to do very soon after my return home. It is thought that General Jones' death was brought about by the complicated responsibilities brought suddenly upon him, without the assistance that I could have given him."[15]

Gregg took pride in surrendering an establishment converted into a fine goods mill, equal to greatly increased production.[16] The company had now a complete mill according to the English mode. It was capable of great flexibility. It would work to the best advantage on yarn of 36 hanks to the pound (2,520 feet to the hank), it could be used profitably to make yarn of 14 or even 6 or 4 hanks to the pound—to make the old style of sheetings or osnaburgs—or it might be run on yarn of 60 to 100 hanks to the pound to be woven into fine cambrics or figured goods. He must have found great satisfaction in saying, "I trust its capacity is equal, if well managed, to the production of the most superior cloths of whatever peculiar stamps we may desire to make." In the twelve months following May, 1865, the mill turned out 61,850 yards per week. After a period of let-down, due to installation of the new equipment, the factory in April, 1867, was producing 98,000 yards per week, and Gregg looked forward to making, when the mill should be in full operation, 120,000 yards. He was satisfied that the whole property, including the real estate, could not be duplicated for a million dollars in currency.[17] Under good management, he thought, Graniteville might yield a profit of from $200,000 to $250,000 a year, or, under bad management, might show a loss as great as $100,000.[18]

Gregg was leaving his work in a state unsatisfactory to him in two particulars. And, for all his effort, his death found both of these matters in worse case than five months before. One was a problem of the dam, and the other of obtaining sufficient working capital. He reported to the stockholders that there was some work about the stone dam and gates which he had intended to have done when the ponds were drawn down in the summer of 1866, but could not. Had Gregg retired when he meant to and gone to the North or back to Europe for a much needed vacation, this dam would not have been the central actor in a great tragedy.

The supply of ready capital called up his old conflict with the company. On May 22, 1865, the company's accounts were balanced to see how it had really fared during the war. It was found that the capital was deficient $221,000 (Gregg said in his report of 1866 the amount was $280,000). Since then the deficiency had been made up, a dividend of $36,000 had been paid, and there was on hand, January 1, 1867 a credit to profit and loss of $1,800—a net gain in 19 months and 8 days of $257,800. During five months of that time, due to putting in new machinery, there was a positive loss on every day's work. At the commencement of the year,

247

the company had a cash mercantile capital, clear of debt, of $55,000—an amount as large as the average cash capital during the decade preceding the war.

That this operating capital was not sufficient to the mill's needs was not his fault, Gregg declared. The blame lay with the board of directors in power in 1864-5, who refused to hold the solid security of 6,000 bales of cotton which he had laid up with the expenditure of the surplus. This cotton had been bought at an average price, in Confederate currency, of 40 cents per pound, when gold was worth more than 20 times as much as Southern paper. Had this cotton been held, and sold in 1865 it would have brought an average of 83.38 cents; had it been sold in 1866 it would have brought 43.20[19] cents. (Both of these prices are in currency; the greenback had an average value of 63.6 cents in gold in 1865 and 71 cents in 1866.)[20] Had the cotton been used in manufacture, the mill would have reaped substantially the same benefit. Gregg went on to quote from the minutes of directors and stockholders, showing their opposition to his policy, and giving chapter and verse.[21]

Notwithstanding the embarrassment of lack of working capital, Gregg was unwilling to see the company become dependent upon commission houses and pressed the claims of his policy of direct sales. These sales should be managed, as he had urged before, by an able treasurer, who, with "a thorough manufacturer and . . . a commanding industrious business man" as superintendent, or agent, could run the business without a resident president, the president to take a minor part, according to Gregg's scheme. On the other hand, it had been proposed (in order to raise the necessary mercantile capital and so conduct the enterprise with the ease that had been possible when sufficient credit facilities rendered forced sales unnecessary) "to engage some mercantile house in New York or Charleston, to furnish capital on our promise to give such house the selling of our goods, and offers have been made to furnish money at seven per cent interest." Gregg's prescience in this all-important particular is testified to by the experience of hundreds of Southern cotton mills after the great development arrived in the eighties, and continuing to the present.[22] His own Graniteville was not to be exempt from the ill-consequences of disregarding his advice. His comment, delivered, one may be sure, with all the earnestness of which he was capable, was: "Any arrangement of that kind I consider most injudicious, if not fatal. It would sink our establishment except in the most prosperous times. . . . I feel quite sure that I will meet the views of every good merchant by advising you, by all means, to sell all the goods you can at home, and to borrow, even at exorbitant rates of interest, rather than hamper your business by giving others, not interested with you, the control of your business."[23] The very fact that the company now had a fine plant, capable of an increased output, added to the need for ready money. All of the sales were made on 30 days time. When sales were made in New York the agents would supply cash immediately, but on sales made from the mill the 30 days must elapse, which necessitated $100,000 of addi-

tional trading capital.[24] It was a blow to Gregg to think
that Graniteville, which was to be an object lesson in
self-reliance, should get these funds from selling agents,
particularly in the North.[25]

Gregg gave some last advice about the choice of a
superintendent, when they should be in need of one.
A freshly imported Englishman, however talented as a
manufacturer, would break down in a year or two because he would not understand and be able to control
the village. And he was certainly judging partly from
his own previous experience when he counseled that if
they "looked among the Yankees" they should not
take the recommendation of any man or set of men
(who might be anxious to get rid of drones), but should
send a competent judge to travel about among the manufacturers until he found the right man. "He will then
have to be bought at a price which his employer will
be unwilling to give. You can afford to do that." He
hoped that no change would be made at present in other
officers than president; he took pains to commend Mr.
Hickman, the treasurer, and Mr. Giles, the secretary to
the company, and with them his son James (who was
now superintendent), "as skillful a manufacturer, and
as able a manager of such a concern as this country
affords."

It was characteristic of Gregg to leave a parting
charge concerning the school. It is to be noticed that he
regarded it frankly in the double light of duty and profit.
"As one of the prominent means of keeping up a steady
working force at Graniteville, I advise, by all means,

that you support the . . . school with a liberal hand. Any
one who has visited it will see for himself that it is a
nursery for the best class of factory operatives. Aside
from a charitable point of view, it is most assuredly a
source of profit to our Company, and the money spent
upon it will produce a rich harvest of results."

The report of Mr. Hickman, the treasurer, shows that
he was at this time fully in accord with Gregg's views
about keeping out of the hands of sales agents.[26] There
seems to have been no dispute about the necessity of
renewing the equipment of the mill. This is where the
money which might have been used for mercantile
capital (had it been possible to run with a broken-down
plant) had gone. The new weave room had cost $30,000,
the new machine shop $3,000, new machinery $233-
315.67, and the new water wheel $7,762.71. The exact
surplus capital to run on was $56,744.56. Hickman
recited that when he came into the treasurer's office,
he found the system of agencies in operation—at New
York, Charleston, Atlanta, Columbus, and Montgomery.
Believing that he could supply the Southern market
direct from the factory at a saving, he discontinued all
but the New York agency. Though he did not say so,
he was, in this policy, simply Gregg's instrument. This
plan had worked entirely to the advantage of the mill.
Though at one time he was able to sell from Graniteville
more goods than all the Southern agencies had disposed
of, the necessity for working capital compelled him to
draw heavily on the New York agent, forwarding goods
there, of course, to meet these obligations. The agent

251

had been very obliging in making large advances, but this meant that the mill was hampered in extending its direct sales to the West. He was opposed to solving the company's problem by a further reliance on this practice.[27]

Gregg was not permitted to retire from the presidency with this meeting of July, 1867. Mr. Trenholm introduced a resolution expressing the stockholders' appreciation of the value of his services to the company, and Dr. Boyce offered another that it was the sense of the stockholders that in the present circumstances of the company its welfare would be seriously endangered by the retirement of Mr. Gregg; his resignation was declined and his continuance in office invited. Both resolutions were passed unanimously. In the election which followed, however, J. J. Blacklock received 381 votes for president; Gregg, with 956 votes, was elected. Votes given Blacklock for president were given to Gregg for director.[28]

William Gregg was now, in important respects, in a position toward which he had been looking forward for years. He was not relieved of the burdens of active administration, it is true, but he had received a strong vote of confidence of the company, the factory was being greatly enlarged and improved and his sons, both of them large stockholders, were closely associated with him in the management of the enterprise—James as superintendent and William as one of the directors. But under the surface all was not propitious. The war, to the immediate stresses of which Gregg had risen

buoyantly superior, was in a real sense his defeat. Few
men could have built up a thriving manufacturing business in the backward agricultural South, but as long as
peace prevailed Gregg was easily equal to this task,
and his plans matured according to calculation. Fewer
men could ride out, as he did, the war period; but still
fewer could adapt themselves to the post-war collapse.

Here was this critical trouble of insufficient working
capital. Gregg wanted, in order to preserve the independence of his establishment, to go on borrowing as
he had done in the past, at higher interest rates if need
be, but the penniless South would not admit of it. The
banks that had been his helpers before had gone down
with Confederate hopes. Individual Southerners with
money which they were willing to lend to home manufacturers were exceedingly few and far between, if they
were to be found at all. And if the North were turned
to, the company's notes would not answer. The mill, to
get money there, must give hostages to fortune. The only
firms in New York willing to supply working capital to
a cotton factory in the prostrate South were commission
houses which would require, in return, almost a monopoly of the sales of the goods produced.

This new, and in many respects unhappy era here
inaugurated, was one which prominently marked the
Southern industry in the next decades, and which has
clung to it in lessening degree ever since. Gregg was
unable or unwilling to make terms with the new necessity. His from the beginning was to be a "domestic industry," a Southern enterprise, and his household gods,

253

like those of a whimsical old-fashioned Englishman, planted a terrible fixed foot. At his age, and with his record for self-sufficiency, he would not bend his neck to the yoke of the times.

All of the new equipment was not yet in working order; the debts of the company, on account of operating capital, grew, and the creditors (not a few of them stockholders in all probability) were about to press for payment. After less than four months of this struggle, August 7, Gregg was under the necessity of calling the stockholders together again in special meeting to contrive a way of getting a steady flow of working funds. But there was not a majority of the stock represented, so the meeting had to adjourn without action. Then he set a second date for a meeting, into the next month.[29] But before this time arrived, a tragic thing happened— not the less mournful because it was a finely fitting close to the drama of Gregg's career.

The dam broke while Gregg was absent in Columbia. (Only six months before, referring to other similar occasions, he had said: "If a dam broke I had to be there in the mud, for no one about could do the work so cheaply and securely as myself.")[30] He was telegraphed for and returned to Graniteville post haste. For two days he was up to his waist in water, and was so busy that during this time of mental strain and physical exertion, he took almost no food. An old Graniteville employe who witnessed the scene gave me a moving account of Gregg in great hip boots, laboring right in with the men, and keeping them up to the work. His was a remarkably strong constitution, even at the age of sixty-seven. He had never had an illness, except once from pneumonia several years before at Kalmia. But this exertion and exposure of closing the breach in the dam was, inevitably, too much for him. He was obliged to take to his bed, with a severe inflammation of the stomach.

Things had reached this pass when the day arrived for the second special meeting of the stockholders. Only one or two came. In the afternoon the treasurer visited the sick room at Kalmia and reported the indifference of the company. The dam was broken, and the business owed $46,500 in gold and more than $86,000 in currency—estimating the gold at 35 per cent premium, the whole loan indebtedness, with interest (much of it as high as 12 per cent) amounted to $156,700. Gregg took the verdict stoically. He told the treasurer he must run the mill if possible, and if not, then they would simply have to close it.[31]

But more than the dam had broken. The floodgates of Gregg's resistance, which had held against so many pressures through the years and impounded power for so much useful work, were giving way now. Knowing how ill he was, the village of Graniteville was hushed. The people sent him their affectionate regard, and he replied with messages of good wishes. He died within the week, September 13, 1867. The mill bell tolled at 9 o'clock, and all knew what it meant. Gregg was buried on Kalmia hill. Every man, woman, and child of the village, unless too infirm or too young to go, attended the funeral, and more came from a wide countryside.[32]

255

Mrs. Gregg remained at Kalmia only about two years after William Gregg's death. She moved in 1870 to Charleston. In those trying times, so soon after the war, it was hard for her to keep up the large place. There remained with her only "Mammy," who when freedom came refused to follow her husband to Chicago, and clung to Mrs. Gregg, whom she called "Miss" and in whose service she was for sixty-years—in Edgefield District, in Columbia, in Charleston, at Kalmia, and then in the concluding years at Charleston again. Mrs. Gregg following her husband's death was her same calm self, accepting all her deprivations with composure, and, despite other difficulties, might have remained at Kalmia but for her health. She was never happy away from that place, and soon after going to Charleston took to her room for the rest of her life. A picture taken at home just before her final removal from Kalmia shows the little old lady in lace cap and mittens, knitting. She was a celebrated knitter of baby socks, and made them for her great-grandchildren.

Little remains to be told. James Gregg, as superintendent, threw his energy into making good his father's expectations so far as the completion and successful operation of the mill was concerned. William Gregg had believed that when all of the new equipment was in readiness, the mill would produce not 62,000 yards a week, but 120,000. The event exceeded his hopes, for within six months after his death the average output was 150,000 yards, and it was thought this might climb to 175,000.

Hickman, the treasurer, called a meeting of the directors at Charleston on October 2, and he was named president pro tempore. Gregg's death had stirred the directors to activity, or it may be one will think it gave them a free hand. Whatever was the case, they authorized Hickman to raise the money necessary to carry on the business, the amount borrowed not to be over $200,000, and the interest not to exceed 12 per cent. Armed with this resolution, he went to New York and reached an agreement with a cotton goods commission house, Wyman Byrd & Company, whereby this firm would raise up to $100,000 by selling its acceptances of the Graniteville Company's drafts, the latter company paying the discounts, and the mill agreeing, in consideration of this service, to send the commission house weekly not less than two-thirds of the production of goods, and all over this amount not sold directly from the plant. This agreement was to continue in force for a year, or longer if mutually agreeable, and the old permission to the treasurer of the company to overdraw his account by $30,000 was to be continued.[33] This was, of course, the relinquishment of Gregg's stout policy of independence. However, the scheme gave the treasurer money with which to pay off other creditors and left enough to enable him to run the mill with ease.[34]

When the stockholders gathered at the next annual meeting, they were sufficiently conscious of Gregg's absence. The treasurer, when he took the chair to preside, declared that "a great and good man has fallen, and the Graniteville Company are not the only sufferers." The

257

formal report of a committee appointed to frame resolutions on Gregg's death, Dr. Boyce being chairman, recorded that "while by the virtues of his private life he has endeared himself to many, by his farsighted sagacity, his untiring energy, and his devoted attention to the interests of this company, he has established a claim upon the gratitude and esteem of all its stockholders, which will never be cancelled." And it was further "Resolved, that his kindness to the poor of the town, his fatherly care of its children, his deep interest in its schools and churches, his earnest efforts for the advancement in morality of its inhabitants have left us a bright example of the fact, that the interests of capital are perfectly consistent with the best welfare of labor, and that gain may be earnestly pursued at the same time that the better ends of life are not forgotten."[35]

After the death of James Gregg in 1876, his mother disinterred the bodies of her loved ones at the Kalmia burial ground and brought them to Magnolia Cemetery in Charleston. However, the shaft which had stood over the grave of William Gregg was appropriately brought back to Kalmia Hill in June, 1926, where it was unveiled by his daughter, Mrs. Chafee. The occasion, in which Graniteville school children, villagers, and officials participated, signalized the enduring service he rendered to that community and to the wider community of Southern industry.[36]

William Gregg was the father of Graniteville, and he wove his thought and his affection into every stone and home and tree and path. Sixty years after his death, the place is redolent with memories of him. The children of the village—grandsons and great-grandsons and great-great-grandsons of other children whom he sent to school and took in his old buggy and delighted with his picnics—play now in William Gregg Park on the edge of the settlement. Before the original factory building, and surrounded by ancient hedges which he planted, is a granite monument to him, as simple and as solid as he was.

But in a larger sense he was the father of the Southern cotton manufacture. The industry has realized, and particularly is achieving now, all that he hoped for in a material way, and more than he ever guessed. In the long years it cannot fail to accomplish what he dreamed of in whole social betterment, its influence telling in universal public education, intelligent use of economic resources, and a fuller life for the average man. Those who are impressed with the story of his life, if they wish to honor him, ought to have a care that this process, on the human side, shall go forward in constant anxiety for justice.

NOTES TO CHAPTERS

CHAPTER I

[1] Albert Cook Myers, *The Immigration of the Irish Quakers into Pennsylvania, 1682-1750*, p. 319, note.

[2] Notation in Gregg family Bible, in possession of Miss Rena Chafee, Aiken S. C. Cf. "Honorable William Gregg, the Founder of Graniteville," in Edgefield (S. C.) *Advertiser*, June 5, 1879; James Henry Rice, Jr., in *The State* (Columbia, S. C.), Jan. 10, 1926, has repeated this. I have not found better evidence for this date of his arrival. A. C. Myers, in his *Quaker Arrivals at Philadelphia, 1682-1750*, does not mention William Gregg in the supposedly exhaustive list of those bringing certificates of removal to the Philadelphia Meeting. If he came over in 1682 it is not indicated where he lived until he acquired his own land three years later. Statements in the newspaper articles cited that Penn and Gregg "bought land adjoining each other in Delaware" and that "their estates adjoined on the Brandywine in New Jersey" should be corrected, of course, to mean that Gregg settled on a part of Penn's grant. William Gregg's name does not appear in the list of those to whom warrants for manors and lands were issued, given in P. W. Sheafer and others, *Historical Map of Pennsylvania*, pp. 22-25. Penn's Manor of Pennsbury, "near the Friends' settlement at the Falls and opposite Bordentown," (Samuel M. Janney, *Peace Principles Exemplified in the Early History of Pennsylvania*, p. 56), was laid out as early as 1683 (Sheafer, *ibid.*, p. 23), and was too far away to adjoin Gregg's acres in Christiana Hundred, but one of the Proprietor's other manors, as for example Rockland in New Castle County, may have done so. William Gregg was one of the company of Friends settled on the west side of Brandywine Creek, Christiana Hundred, New Castle County (near the present village of Centerville), who in 1687 were granted permission to hold their own meeting in the winter months, instead of going to Newark Meeting, "by reason of the dangerousness of ye ford. . . ." (Myers, *Immigration of the Irish Quakers*, pp. 122-3.)

[3] The article in the Edgefield *Advertiser* has it that "they traveled together in England and Germany," and Mr. Rice (see note 2) says, "they were fast friends" and "had mutual interest in a lead mine." Neither of these notices, two of the few which have appeared on Gregg's life, is apparently based on documentary sources, and both contain inac-

curacies, the first giving the name of the immigrant as John. Myers says (*ibid.*) : "It is presumed by the writer that William Gregg came from the north of Ireland with the Hollingsworths, Dixsons, Sharplys; but no doubt the point could be fully proven if a diligent investigation were made in Ireland." He cites the residence of other Greggs in Tober-head Meeting in 1700, 1702, and 1714. Valentine Hollingsworth, Adam Sharply, and other Friends arrived "about 1682 . . . and settled near each other on the east side of Brandywine Creek, in New Castle County" (now Delaware, but then among "The Territories" or "Lower Counties" of Pennsylvania) (*ibid.*, pp. 118-119). It is possible that William Gregg belonged to the English branch of the family, which was settled in Derbyshire and had a later coat of arms than the original Scotch branch. Myers notes that "Quite early, meetings were established at Coleraine, Ballynacree, Lisburn and other places in Antrim, but they were not as large as other meetings without the pale of the Scotch," and inclines to believe that "the great majority of the Quakers in Ireland were English, or of English descent." And further: "The certificates of removal which the Irish Friends brought to Pennsylvania show that many of the emi-grants were natives of England and had lived but a few years in Ireland." (*Ibid.*, pp. 36-37.) Myers' book contains many references to settlers of the name of Gregg.

[4] Gregg family Bible; for a brief description of Concord Meeting, see Myers, *Immigration of the Irish Quakers*, pp. 116-117.

[5] Myers, *ibid.*, pp. 129-130. He paid 3s 4d, which was about the average for the nine Irish Friends; the richest, Ezekiel Harlan, paid 12s 6d. In all, 43 persons were taxed in Kennett in this year.

[6] DeBow's *Review*, X, 348 ff. The name is spelled *Hinchy* in DeBow, and this spelling is repeated in the Edgefield *Advertiser* article cited. *Hinkey* is the form in the family records.

[7] Edgefield *Advertiser*, June 5, 1879.

[8] DeBow's *Review*, X, 348 ff. William Gregg probably settled at Hope-well in the Shenandoah Valley (originally Opequan Meeting) ; it is possi-ble that his father, Herman, had drifted southward from York. For more than a generation Friends from this migration had been moving into southern Virginia and on to North Carolina, and by the time of the Revolution meetings had been founded in South Carolina. (Myers, *ibid.*, pp. 178-179.) "Our" swamps would indicate, along with other details, that the account which DeBow published was based on a memo-randum furnished by William Gregg the son, subject of the sketch. The laudatory passages and some characterized by "fine writing" were certainly the work of DeBow. Mrs. Chafee remembers writing letters to

DeBow for her father, but at this date naturally does not recall any of the contents.

⁹ The early accounts say he went to "Monongahela County, Virginia." The present spelling, a corruption of Monongahela, is of course Monongalia. His return to Pennsylvania was doubtless due, as with numbers of others of the sect, to dislike of the institution of slavery. From Pennsylvania he followed the westward migration of Friends, which by this time was moving by well-worn trails through Shippensburg, and going thence either by the Cumberland and Potomac valleys and so over Braddock's route, or taking the more mountainous course by Fort Littleton and Bedford, diffused itself in the Redstone region, afterwards Monongalia. William was not the first Gregg to go into this Western country, for one Thomas Gregg, of Kennett, had settled near Redstone by 1773. (Myers, *ibid.*, pp. 177 ff.) Professor James M. Callahan, of the West Virginia University at Morgantown in this county, and chief authority on the history of the section, to whom I am indebted for many particulars, writes: "I am not sure whether any of the Greggs at that early date resided south of the Pennsylvania boundary line which was finally established by surveys of 1784. The early records of Monongalia County were destroyed in 1796 and many deeds to land before that date cannot be found on our county records." The earliest deed of land to a Gregg, so far as the records show, was that of Samuel Camby to Elizabeth Gregg *et al.*, Dec. 10, 1814. This Elizabeth could not have been William Gregg's mother. The oldest Gregg will recorded in the county is that of Thomas Gregg, dated July 8, 1818, proved at the April term of court in 1819. The present county clerk is Mr. John M. Gregg, whose grandfather was John B. Gregg, and whose uncle was William H. Gregg; this is undoubtedly the same family, these Christian names being familiar ones.

¹⁰ James M. Callahan, *Centennial History of West Virginia*, pp. 33-34, 49.

¹¹ The old accounts make no mention of the childhood years in the neighbor's family, making it appear that immediately after his mother's death he was taken by his uncle. Mrs. Chafee thinks her father was only two years old when his mother died.

¹² Mrs. Chafee heard her father repeat this.

¹³ DeBow's *Review*, X, 348 ff.

¹⁴ The date is given in the *Review* as 1810, though it may have been a little later, since Mrs. Chafee has the impression her father was a "good big boy" when he went to Georgia. No independent record of a manufactory of cotton spinning machinery at Alexandria has been found.

NOTES TO CHAPTER I

Jacob Gregg must have supplied very small establishments, probably mostly in the South, with crude machinery made in hardly better than blacksmith fashion, though it is possible that the precision of the watchmaker entered more largely into Gregg's product than was usual in the South at that day.

[15] "It was at the cotton factory in Georgia . . . that our young friend first learned to *love* and *understand* machinery." (Edgefield *Advertiser*, June 5, 1879.)

[16] DeBow's *Review*, X, 348 ff.

[17] Cf. J. W. Speake in Augusta (Ga.) *Chronicle*, June 20, 1926.

[18] This date is given by DeBow, and is probably accurate. The Edgefield *Advertiser* gives 1827.

[19] Edgefield *Advertiser*, June 5, 1879. This is not included in the version in DeBow, which appeared in Gregg's lifetime—another evidence that he furnished the main data for the earlier article himself.

[20] *Ibid.* The printed accounts make no mention of a Mr. Young, of Camden, whom Mrs. Chafee remembers as having been a partner of Gregg in Columbia.

[21] Two of the horses were sold before they returned, Gregg deciding he had put on a little too much style, since feed for the horses was hard to purchase in the thinly populated West.

[22] Mary Virginia was born in 1830 and died in 1834. Another daughter, Sarah Elizabeth, born in 1852, died when eighteen months old, just before the final removal of the family from Charleston.

[23] William Gregg, *Essays on Domestic Industry*, p. iii. The wording of the following passage may have been supplied by him: "Having amassed a moderate fortune, and being in delicate health, he retired from business, believing that he possessed the means of providing his children with a good education, yet, at the same time, not such a superabundance as would lead them to believe that they were raised above dependence or self-exertion, which in so many instances proves the ruin of the wealthy." (DeBow's *Review*, X, 348 ff.)

[24] *Domestic Industry*, p. 34.

[25] DeBow's *Review*, X, 348 ff.

[26] Edgefield *Advertiser*, June 5, 1879. This article has the name *England* for Eyland, a mistake.

[27] *Ibid.* After a time, probably because Gregg invested more heavily, the name seems to have been changed to Gregg, Hayden & Co., "known throughout the South as extensive importing merchants." Mr. Nathaniel Hayden afterwards went to New York and was president of the Chatham Bank until his death. His niece, Miss Emma Hayden, of St. Michael's

Place, Charleston, could tell me little about the firm or about Gregg.
The business was located at the corner of Hasell and King streets. The
handsome paneling of the store has been moved to a shoe store on
King Street near George. Hayden & Gregg silver is still to be found in
many Charleston homes. With no difficulty I turned up two teaspoons
in the old-silver box of one of the jewelers. They are of simple pattern
and worn thin with age, but bear the hall mark of the firm very clearly.

[28] *Ibid.*

[29] In the possession of Miss Rena Chafee, Gregg's granddaughter,
Aiken, S. C.

[30] There have been few changes in the place since Gregg's time. The
downstairs hall has been partitioned in the center, and the cisterns, one
of which, big enough for a dungeon keep, Gregg installed, are no longer
used. Always anxious to make improvements, Gregg built on a little
kitchen as a part of the house (instead of continuing the inconvenience
of a kitchen in a building in the yard) and included a dumb waiter running to the dining room floor. Here Aunt Dolly, "a little bit of a yellow
woman from Virginia," was cook. Gregg contrived that water from the
cisterns should run through kitchen and pantry. In a small room in the
ample attic, with the kind assistance of the present owners, I found
copies of old Southern periodicals, such as the *South Carolina Rose* and
Southern Literary Messenger, but all bore names of the Rutledges who
took the house from Gregg and owned it for seventy years, and I could
find nothing that connected with the subject of this essay.

[31] The Edgefield *Advertiser*, June 5, 1879, called him "a prominent and
honored citizen of Edgefield District." The traveler on the old road between Aiken and Newberry passes through the little village of Ridge
Spring, and near the graves of Colonel Jones and his wife.

[32] Gregg, *Domestic Industry*, p. 33. Vaucluse is said to have got its
name from a colony of French who settled at the place and named it
after their village in the old country, near Avignon. The situation is
charming, with low heavily wooded hills gliding into one another and
forming a principal valley through which the creek slips on its
way to Graniteville and beyond.

This factory was on the site of an older one which burned. (See
Gregg's account of Vaucluse in DeBow's *Review*, XXIX, 494.) The
corner stone of this second mill, deeply cut with the date 1832, is
preserved in the foundation of the present factory, which appears to
be the third in the place, that of McDuffie and King having been burned
about 1866. (Aiken, S. C. *Journal and Review*, Sept. 29, 1920.) The
original factory, according to tradition, was of logs on a stone foundation,

and this foundation, as indicated by recent excavations at the place, probably ran at a right angle to the present one. The building completed in 1833 was of hewn granite, four stories and an attic. (Gregg, *Domestic Industry*, p. 60.)

[33] Gregg, *ibid.* R. F. W. Allston, in the Report of the Secretary of the Treasury for 1845 (quoted in DeBow's *Review*, VI, 288; cf. *ibid.*, II, 417) spoke of several cotton factories in the State "operating on a small scale"—Vaucluse in Barnwell, Saluda in Lexington, that of Col. Williams at Society Hill, one recently abandoned at Marlboro, and others in Pendleton and Greenville districts. "Limited as is the number of these factories," he continued, "it is believed they are not dependent for their profits on the present duties; but it cannot be doubted that a number of them were brought into existence by the patronizing countenance of government, and stimulated by the temptation to share a portion of the immense profits derived from their peculiar *tariff protection* by the similar establishments at 'Lowell,' Fall River, Paterson and elsewhere." A North Carolina newspaper in the thirties declared that should a protective tariff measure pass Congress, the people of the Carolinas must "join in the scuffle for the benefit anticipated from this new American system, and they will have to bear a portion of its burdens and buffet the Northern manufacturer with his own weapons." (M. R. Pleasants, *Manufacturing in North Carolina Before 1860*. MS; cf. the present writer's *Rise of Cotton Mills in the South*, pp. 16-26.) It is difficult to say in how far the cotton mills set up in the South in the late twenties and early thirties sought to take advantage of protection and in how far they were, as industrial manifestations of the nullification spirit, efforts to free the South from dependence upon the North. Mr. Clark (in *The South in the Building of the Nation*, V, 316 ff.) has taken the latter view: "During the decade ending with 1833, when hostility to the tariff made the Southern people bitterly resent economic dependence upon the North, there was a second movement towards manufactures, especially in South Carolina and Georgia, directed mainly towards the erection of larger and more complete factories."

[34] Cf. Aiken *Journal and Review*, Sept. 29, 1920, for the statement, loosely made, that the mill produced only negro cloth.

[35] p. 34. In the preface to the pamphlet edition of the *Essays*, which carried Gregg's name, he wrote of this episode in the first person. From this it appears that he did not begin to buy Vaucluse stock until he gave up his business in Columbia in 1837, and he could have been interested in the company but a short time before he took charge in person in the summer of the same year. This leaves a break in the history of Vaucluse

from the time of the incurring of the deficit (say the summer of 1835) to that of Gregg's taking hold. I tried to find out from Mrs. Chafee when her father was first identified with Vaucluse, but the best she could tell me was that "he seemed to have an interest in that place from my earliest childhood." Gregg must have bought his shares from an a priori conviction that the factory ought to succeed, for by his own statement it was not until he acquired considerable stock that he "looked into matters" narrowly. Since his agitation resulted in the offering of the mill for sale, it is not unlikely that he stood ready to purchase it himself; certainly this must have been in his mind after he had proved that the enterprise, when properly conducted, could make money. It was his ill-health, he said in the preface, which prevented his purchasing the establishment when it was sold late in 1837. The shares, 54 1-2 in number, had originally been worth $1,000 each, and the sale found them reduced to $750 each. Gregg's success in the emergency management of the unwisely equipped mill was a tribute to his skill, and gave him confidence, if he needed any, for further adventures at Graniteville. (*Ibid.*, p. iii.) It may be conjectured that in the eight months of his first management of Vaucluse he occupied the largest of the cottages at the mill; it stands on a slope opposite the factory site, was for years the home of General Jones, who played a conspicuous part at Vaucluse and Graniteville, and is now the residence of the village clergyman and schoolmaster. It would appear, however, that despite the tradition that this house comes down from 1833, it was erected a decade later when Gregg and Jones bought Vaucluse, for Gregg remarked in 1845, anent the fine manufacturing establishments near Boston, "I do not certainly exaggerate, when I say, that the most indifferent overseer's house in Lowell, at least such as I saw, cost more than the whole village of Vaucluse, containing upwards of 200 inhabitants, including a comfortable dwelling recently built as a residence for one of its owners. . . ." (*Ibid.*, pp. 35-36.)

[36] *Ibid.*, p. iii.

[37] *Ibid.*, pp. 34-35. I have not discovered who this owner was. Mrs. Chafee's recollection (gained from report) is that the old stone or wooden mill was owned by a German or Frenchman; it may be, however, that what was told her referred to a still older mill near Vaucluse. The minutes of the Graniteville Company, 1846, refer to "the mill site known as 'Richardson's old burt mill' on Bridge Creek, but this would be nearer Graniteville than Vaucluse; Mr. George H. Leitner, of Graniteville, told me that in building a dam on the company's property he unearthed the remains of a very early mill, probably a saw mill;

and Professor G. C. Williams, of the University of S. C., has always heard that there was a mill of some description in the vicinity of Vaucluse before the 1833 factory was built.

[38] James Jones was a brother of Mrs. Gregg. In 1848 Jones must have been in active direction of Vaucluse, for DeBow, in listing the cotton mills in South Carolina, spoke of "Vaucluse factory, near Hamburg, under management of Col. James Jones." (*Review*, V, 189-190.) A MS list of stockholders of the Graniteville Company, Mch. 19, 1847, gives the residence of Jones as Aiken. He held two shares of Graniteville stock, was one of the original directors, acted as secretary of the first stockholders' meetings, and was elected treasurer the year of his death, 1865. Mr. August Kohn has a pamphlet, *Memorial in Relation to the Charter Granted by the Legislature of South Carolina to Messrs. Jones and Kennedy, 1853*. The matter related to a bridge in which Jones' was interested.

[39] *Domestic Industry*, p. iii. Since he was writing in January of 1845, he must have commenced manufacture at Vaucluse as soon as he acquired an interest in it; he probably took it over as a going concern, with a large tract of land attached (letter of Coles Phinizy to G. E. Senn, gives the "original Vaucluse tract" as 3,000 acres). Gregg went on to picture the regeneration of the State which he believed, from his experience at Vaucluse, cotton manufactures would inspire; he hinted at Southern separation from the Union in believing that these improvements "would place us in a condition to meet any emergency that might arise."

[40] *Domestic Industry*, pp. 33-34. "Its size forbids its being brought under the same system, and producing similar results, as the Massachusetts mills, and however profitable it may be to its present owners, it can never be considered a fair test of what cotton manufacturing can be, when properly introduced in this State." (*Ibid.*, p. 35.) He must have made the changes at Vaucluse only after fullest investigation. They were in accord with the admonition to the proprietors of the Saluda Factory that they should have sought New England advice and made one standard article only. (*Ibid.*, pp. 31-32.) Twenty years later he told his Graniteville stockholders that great caution must be used in changing machinery lest money be thrown away. As illustration he used among others the Saluda Mill, with which he had long been acquainted. Gregg had recommended an overseer to the mill with the warning that he should not be allowed to buy new machinery. "I advised that the overseer be required to run the factory just as it was, and make the most of a mill that had cost $250,000 and had been sold to the present owner for

$20,000. The warning was disregarded, with the result that $30,000 was spent fruitlessly and the overseer lost his position." (MS *Stockholders' Minutes*—hereafter referred to simply as *Minutes*—Jan. 22, 1859.)

The Edgefield *Advertiser*, June 5, 1879, in its sketch of Gregg's activities, made no mention of his second connection with Vaucluse, beginning in 1843.

CHAPTER II

[1] *Domestic Industry*, pp. 48-49. "I trust that enough has been said on the subject of Cotton Manufactures to prove the practicability of engaging in them in South-Carolina, in competition with any other country. To the thinking part of the community, it is hoped, arguments are not now necessary, to show the necessity of *changing our industrial pursuits*, in order to close up the flood gates—that are draining our State . . . and sweeping off millions of . . . capital, to build manufacturing towns at the North." (*Ibid.*, p. 50.)

[2] The dates of all of the articles were as follows: Sept. 20, 21, 30, Nov. 22, 26, 30, Dec. 4, 6, 10, 11. The long break after the third article was probably because Gregg wanted to gather more material to continue the series after having prepared a few numbers in advance. Each article had a few lines of introduction tying it to what had gone before.

[3] *Courier*, Charleston, S. C., Dec. 11, 1844.

[4] Dec. 24, 1844.

[5] *Ibid.*

[6] Jan. 28, 1845. It was thought wise to state that "The views of the author are urged without any reference to a protective tariff, being based on our possession of the raw material. . . ."

[7] The pamphlet bore the full title, *Essays on Domestic Industry*, or, *An Inquiry into the Expediency of Establishing Cotton Manufactures in South-Carolina*. Originally published in the Charleston *Courier* and now re-published at the request of several gentlemen of Charleston. 1845, Charleston, Burges & James. 63 pp. It was to be had at the bookstores of Messrs. S. Hart, Senr., Babcock & Co., G. Oates, McCarter & Allen, and A. Head. Copies of the pamphlet are rare, though not as rare as certain others of his writing. I know of only seven. D. A. Tompkins reprinted the *Domestic Industry* as an appendix to his volume *Cotton Mill, Commercial Features*, 1899, saying in introduction that he had not known of Gregg's work until he had finished his own, and declaring "his arguments are as good today and for our time, as for the time in which they were written and published." (pp. 205-206.)

[8] *Domestic Industry*, pp. iii-iv.

[9] Of the meetings at Carey's home Robt. Ellis Thompson said: "Whatever visitor of notable worth or name was to be found in our city, was sure to be carried thither, to meet not only Mr. Carey, but one of the most remarkable assemblages of character and intelligence to be found in any American city. . . . desirable and pleasant people of all sorts, artists, authors, journalists, men of business, met on a free and friendly footing." (*Penn Monthly*, X, 831-2.) Graniteville was frequently mentioned with pointed approval in *The Plough, the Loom and the Anvil*, which was in reality Carey's magazine. Cf. H. C. Carey, *The Harmony of Interests*, I, 137.

[10] *Domestic Industry*, pp. iii, v.

[11] *Ibid.*, p. 7. Gregg particularly deprecated current use of the failure of certain cotton manufactures in South Carolina as a text from which to preach general discouragement of industry as opposed to agriculture. Cf. Victor S. Clark, *History of Manufacturing in the United States, 1607-1860*, p. 556. General George McDuffie, who had made capital of his failure at Vaucluse—a factory which Gregg had rescued—came in for frankest dislike. "Oh! fie, Gen. McDuffie, why are you not engaged in the great cause of reforming the habits of your countrymen? You once counted the profit of Cotton-Spinning. . . . Why did you permit the establishment to dwindle, sicken and die, purely for the want of that attention, which you well know is essential to the success of your cotton plantation?" (Gregg, *op. cit.*, p. 8; cf. p. 12, and the writer's "Southern Spindles," in *Yale Review*, April, 1925.) Gregg continued: "Lamentable, indeed, is it to see so wise and so pure a man as Langdon Cheves, putting forth the doctrine to South-Carolina, that manufactures should be the last resort of a country. . . . I will venture the assertion that a greater error was never committed by a statesman." (*Op. cit.*, p. 14.) "Even Mr. Calhoun, our great oracle . . . is against us in this matter; he will tell you, that no mechanical enterprise will succeed in South-Carolina . . .—that to thrive in cotton spinning, one should go to Rhode Island. . . ." (*Ibid.*, p. 19.) Gregg was sure that "the failures which have taken place, ought not to deter others from embarking in the business, they being the result of unpardonable ignorance, and just such management on the part of those interested, as would prove ruinous in any other undertaking." (pp. 19-20.) Gregg was rightly conscious of his own superior statesmanship, flowing from practical experience in these matters.

[12] *Ibid.*, p. 14 and note.

[13] *Ibid.*, p. 7. He asked why McDuffie had not followed "the patriotic example of the Lowells, Bootts, Jacksons, Appletons, and Lawrences, of Boston? who, after fighting for years with their native State against the protective system, and finding it fastened upon her, did not stop to preach the doctrine of State resistance," but launched upon manufactures which "elicited every energy that the State is capable of exerting." (pp. 8-9.) Already, he thought, "those . . . engaging in this branch of business, are not looking to Government for laws to enhance the price of their goods," as was proved, he considered, by the fact that a large surplus of American cotton manufactures found a profitable market abroad in competition with English goods. (pp. 12-13.)

[14] In this it is not at all likely that he was influenced by reliance, for South Carolina manufacturers, upon a local market secure against foreign competition. It is true that he said, "Let South-Carolina be true to herself, let her go to work with a determination to resist the Northern tariffites, by resolving not to purchase or use their articles of manufacture," (p. 11) but he meant for Southern industry to grow. "I firmly believe," he declared, "that our advantages are such as to enable us to compete successfully with any country, now engaged in the manufacture of *Coarse Cotton Fabrics*." (p. iii) ; and he mentioned with pride that already much Southern-made goods was exported to New York and perhaps to the East Indies. (p. 11.)

[15] *Domestic Industry*, p. 8; cf. pp. 9-10.

[16] *Ibid.*, p. 18. "No good is without its evil, and I am free to confess, that when a people become so infatuated with the spirit of manufactures, as to undertake to force large establishments into unnatural existence, at the expense of other pursuits, they are committing an error by making an evil of that, which would otherwise be a great blessing." Gregg's own successful orcharding and active membership in the Beach Island Farmers' Club testify to the sincerity of the remark next following: "I admit . . . that agriculture is the natural and 'blessed employment of man;' but, that a country should become eminently prosperous in agriculture, without a high state of perfection in the mechanic arts, is a thing next to impossible. . . ." (p. 14.)

[17] *Ibid.*, p. 21.

[18] *Ibid.*, p. 22. On the employment of poor whites as a motive in mill building, see *Rise of Cotton Mills in the South*, pp. 132 ff., p. 168 ff. On the subject of slaves as operatives, *ibid.*, pp. 209-213, and on Negroes in mills after the Civil War, pp. 213-221.

[19] *Domestic Industry*, p. 24. "It is a well established fact, that capital employed in this State, in the culture of cotton, does not, with ordi-

nary management, yield more than 3 or 4, and in some instances, 2 per cent; this being the only mode of employing our capital, except in the culture of rice, how can we expect to retain men of *capital* and *enterprise* among us?" (p. 18.)

²⁰ *Ibid.*, p. 16; cf. pp. 10-11. "Unless we betake ourselves to some more profitable employment than the planting of cotton, what is to prevent our most enterprising planters from moving, with their negro capital, to the South-West? What is to keep our business men and moneyed capital in South-Carolina?" (p. 18; cf. p. 24.)

²¹ *Ibid.*, p. 25; cf. Clark, *History of Manufacturing*, p. 556.

²² *Domestic Industry*.

²³ *Ibid.*, p. iv.

²⁴ *Ibid.*, pp. 25 ff.

²⁵ *Ibid.*, pp. 27 ff. One plant given separate examination exhibited "a fact that cannot but strike a *cotton planter* with great force, viz: *that 174 hands in 12 months convert 4,329 bales of cotton, 345 lbs. to the bale, into cloth—about 24 3-4 bales to the hand; thus adding over $40 to the value of each bale.*" (pp. 29-30.)

²⁶ *Ibid.*, p. 30.

²⁷ *Ibid.*, p. 31.

²⁸ This was of the nature of the Nullification movement, of course.

²⁹ *Domestic Industry*, pp. 31-35.

³⁰ *Ibid.*, p. 49.

³¹ *Ibid.*, pp. 36-40.

³² *Ibid.*, p. 43. Nor need English competition be feared. "Let us remember, that the article which is produced by the English *six penny* labor is taxed a *shilling*, for the support of an extravagant government." Sending raw cotton to England to be spun made the product cost four times as much as if made up in the South. (pp. 43-44.) In this connection Gregg quoted McCulloch, Dr. Ure, and Kirkham Finlay.

³³ *Ibid.*, pp. 41-42. When the Boston merchants embarked in cotton manufacture "they were as ignorant as we are, while the Rhode Island people were eminently skilled in it; but this did not deter the former when driven from their favorite occupation, [as he conceived Southerners were being driven from cotton culture] from engaging in it. These gentlemen, not unlike our merchants and capitalists, and very similar to our intelligent cotton planters, embarked immediately in cotton manufactures, which have indeed yielded them golden harvests. They are not the men to take off their gloves and perform manual manipulations, but they look on with their hands in their pockets, precisely as a cotton planter would do, and depend on the skill of an intelligent overseer, to produce good, practical results." (*Ibid.*, p. 35.)

[34] See Elizabeth Merritt, *James Henry Hammond*, p. 85, note; Miss Merritt says letters by Gregg appear in the Charleston *Evening News*, Mch. 6, 11, 31, 1846, Oct. 16, Dec. 13, 16, 19, 1847, and in the *Mercury* (Charleston) April 8, 1848 ff. Clear signs of the same thought put forward by Gregg appeared elsewhere at the time of publication of the *Domestic Industry* and just afterwards. Thus in the fall of 1844 the State Agricultural Society of S. C. urged a combined system of agriculture, commerce, and manufactures, recommending "a system of household manufacture in every article where domestic skill can be made available," and also proposed home production of flour, pork, and hay. (*Niles' Register*, LXVII, 116.) The Montgomery *Independent* instanced the export of yarns by a little mill at Tallapoosa, and remarked: " . . . we hope to see the day when Alabama will not only use her own fabrics, but will be able to send the manufactured cottons in all varieties abroad.—That is the true, safe, and effectual remedy against all oppressions of the tariff, real or imaginary." (Quoted in *ibid.*, LXIX, 188.) There were also arguments against home industry, mostly blaming the tariff for the unprofitableness of cotton culture (see *ibid.*, LXVIII, 54-55); or declaring, on the contrary, that the Southern cotton planter should not think of manufacturing his staple, but should support a high tariff as furnishing him a good market for his product in the Northern textile centers. (See *ibid.*, LXX, 28 ff.)

[35] It is not amiss, since they bear testimony to the effects of Gregg's advocacy, to give some hint of the contents of these articles. An editorial in the *News*, Mch. 6, 1846, referred to a preference, shown at a recent meeting in Charleston, for water power over steam as the means of driving mills. But Charleston capitalists, instead of building up other localities, should consider what steam had to offer for factories right there. Newburyport, Mass., showed the superiority of steam. Were Lowell being built anew, steam might be used there. Charleston would have other employments for inflowing labor which was unsuited to factory work. The large surplus capital in the Charleston banks, not earning over 5 per cent, should be diverted to industrial development. Such a transfer of money would increase the value of real estate. If some of this might have sounded inimical to Graniteville (which, however, was not directly mentioned), the doubt was removed by the remark that no backset to country adventures in the new manufacturing was meant. The same paper on Mch. 11 said the State was behind the rest of the South in turning to manufactures: "In Charleston very recently the newspaper press teemed with essays illustrative of this subject. The

public mind appeared to be highly excited by it, if not solemnly impressed, with its importance. The Legislature was invoked on the subject. Prodigious efforts were made to subdue certain prejudices—to enlighten public opinion—to awaken dormant energies—to arouse self interest—and appeals even made to selfish instincts." Then came a hint of reproach to Gregg: "Well, charters were obtained. Those who wanted them were satisfied. Charleston was to feel the beneficial influence, forthwith, of industry awakened from its torpor. . . . But paralysis seems to have succeeded to all this salutary excitement." On the subject of the tariff the writer felt about as Gregg did at the outset. There was no real repugnance between manufacturing pursuits and the doctrine of free trade. In the South coarse cotton manufactures required no protection and better grades would thrive on a revenue duty of 20 per cent. Another article, Mch. 31, in order to stir South Carolina to action equal to that of sister States, cited the cotton factories in and about Fayetteville, N. C.; six mills had been built there in the late thirties and early forties. The next article, Oct. 16, was plainly influenced by Gregg, praising the arts as opposed to the professions, and showing how one manufacture would lead to another. The *Mercury*, of which John E. Carew was editor, carried a series of articles by C. T. James, of Rhode Island, in the spring of 1848. The arguments are about the same as presented by this author and promoter elsewhere: South Carolina, without reducing the quantity of her agricultural products, might supply twice the number of people for cotton manufacturing as were engaged in this industry in Massachusetts (Apr. 10); Charleston, as the seaport of a cotton producing country, possessed unique advantages for cotton manufacturing (Apr. 20). Much of this writing has the ring of the post-war advocacy of cotton mills. However, there is no doubt that the political articles being published by the same papers, heralding sectional strife, were less forced. See, for example, Charleston *Mercury*, May 1, 1848, quoting Calhoun in the senate as he threatened the consequences of trampling on the Constitution, or *ibid.*, May 8, suggesting that a suspected Abolitionist then traveling through the State be given short shrift.

CHAPTER III

[1] See Edgefield *Advertiser*, June 5, 1879.

[2] Merritt, *Hammond*, p. 85.

[3] *Statutes at Large of South Carolina*, 1845, XI, 357-358, No. 2954. See also *Charter and By-Laws of the Graniteville Manufacturing Company*, Charleston, 1846. This pamphlet was printed by the company. The by-

laws contain nothing of special interest. On the back of the title page, however, is a MS list of stockholders, made at the time when there were 600 shares of $500 each. (Library of Congress copy.) The committee of the legislature on manufactures recommended the passage of the act of incorporation by a majority of one vote. A friend of Gregg's said years afterwards that only the confidence which the chief men of the State had in him, and his pledge to subscribe to at least half the stock, secured the granting of the charter. (August Kohn, *The Cotton Mills of South Carolina*, pp. 17-18.) Gregg did not subscribe to half the stock, nor was he the largest shareholder.

[4] A number of incorporations of cotton manufacturing enterprises promptly followed this of Graniteville. The very next act chartered the Ashley Manufacturing Co. with a capital of $200,000. Of more interest is that of Dec. 17, 1847, chartering the Charleston Cotton Manufacturing Co. (*Statutes*, XI, 486), incorporators being J. H. Taylor, Jr., Henry Cobia, James T. Welsman, and Joseph Prevost. Unlike Graniteville, this company was given power to increase its capital of $100,000 to $500,000 on decision of the stockholders or directors after proper advertisement. The legislature by this date had made progress. Up to the time of the Graniteville charter, incorporations in South Carolina were mostly of churches, benevolent societies, fire companies, rifle companies, villages, ferries, bridges, etc. Now, learning from experience, was passed "An Act to Define the terms upon which manufacturing companies shall hereafter be incorporated" (*ibid.*, pp. 465-468). This general act followed the lines of the Graniteville charter, providing particularly that manufacturing corporations should not engage in banking; it also prescribed the method of opening books and organizing the corporation. In 1848 the Laurel Falls Manufacturing Co., Lexington District, was incorporated (*ibid.*, pp. 497-498). In 1850 came the Wateree Manufacturing Co., with capital of $200,000 (*ibid.*, XII, pp. 46 ff.). The incorporation of companies to build plank roads, which took place in these years, and which went through the same progress from specific acts to a general provision, is spoken of elsewhere. *The Southerner* (published at Richmond) said that southern legislatures in the winter of 1848 incorporated upwards of ninety companies for manufacturing and kindred purposes; ". . . it shows that the time is coming when public men will be forced to establish and maintain, as an *American, national* policy, a system, under which we shall have *concentration* instead of dispersion." (Tuxedo in *The Plough, the Loom and the Anvil*, I, 47-8.)

[5] *Charters of Incorporation*, p. 3.

[6] *Ibid.*, p. 4.

[7] *Ibid.*, p. 6; cf. pp. 13-14.

[8] *Ibid.*, p. 6; cf. pp. 9-10. "About three-fourths of the manufacturing of the United States, is carried on by joint stock companies. . . . We shall certainly have to look to such companies to introduce the business with us, and those who are desirous of seeing a change in the condition of our State, are earnestly called on to waive their objections, and permit those who choose to embark their capital, to make a fair experiment. Such establishments, to say the least of them, will serve as schools, in which our sons will be taught the art of converting our raw material into merchantable fabrics. . . ." (*Ibid.*, p. 7.) Gregg in many places stressed the fact that in order to introduce an industry of the complication of cotton manufacturing into an agricultural community such as South Carolina, it was necessary to put reliance in expert technicians. "In order to make a successful experiment, we must begin right; and to begin right, we must secure the services of men, successfully engaged in prosecuting similar works, in other countries; to secure them, we must rear such establishments as will enable us, not only to pay the highest wages going, but to satisfy the ambition of such as have set themselves out to establish their fortune and fame, by rendering such establishments productive" to the capitalists concerned. (*Ibid.*) No one in South Carolina should think of building a cloth mill of less than 5,000 spindles unless he meant to apprentice himself to the business and assume personal management. "A young man, reared in one of these fine New England establishments, would consider it almost an insult, to be offered a situation in a 1,200, or 2,000 spindle factory, in South-Carolina. Such men could not be induced . . . to take charge of anything short of a *first rate* establishment. . . ." (*Domestic Industry*, p. 53.)

[9] *Charters of Incorporation*, p. 9.

[10] *Ibid.*, pp. 9-10. Similarly, while an individual might easily underestimate the cost of erecting a plant and starting it in operation, and so be ruined at the outset, a chartered company was more apt, through the calculations of several, to be circumspect in providing sufficient capital and was sure to have more resources should additional funds at any time be needed. (*Ibid.*, pp. 7-8.)

[11] *Ibid.*, pp. 11-12. The years of depression, 1837-42, had given the public sufficient experience of catastrophic business wind-ups; Gregg instanced especially men enjoying abundant credit who were suddenly discovered to have lost everything in cotton speculations—a phenomenon all too familiar in South Carolina.

[12] Gregg's modernity, and at the same time his very natural limitations, come out strikingly in a passage here. "In the Merrimack Company of Lowell, $60,000 of its capital is owned by its own operatives. In this way, every industrious man, who is disposed to save his money, may become an owner and co-partner in the concern, which gives him employment, and thus become personally interested in its producing good results. By this means, the immense gulf, which would otherwise separate the owner and operative, at once disappears, and although lines of distinction will always be seen, yet they will be so modified as scarcely to be felt; while the owner and operative, engaged in carrying on great business pursuits, will constitute two . . . distinct classes, they will be so harmoniously blended together, as to form a community, though widely differing in rank, yet all working for the good of the whole. . . . Deplorable indeed, will be the condition of the poor, when the business of manufacturing shall be confined to the great capitalists of the world; they will indeed be ruled with a rod of despotism. . . ." Charles Dickens, if no other, had familiarized America with the plight of the English cotton mill worker, and Gregg had seen at Lowell the contentment (though it was, in truth, not too well founded), which the novelist admired on his visit to this country. "While the manufacturing population of Great Britain," said Gregg, "are in the hands of great capitalists, and in a worse condition than slaves, we find the same class of persons in New-Hampshire, Maine, Massachusetts, Rhode Island and Connecticut, the most free and happy people on the face of the globe." (*Ibid.*, pp. 12-13.) Gregg probably had the writings of Thomas Skidmore and agitations of the Workingmen's Party in mind when he said (surely with safety!) that "South-Carolina possesses little, or none of the agrarian spirit which pervades Pennsylvania and New-York, where the poor are ready to wage war against the bread of their existence, because it is procured through the aid of capital which pays interest to its owner, and enables the rich to live without laboring." (pp. 9-10; cf. p. 14.)

[13] Mr. Coles Phinizy, of Augusta, who has been interested in Gregg's history, believes that he tried for several years to buy the old Vaucluse Mill before he succeeded in 1843. During this time he must have thought of establishing his own plant if he failed in securing Vaucluse. Mrs. Chafee, evidently neglecting any early connection of her father with Vaucluse, said that his attention was first directed to the Graniteville location when he passed one or two summers at Aiken. This was on the South Carolina Railroad and a convenient retreat for Charlestonians

in the hot months. Mrs. Chafee said that in driving about the country-side he was attracted by the two strong creeks in the valley and thought they would make good mill streams.

¹⁴ *Domestic Industry*, p. iv. A statement of Gregg's that the land was acquired in 1845 refers to himself and Boyce rather than the Company as such. (*Reports of the President and Treasurer, Graniteville Manufacturing Co.*, April 18, 1867, p. 4; this pamphlet is hereafter referred to as *President's Report*, April 18, 1867. Deeds to the Graniteville property were destroyed in the Barnwell Court House fire, Graniteville lying originally in that District.

¹⁵ William Gregg, *Speech on Blue Ridge Railroad*, p. 30.

¹⁶ *MS Minutes of Stockholders' Meetings*. The large, securely bound book was made and sold by Joseph Walker at Stationers' Hall, 89 East Bay, Charleston. These records were perused by DeBow, judging from an article in his *Review*.

¹⁷ One of Gregg's old operatives spoke of such a saw mill, but thought that a Mr. Bauskett was Gregg's partner. Col. Bauskett once owned the Flat Rock dam, which helps to impound water for Graniteville, and also the dam at Vaucluse above—with the land for four miles on both sides of the creek. (August Kohn, *The Water Powers of South Carolina*, p. 56), but there is no evidence that Bauskett and Gregg were in partnership. Gregg later complained that lumbering along the line of the South Carolina Railroad was not encouraged because western freights were preferred; hence timbered lands sold for little and the railroad satisfied its requirements for timber at prices which barely paid for the labor of getting it out. A competing road was badly needed, he said. Perhaps his own lumbering interests had taught him to appreciate this argument against the monopolist.

¹⁸ *Minutes*, Mch. 10, 1846.

¹⁹ *Ibid.*, Jan. 14, 1846; Kohn, *op. cit.*, p. 55.

²⁰ *Minutes*. Of the 23 subscribers, no less than 15 were from Charleston—Ker Boyce, 60 shares; William Gregg, 50; C. K. Huger, 10; Edward Sebring, 10; Robert Martin, 10; E. Geddings, 10; T. Street, 10; Howland & Taft, 20; Otis Mills, 10; Alex. McDonald, 2; James Lamb, 10; S. S. Farrar, 5; W. H. Gilliland, 5; William Bell, 10. Gregg was constantly saying that Charleston had ample capital, if only she could be brought to use it for improvements within the State (see, for example, *Domestic Industry*, p. 50; *Blue Ridge Railroad*, pp. 7-8, 29 ff.). The list of the original Graniteville stockholders shows that he practiced what he preached, by enlisting the strong support of Charleston investors. Two subscribers were from York District—John Springs, 20 shares, and

William Wright, 20; two were from Abbeville District—Joel Smith, 20 shares, and John McIlwain, 2; and two more from Hamburg— Hiram Hutchinson, 50 shares, and John J. Blackwood, 10 shares. Completing the list were A. W. Thompson, Union, 10 shares, and James Jones, Aiken, 2 shares. The largest stockholders were thus Boyce, $30,000, and Gregg, Hutchinson, and Smith, $25,000 each.

[21] At the time Graniteville was set going, there was only one house, known as the Morris farm house, between the mill and Graniteville depot, now called Warrenville. The young people of the new village, fresh from the country, used to think it a treat to walk to the depot to see the train pass. An old map of 1832, about the time of the building of Vaucluse but fourteen years prior to the erection of Graniteville, shows the South Carolina Railroad running from Charleston via Summerville and Murrayville (there was no Branchville at this time) to Aikenville, and thence west for a few miles before turning southwest to Hamburg. The point of this last turn, one mile from the Graniteville factory, became the Graniteville depot and the point of shipment for the mill. The settlements in Edgefield District are given as the Court House, Hamburg, Campbellton, North Richmond, Martin Town, and Richardsonville, and the streams bear the names of Little Saluda River, Cuffytown Creek, Turkey Creek, and Steven's Creek. A main wagon road is shown running from the Court House to Hamburg and thence to Barnwell Court House; from this point there is a winding lesser road to Orangeburg. In 1820, according to the census figures given with the map, Edgefield District had 12,764 whites, 57 free blacks, 12,198 slaves— a total population of 25,119. In 1830 the population was 30,511. (S. Augustus Mitchell, *Map of North and South Carolina and Georgia, Constructed from the Latest Authorities*. Philadelphia, 1832.) Five miles above Vaucluse, at shoals on the Edgefield branch of Horse Creek, a pottery was conducted for many years prior to the establishment of Graniteville. The original Flat Rock dam, which was incorporated into Gregg's works for Graniteville, appears to have been built in 1817, and was used first for a flour mill, and later for a saw mill. (Kohn, *Water Powers of South Carolina*, pp. 56, 57.) Mr. Kohn says the Indian name for Horse Creek was Cussaboe, meaning a place of small canes.

[22] *Minutes*, June 22, 1859. Regarding engagement of experts, see *Domestic Industry*, pp. 25-26, 35, 53. Gregg's report to the stockholders, April 18, 1867, would indicate that he very quickly dismissed any notion of employing an outside engineer. He was speaking of informal arrangements when he used 1845 as the date when "We purchased the land we occupy, obtained a charter and formed our Company. . . ."

[23] *Minutes,* Jan. 29, 1859.

[24] *President's Report,* April 18, 1867. Quite aside from his own stock subscription, Gregg felt extraordinary responsibility as the prime agitator in a novel undertaking. If Graniteville failed it would carry down with it all his hopes of a cotton manufacturing development in the South.

[25] Mrs. Chafee said that a Col. Tomanis was superintendent of the building construction at Graniteville. Judging from Gregg's remarks, however, it must have been a minor place which he occupied.

[26] He had said in the preface to his *Domestic Industry* that cotton manufactures would initiate a force that would "shake the very foundation of the beds of *granite* that abound in all parts of our State . . ." (p. iii). The old quarry has since been known as the "log wash hole."

[27] Mr. J. E. Sirrine, Greenville. In the appendix to *Domestic Industry,* Gregg set forth the proper equipment of mills of different sorts, with the cost as obtained from Northern manufacturers (pp. 59-61). He observed all of the physical characteristics of the New England industry with great care during his tour in 1844, and took pains to report as much necessary information as possible in the hope that it would be availed of in the South.

[28] "This is a high estimate for the building [$25,000] and water-wheel, [$17,000 with gearing and belting] for our back country. The Saluda Factory's building, of granite, 4 stories and an attic, 200 by 40 feet, cost only $20,000. The Vaucluse, of hewn granite, 4 stories and an attic, 80 by 40 feet, with wheel-pit and water-wheel, cost only $17,500." He gave further evidence of his anxiety that home industry should be patronized by adding, after giving estimates from a Bridesburg, Pa., machinery maker, that all the castings might be obtained at several places in Charleston; he had had them made as cheaply by Thomas Dotterer. (*Ibid.,* p. 60; this would be for the Vaucluse Mill; *ibid.,* p. 47, note.) Montgomery's book is *A Practical Detail of the Cotton Manufacture of the United States* (Glasgow, 1840).

[29] As to the changes in wheels, see *Report of President and Treasurer, Graniteville Co., for year 1854,* p. 5. In the mill yard is part of the capstone from the wheel pit at the upper end of the mill, showing the holes drilled for the bolts.

Clark says the mill was driven by a turbine wheel of 116 horse power. He may have confused the installation of 1866 with the original wheel. (Victor S. Clark, *History of Manufactures in the U. S., 1607-1860,* p. 557.)

[30] Dr. Cook, at a meeting of Gregg's friends soon after his death, said: "When we consider all the circumstances of the case, the almost entire

ignorance of our people on this subject, their prejudice against it and the consequent difficulty of enlisting capital in its favor, the conversion of a barren wilderness into a beautiful village with its neat cottages, its flower gardens, and beautiful grounds, its churches, its factory structure built of solid Granite obtained on the spot, the beautiful and perfect machinery; all these things, never before seen, or dreamed of, by the natives, seemed as if created by magic." (Quoted in Edgefield *Advertiser*, June 5, 1879.)

[31] See *Domestic Industry*, p. 46 and p. 47, note.

[32] I talked with the son of a man who came in to work on the mill. The father lived on a few acres at Minerva, eight or ten miles above Graniteville, at the head of Horse Creek. When the mill was started older sons and daughters, including my informant (now a man of 80), came to Graniteville as operatives. Later, at the death of the father, the whole family moved to the factory village, leaving the cabin in the country to decay. This happened with scores of others.

[33] Mrs. Chafee, Gregg's daughter.

[34] The saw mill cost $5,000. "When the factory went into operation, this mill was abandoned and its cost charged to the lumber we had cut, which brought its prime cost, including loss on the saw mill, to 4 33-100 dollars per thousand feet." (*President's Report*, April 18, 1867, p. 5.)

[35] The masonry contractor asked the court for a judgment against the company of $10,000. "We justly owed about five hundred. The suit was compromised by our paying one thousand dollars." Gregg thought that a master mason who supervised the work deserved to be remembered in the chronicles of Graniteville: "For good stone walls, we were indebted to Wm. Murdoch, a faithful stone mason, who has since made a fortune by his skill and integrity. He was employed at three dollars a day, to stand on the walls and see the contract strictly complied with." After the contracting mason quit, the work was, apparently, completed with day labor, Murdoch probably being in charge. Bad work by the carpenter-contractor necessitated the re-laying of all the floors and the rejection of the window sashes, costing about $4,000. (See *ibid*.)

[36] *Minutes*, June 22, 1859.

[37] *Ibid.*, Mch. 9, 1847. A. R. Taft, of the firm of Howland & Taft, of Charleston, mercantile agents of the Graniteville Company, was treasurer during the time of erecting the mill. (*President's Report*, April 18, 1867, p. 5.) He came to Graniteville only occasionally.

[38] The newcomers were B. McBride, of Hickory Hill; R. H., Joseph J., and W. A. Wardlaw, Abbeville C. H.; William Smith, of the same place; Hugh R. Banks, Charleston; John W. Lewis, Charleston; Joseph

281

Lyon, Abbeville; E. M. Beach, Charleston, and Jas. G. O. Wilkinson, Aiken. (It may be noticed in passing that the stockholders listed in the Aiken *Journal and Review*, Sept. 29, 1920, as the original investors, were rather those as of Mch., 1847, taken from the paper referred to, which is, by the way, in the handwriting of James Jones, who recorded the early minutes.) The only large investor in this new group was McBride, owning 36 shares. A number had considerably increased their holdings—Boyce from 60 shares to 80 shares, Joel Smith from 20 to 80, Gregg from 50 to 60, Hutchinson from 50 to 80, Wright and Springs from 20 to 30 each, and Martin, Howland & Taft, Lamb, and Bell from 10 shares to 20 shares each. This list was prepared at about the same time as that found in the Library of Congress copy of the charter. The Charleston *Mercury*, (Mch. 23, 1848) was mistaken, apparently, in saying the whole capital of $300,000 was subscribed within a few weeks after books were opened.

CHAPTER IV

[1] *Mercury*, Mch. 23, 1848.

[2] DeBow's *Review*, VI, Nos. 4-5, 370 ff., quoting from Tuscaloosa *Monitor*.

[3] *Hunt's Merchants' Magazine*, XXI, 671-672; Gregg wrote at Kalmia, Oct. 22.

[4] See DeBow's *Review*, VII, 456. Robinson was a well known journalist of the time, and the author of the popular book, *Hot Corn*. Born in Connecticut in 1803, he was successively carpenter, pedlar, and writer. He was for a time agricultural editor of the New York *Tribune* and later was interested in social conditions of cities. Toward the end of his life he bought a farm in Florida, where he died in 1880. In the case of Graniteville he proved himself a useful reporter. (*See National Cyclopaedia of American Biography*, III, 454.)

[5] Gregg had said "We turn out daily about 12,000 yards of cloth, sheeting, shirting and drills, of No. 14 yarn, according to the judgment of the merchants of Charleston, New York and Philadelphia, equal in point of quality to any of the kind made in the United States or any other country."

[6] Robinson recorded the following itemized statement of cost:

Real estate	$ 12,222.35
Canals, dams	9,505.46
Buildings (factory)	60,144.57
Water wheels, flumes	6,949.12

Shafting, gearing	$ 12,663.99
Machinery	121,754.03
Fire and steam apparatus	5,947.65
Starting up mill, and furniture	3,587.96
Saw mill, machine shop, etc.	9,079.86
Card clothing	3,010.00
Dwelling houses	43,293.18
Streets and fences	1,998.80
Contingencies	3,307.49
Margin left	6,539.67

[7] DeBow's *Review*, VII, 456.

[8] See DeBow's *Review*, VIII, 24 ff. An engraving of Graniteville published in Mch., 1851, is much like the scene today, except that this old picture is bare of shrubbery and in it the forest closes in about the main buildings. In the foreground is a fenced road, with the canal beyond it. A small arched bridge leads over to the enclosure surrounding the mill; there are two warehouses and two small buildings besides, and a trackway into the picker room for conveying cotton. (See *ibid.*, X, 348.)

[9] *Hunt's Magazine*, XXI, 671-672.

[10] Of the Lowell establishments he had written that "the boarding houses for the accommodation of their operatives, are what we in Charleston, would call fine houses, not inferior in quality and appearance to the best buildings, in the newly built portions of our city." And again he said that these houses were "quite as elegant—fully as costly, and afforded as much room as all the buildings on both sides of King-street, between Market and Hasel-streets." (*Domestic Industry*, p. 35, p. 36, note.) Certain streets of these operatives' boarding houses in Lowell, as for instance that containing the Arkwright Club, still testify to the correctness of Gregg's description, being quite as good as the houses he mentioned in Charleston. The plan of boarding farmers' daughters under the strict supervision of matrons for each "tenement" in New England cotton mill towns of this period has often been described.

[11] DeBow's *Review*, VIII, 24 ff.

[12] p. 22.

[13] DeBow's *Review*, VIII, 24 ff.

[14] Potatoes and peas were other crops, but nobody in that district, with the exception of a few large slaveholders, grew cotton; guano, thought essential for cotton culture in this part of the State, was not brought in until after the Civil War.

[15] The New England cotton manufactures, of course, had well-developed villages at least three decades earlier; Lowell had operatives' cottages and a stone school house at his works at Waltham as early as 1813, and Gregg, as has been noted, found much to admire in the town he later built at the place bearing his name. In the South also there were company villages before Graniteville. The Saluda Factory had quarters for its slave operatives, and Vaucluse had its little community of homes and school, all operatives living in company houses rent free and cultivating all the land they chose to fence. (See DeBow's *Review*, VII, 456 ff.) The DeKalb Factory, near Camden, founded in 1838 with 1,000 spindles (with a grist mill and shoe factory in connection), had its own village, as was advertised by the local paper when Graniteville was receiving so much attention a decade later: "The Factory Village, where the operatives reside, is pleasantly situated. One hundred and fifty-four constitute the white population, and their neat cottages and thriving gardens present a handsome appearance, indicative of comfort and contentment. The moral and mental culture of these families receive great attention. A daily school for their children is kept through the week, and . . . every Sabbath morning members of the various churches in town meet them in Sunday School. . . . We are told that this little *Village* can well compare, in point of morals and good order, with any in the Union, of the same size. . . ." (Camden *Journal*, quoted in *ibid.*, pp. 372-373.) This company had formerly employed many negroes, and may have built the village for the slaves. After Graniteville was built, however, there was a crop of cotton mills in the South, a number of which at the start erected villages with certain "welfare facilities" for white operatives who were to be drawn in from the countryside. Thus the factory at the new place of "Fulton" near Mobile, which was being completed in 1850, would contain 5,040 spindles and house 200 operatives in the village. (DeBow's *Review*, IX, 431.) The Autaugaville Factory, Alabama, started in 1848, contained 3,000 spindles, 110 looms and 42 cards, and employed in 1850 some 80 operatives, mostly women and girls. "Autaugaville," it was said, "has grown up in the woods during two years past. It now has a population of 250 souls—four mercantile establishments—two churches, and a third is soon to be built, and two good schools. The village is situated some two or three miles from the Alabama River, and about the same distance from Prattville, and Vernon, and is rapidly increasing in population. . . ." (*Ibid.*, p. 461.) Of the village of the Howard Mill, Columbus, Ga., it was said: "The hands, male and female, had a general appearance of cleanliness, health and contentment. The proprietors of the manufactories have made arrange-

ments for preaching, Sunday schools, and . . . daily free schools for the operatives and their families."

[16] *President's Report*, 1854, p. 11; cf. *Domestic Industry*, pp. 22, 46.

[17] *Plough, Loom and Anvil*, II, 197 ff. Gregg organized a sick fund, to which each family made a trifling contribution, and from which the doctor's fees were paid. He also inaugurated a small library, with a self-taught operative as custodian of the books.

[18] DeBows's *Review*, VII, 456 ff. Gregg (*Domestic Industry*, Appendix E) gave tables of wages, exclusive of board, in Lowell and in South Carolina mills in 1845; the average per day for the former was 59 cents, and for the latter 42 cents; the lowest wage in the Northern mill was 35 cents, but in the Southern mill 30 boys and girls were receiving 20 cents and under. At Lowell, the next year, the average weekly wage of women operatives was $2, exclusive of board. (Niles' *Register*, LXX, 29.)

[19] DeBow's *Review*, VIII, 27-28.

[20] Interview with Mr. Jule Overstreet.

[21] The pay roll of the company (not including, presumably, the superintendent) averaged, in 1848, $37.85 per day of 12 hours. Making 8-ounce osnaburgs and bundle-yard, the labor cost was 2 cents 9.361 mills per pound for cloth and 1 cent 9.62 mills per pound for yarn. Apparently the old British system of master spinners employing their own spinners prevailed, for it was said that "All the hands, except a few men who are unmarried, and all that can, work by the piece." Unmarried men evidently could not employ children, all working by families. At the DeKalb Factory the white hands, constituting two-thirds of the force, received from 13 to 26 cents per day for 11 3-8 hours, and weavers on piece work got 18 cents a cut for 33 yards, averaging 3 cuts per day, or a monthly wage of $9.90 to $18. The hired blacks got 18 3-4 cents per day and boarded themselves. At the little Marlboro Factory near Bennettsville, spinning the coarsest yarns, some of the 35 hands were boys and girls 10 years old; including 5 slaves counted at $8 a month and a machinist at $9 a week, the operatives averaged in wages $1.90 a week, none of the work being by the piece. (DeBow's *Review*, VII, 456 ff.) In 1849 all the weavers at the DeKalb Factory were white females "receiving wages from twelve to twenty dollars per month—an amount far greater than they realized before their connection with the Factory, and sufficient to secure the necessary comforts of life, and create a small sinking fund if desired." (See *ibid.*, pp. 372-373.) In 1850 the Coweta Falls Manufacturing Co., Columbus, Ga., paid its superintendent $1,000 a year, overseers from $30 to $60 per month, and weavers $15, carders $8, and spinners $7.50 per month. At the Howard

Mill at the same place the superintendent received $900 per year, and common hands from 12 to 75 cents per day, none of the hands being younger than 12 years. (*Ibid.*, IX, 431.)

[22] An official of the Graniteville Company, who has grown up in Southern mills, said that when he was a boy he began work at 6:30 in the morning and quit "eventually."

[23] Until the age of twelve, children must be kept in the school; see *Hunt's Magazine*, XXI, 671-672.

[24] *Ibid.* The New England superintendent or overseer was common in the Southern mills of the period. Gregg counseled it. The Saluda Factory had a Lowell weaver in charge; cf. DeBow's *Review*, IX, 432-433.

[35] *Hunt's Magazine*, XXI, 671-672.

[26] *Ibid.*, XXII, 107. Solon Robinson (*ibid.*, pp. 350-351) seconded these observations of Gregg with excellent understanding. A cold calculation of low money profits to be made in the business by new mills rising in the South did not tell the whole story of the advantage to the section. "The lower class of New England population are possessed of energy, inventive genius, and go-ahead industry, with intellects brightened by a plain education; while the same class here are as inert as indolence and poverty and total want of education for ages can make a people; and the change wrought upon such a population, by transposing them from their miserable log-cabins in the pine woods, and equally miserable food and raiment, to the state of civilization that they meet with in such a beautiful manufacturing village as Graniteville, must be seen to be appreciated. It is no wonder that Mr. Gregg estimates the benefits to the body politic so highly. The whole tract around Graniteville, three years ago, was a wild barren waste, and the greater portion of the operatives as wild as the aboriginees—living a sort of vegetable life, of little profit to themselves or others."

[27] See the writer's *Rise of Cotton Mills in the South*, pp. 151 ff. Cotton mills erected soon after Graniteville at Augusta, New Orleans, Memphis, and Mobile have been attributed to Gregg's example. (See Clark, *History of Manufactures in U. S.*, p. 557). If one wishes to go back far enough, he can find tiny cotton mills, with individual proprietors, erected in the South in the thirties, and their example encouraged with arguments similar to those used afterwards. Such was Malletts Mill, 500 spindles, built at Fayetteville in 1836. (*Niles' Weekly Register*, I, 378.)

[38] *Niles' Register*, LXVIII, 179.

[29] *Ibid.*, p. 311.

[30] Quoted in DeBow's *Review*, IX, 214 ff.

[31] *Ibid.*, X, 461.

[32] *Ibid.*

[33] See as to those in the West, *ibid.*, IX, 328-329, and as to those of Tennessee, Alabama, Georgia, and South Carolina, *ibid.*, pp. 214 ff., 431, and *Niles' Register*, LXXII, 260. Most were small factories, only one having more spindles than Graniteville.

[34] Augusta *Chronicle and Sentinel*, quoted in *Hunt's Magazine*, XX, 114.

[35] Quoted in DeBow's *Review*, IX, 327-328. "It has often been asserted of southern industry, that it was not persistent or enduring; that our climate was enervating, and productive of lassitude, indolence and feebleness; and that if cotton mills were started they could not be carried on by southern operatives. . . . Again, it was urged that the business was one unsuited to our tastes and pursuits, and could not successfully be introduced among us. . . . While the mills at the north are running short time, or stopping work altogether, we are pleased to learn that the Charleston mill is driving every loom to the utmost capacity, and that its product per loom is now equal to the best mills in the country." In twelve months it had been awarded three first-class premiums for its goods.

[36] Charleston *Post*, quoted in *Niles' National Register*, LXVII, 288 (Jan. 4, 1845).

[37] Charleston *Courier*, quoted in *ibid.*, LXXII, 260.

[38] *Niles' Register*, LXXIII, 115.

[39] *Review*, VII, 454. Later (1852) in an editorial on manufactures at the South, DeBow gave arguments probably inspired by Gregg, whom he elsewhere acknowledged as the champion of this movement. "We are not without hope," he said, "that the interest which has been excited in this subject will not be profitless." He estimated that already Georgia had 40 cotton mills, with 80,000 spindles; Tennessee 30 mills, with 36,000 spindles and 700 looms; Alabama 12 mills, 12,580 spindles and 300 looms. Thus in four States there were 98 mills, with others building. If they continued increasing for the next five years as they had in the last five, the South could look for mills consuming 200,000 bales of cotton and employing 30,000 operatives. (*Ibid.*, XII, 92.)

[40] The article of James which attracted the fire of Lawrence was "The Production and Manufacture of Cotton: With Reference to its Manufacture in the Cotton-Growing States"; this appeared in *Hunt's Merchants' Magazine*, XXI, 492-502 (Nov., 1849). It is similar in matter and viewpoint to another brief of his ("Cotton and Cotton Manufactures at the South. Comparative Cost and Productiveness of Cotton, and the Cost and Productiveness of its Manufacture") which

appeared in installments in DeBow's *Review*, as follows: VII, 173-176 (Aug., 1849); *ibid.*, pp. 370-372 (Oct., 1849); VIII, 307-311 (March, 1850). Thus two installments had been printed in DeBow's before his article in Hunt's, but the *Southern Review* was probably not seen by Lawrence.

[41] He was major-general of the Rhode Island militia and, after a term in the U. S. Senate, gave chief attention to perfecting a rifle cannon and projectile, dying in 1862 from injuries received in his experiments. See *National Cyclopædia of American Biography*, III, 324; *Hunt's Magazine*, XXII, 456.

[42] See the writer's *Rise of Cotton Mills in the South*, pp. 109-110, 117, and note.

[43] *Hunt's Magazine*, XXI, 494; for a more detailed calculation, see p. 496.

[44] See for some expressions at this and later dates the writer's *op. cit.*, pp. 115 ff.

[45] DeBow's *Review*, VIII, 312; cf. *ibid.*, pp. 3 ff.

[46] Southerners "should continue the production of cotton, and the great staples indigenous to their soil and climate, and at the same time introduce such branches of manufactures as promise even a moderate remuneration for the capital invested. The influence of such a course will tend to equalize and improve the condition of the entire people, and cement our Union, by bands that will 'grow with the growth, and strengthen with the strength,' of a common interest and a common industry." (*Hunt's Magazine*, XXI, 677 ff.; cf. XX, 114.)

[47] See the writer's *op. cit.*, pp. 117 ff.

[48] The Massachusetts Mills, Lowell, in the years 1841 to 1849 inclusive, earned as follows: 0, 3, 4, 14, 20, 20, 19, 6, 6; the Appleton Mills from 1845-49 made earnings of 12, 12, 3, 5, 3a6; Tremont in the same years, 18, 16, 7, 2, 3. With par of 1,000, Massachusetts stock sold at 900, Appleton at 800, Tremont at 875. Merrimac and Otis stocks were above par (1,120 and 1,050), but Chicopee sold for 600 and Atlantic 670. (*Hunt's Magazine*, XXI, 628 ff.)

[49] *Ibid.*, XXII, 184 ff., 290 ff. The Charleston *Mercury*, in a note concerning the Charleston Cotton Mill, explained that this was "one among many others which that eminent engineer, Gen. Charles T. James, has erected within the last few years in the South and West. We learn with much satisfaction that his highly liberal offer to subscribe for half the stock of a $300,000 cotton mill, will ensure at an early day the erection of a factory in our city on an enlarged scale. . . . The remarkable practical genius of Gen. James, his wide experience in all that concerns the

cotton manufacturing, and his careful study of all the questions connected with its successful introduction into the Southern States, give great value and interest to the conviction he has expressed and so strongly backed, in favor of the adaptation of Charleston for the prosecution of this department of industry on an extensive scale." (Quoted in DeBow's *Review*, IX, 327-328.) The new factory here spoken of was to be an enlargement of the Charleston Mill, which had a high unit cost of production due to its small size, 3,300 spindles and 100 looms. (See J. H. Taylor in *ibid.*, VIII, 29.) The plan did not materialize.

[50] *Ibid.*, p. 550 ff.; see also Smith's paper on the relative cost of steam and water power in *ibid.*, VII, 128 ff.

[51] Lawrence had asserted, among other counts, that the South had not the requisite labor and skill to compete with Northern cotton manufactures. "A full contradiction of this averment," Smith rejoined, was to be found in Gregg's letter in *Hunt's Magazine;* here it was shown that, if 4,500,000 yards of domestics was a large yield for a mill of 10,000 spindles, as Lawrence had said, the Graniteville Mill, operated by home labor, came well up to the standard, producing at the rate of 4,420,000 yards for a 10,000 spindle mill. "This labor," Smith added, "that seems to approximate very nearly to your standard, is stated to cost 20 per cent less than the Massachusetts rate." Hunt prefaced the letter by saying "we rejoice to find our southern friends advocating the importance of 'bringing the cotton mill to the cotton field.'" This is the earliest use known to me (1849) of a slogan which was the rallying cry in the "cotton mill campaign" that signalized the great burst of cotton factories in the South in the eighties.

[52] Gregg promised to write more fully later, especially as to Graniteville, and meantime sent his address delivered before the South Carolina Institute, with permission to print it. The editor added that since receiving Gregg's letter, the Graniteville Factory had been awarded first premium by the Franklin Institute of Philadelphia for sheetings, shirtings, and drillings—"quite a triumph for our Southern friends." (*Hunt's Magazine*, XXI, 671-672.)

[53] XXII, 107; the letter was dated Charleston, Dec. 20, 1849.

[54] Cf. Edward Ingle, *Southern Sidelights*, pp. 81-87 for references to this controversy.

[55] DeBow's *Review*, VIII, 24 ff. Two other articles, among many contributed on this general subject, deserve mention here—that of S. R. Cockrill on "Manufacturing of Cotton by Its Producers" in *ibid.*, VII, 485 ff., and J. H. Lumpkin's "Industrial Regeneration of the South," *ibid.*, XII, 41 ff. The former gave a good expression of the view, repre-

hended by Gregg, that farmers should put up small rude mills as aux-
iliaries of the plantation. For a forecast, in 1850, of successful competition of Southern against Northern mills, which is being exactly borne
out today, see *Hunt's Magazine*, XXII, 311.

⁵⁶ *Hunt's Magazine*, XXI, 629 ff.

⁵⁷ *Ibid.*, pp. 671-672.

⁵⁸ *Ibid.*, XXIII, 679.

⁵⁹ "We turn out daily," said Gregg, "about 12,000 yards of cloth, sheetings, shirtings and drills, of No. 14 yarn . . ." (*Ibid.*, XXI, 671-672).
In 1852, Southern cotton mills were still throttled down. Only half the
spindles in Virginia were in operation, and many of these on part time,
with a 25 per cent reduction in wages. Of 28 mills in Maryland, only
2 were constantly employed, and 8 were entirely idle. Overproduction of
coarse goods was principally blamed for the depression in the industry.
In 1850, imports of cotton goods into the United States amounted to
$19,685,986 as against $15,182,518 in 1849. (DeBow's *Review*, XII,
359-360.)

CHAPTER V

¹ *Domestic Industry*, p. 22.

² *Hunt's Magazine*, XXI, 671-672. The first accounts of Graniteville,
by Thomas Maxwell and Solon Robinson (1849), make no mention of
the school, though it was probably in operation by the time the latter
wrote. In 1850 Robinson noted "Here the children *must attend*
school . . ." (*Hunt's Magazine*, XXII, 350-351.)

³ DeBow's *Review*, VIII, 24 ff.

⁴ Another pupil told a similar story. She was brought up close to
Graniteville, and when her father was killed in the war, Gregg included
the children in the school and in all of the outings in which he took such
delight.

⁵ However, he did not keep his promise, nor could any one know the
tragic end his truancy would lead to. One day he ran away from school
and down to the mill. In playing with a piece of rope on the shaft from
the picker-room which ran the saw mill he was caught, wound about the
shaft, and his body broken in a hundred places.

⁶ It was added by my informant that Fagin stood in need of the
bath. Fagin was found at the spring one winter morning, frozen to
death in the snow.

⁷ See *Hunt's Magazine*, XXI, 671-672. Mr. Taylor, the company's treasurer, set it forth that "Graniteville is strictly a temperance town.
There is no liquor sold, and if it is known that any one brings it into

the place to drink, he is expelled, driven off in disgrace. The consequence is, there is no noise or disturbance, and but little of any kind of immorality . . ." (DeBow's *Review*, VIII, 24 ff.)

[8] *Hunt's*, XXII, 350-351.

[9] MS letter to James Montgomery, Charleston, 31st Dec., 1850.

[10] These stories of Dawse and his jug were told me by many persons at Graniteville; it may easily be that the lapses of others have been identified, as the years have passed, with this single individual.

[11] The name of the place was afterwards changed to Madison. Wooley's hat factory was near what is now Carpenter's Garage.

[12] MS letter to Montgomery, Charleston, Mch. 20, 1851.

[13] Resolutions adopted by the church at his death said: "Though a member of a congregation of a different order from our own, yet from the earliest foundation of our Church . . . he was identified with its interests, as its unwavering friend, and constant benefactor. He had its welfare so much at heart that his generous contributions to its funds were a perennial stream." (MS in possession of Mrs. Chafee.)

[14] Edgefield *Advertiser*, June 5, 1879.

[15] Wilkinson was not one of the original Graniteville stockholders, but in a list of 1847 he appears as the owner of two shares, his residence being put down as Aiken.

[16] This was believed by many of the village people to be a vault where Gregg kept the company's money, but the only excuse for this notion was the churned gold it housed.

[17] The iron grill work which stood outside the library windows has in recent years been moved to the Hofmann house in Aiken, where it encloses the portico.

[18] Gregg to Hammond, (Kalmia, Feb. 16, 1857) *J. H. Hammond Papers*, (Library of Congress) XX.

[19] Aunt Maria was Mrs. Gregg's maid. Gregg in his diary made note of her marriage in 1856. Aunt Hester had been the cook in the Jones family. "General" was Gregg's body servant. Gregg on the eve of the Civil War gave his only emphatic expression of a belief in slavery as "rooted in nature, and sanctioned by the Bible." (DeBow's *Review*, XXX, 103.)

[20] The hilltop is now being divided into building lots for a suburb of Aiken. The site of the house showed, at Christmas 1925, just a tumble of broken bricks fallen from the low pillars which had served for foundation. Embedded in the refuse was some piping and a tank which may have formed part of the gas plant which Gregg installed. The small cellar of an outbuilding, probably that occupied by the ser-

vants, has sizable pines growing in it. The sweeping terraces are overrun with underbrush and vines, but their plan is still discoverable in the arcs of larger trees which Gregg planted. The garden, once filled with roses, has for many years been neglected. Live oaks have sprung up in all directions from an original three which Gregg set out with his own hands. The magnificent view over the hills down into the valley, with a distant peep of Graniteville, is the same as in his day. (An oil painting of this prospect, made in Gregg's lifetime by an artist who did not exceed the fact, now hangs in the mill office, testifying to an old and never-changing loveliness.)

CHAPTER VI

[1] *Minutes*, Mch. 14, 1848. Sixteen stockholders were present in person and eight by proxy, representing 530 shares.

[2] *Mercury*, Mch. 23, 1848.

[3] *Minutes*, Oct. 16, 1848.

[4] *Ibid.*, June 22, 1859.

[5] *The Plough, the Loom and the Anvil*, II, 197 ff.; *President's Report*, April 18, 1867, p. 5.

[6] *Minutes*, Mch. 13, 1849. The time of the annual meeting was changed to the last Wednesday in April. The majority of stockholders living in Charleston, attendance on meetings at Graniteville was difficult, so it was provided that five actually present and representing, in person and by proxy, a majority of the stock should constitute a quorum for the transaction of all business, whether specifically mentioned in the call for the meeting or not. The officers and directors were reëlected.

[7] *Ibid.*, Apr. 24, 1850.

[8] *Ibid.*, June 22, 1859.

[9] *President's Report*, Apr. 18, 1867, pp. 5-6.

[10] *Ibid.*, p. 6. Montgomery simply signed leases and certificates; B.C. Hard did the bookkeeping. Mr. Montgomery was a Scotchman, and had worked his way forward from the time when, as a small boy in a cotton mill at home, he had attended the same night school with David Livingstone. (Aiken *Journal and Review*, Sept. 29, 1920.)

[11] *Minutes*, June 22, 1859.

[12] "At one time our dam broke and I was telegraphed to Charleston; Wheelbarrows were wanted and could not be purchased in that city; I went to Fort Sumter, then in process of erection . . . and borrowed fifty barrows from the government. Mr. Connor generously let me have a hundred railroad hands, and with other forces we soon closed

a breach that for the want of management might have cost us **many** thousands of dollars by the stoppage of the mill." (*President's Report,* Apr. 18, 1867, p. 6.)

[13] *Ibid.*

[14] *Domestic Industry,* p. 34.

[15] For these facts see MS. *Minutes of Stockholders,* 1849-53. It is strange to find manufacturing supplies charged to the contingent account. However, at the Vaucluse Mill so near by and with which Gregg had been so intimately identified, in spite of the careful cost accounting system, "contigencies" included some items of "materials," though flour for sizing was separately charged to manufacturing cost. (See DeBow's *Review,* VII, 456.)

[16] *Minutes,* 1854-56.

[17] *Statutes at Large,* S. C., XII, 48-49. The charter was continued in force for thirty years after passage of this act. The company might increase its capital stock to any amount not exceeding $1,000,000, but at any one time it should not be increased less than $50,000; such additional stock was to be divided rateably among the stockholders in proportion to their shares at the time of the increase, but there were to be no assessments to make up the new issues of stock.

[18] *Minutes* Apr. 23, 1851. Hiram Hutchinson refusing to be re-elected director, Joel Smith was put in his place.

[19] *Ibid.,* July 14, 1852.

[20] *President's Report,* 1854, pp. 4, 13.

[21] See *Ibid.,* p. 3.

[22] Mch. 16, 1853. In nine months of 1849, forty marriages took place (*Plough, Loom and Anvil, ibid.*).

[23] *President's Report,* 1854; *Minutes,* Mch. 15, 1854. Mr. Kohn has dug up the fact that in 1853 two proprietors of saw mills above Graniteville sought in the courts the right to navigate Horse Creek with lumber rafts by operating the sluices of the dams. Gregg in a petition to the legislature showed that such an attempt would be ruinous to the water powers and impracticable for the lumber men. Both suits against Graniteville were dropped. (*Water Powers of S. C.,* p. 56).

[24] *Minutes,* Mch. 15, 1854. Five years later, when some of his policies were being called in question, Gregg referred to his having served the company for nothing during the arduous years of launching. One senses in his words no bitterness, but an affection for the enterprise and a certain loneliness in his effort. "In January 1846," he reminded the stockholders, "I took charge and gave the Company's service my undivided attention, acted the part of Engineer and General Agent. I

293

worked for you eight years of the prime of my life, devoting my entire energies to your service without charging you a cent. . . . The first compensation I took from you was $1,500 in 1854, then $2,500 in 1855, 6 and 7, and $1,500 in 1858. I repeat, that I have been worth to you $5,000, and I say it without the fear of being charged with vanity, that when I leave your service, you will be a fortunate Company, if you get a man to do your work so well for $5,000 a year and you may make up your minds now on that point, while you have me to advise you. If the goods be not uniformly well and cheaply made, no merchant can sell them and make you money and a reputation." (*Minutes*, June 22, 1859.)

[25] *President's Report*, April 18, 1867, p. 8. Ker Boyce having died, J. G. O. Wilkinson was elected to succeed him on the board of directors.

[26] This was presented to the meeting of Mch. 14, 1855; seven stockholders were present in person; the name of William Gregg, Jr., appears for the first time, his father holding his proxy; he was later to be useful to Graniteville, but an unwilling occasion of discord, too. F. L. Olmstead noticed at some length this report of Gregg's, generally with great approval; cf. *The Cotton Kingdom*, II, 286 ff.

[27] *President's Report*, 1854, p. 3; *Treasurer's Report*, 1854, p. 17.

[28] *President's Report*, 1854, pp. 3-4. If 1855 should prove as profitable as 1854 (and Gregg believed it would be more so), the company would have made a sum sufficient to bring the average earnings up to 9 per cent, and the president felt that long before the factory was depreciated by wear the stockholders could say that they had not only received their interest, but had their capital back again.

[29] *Ibid.*, pp. 4-5.

[30] *Ibid.*, p. 5; he made a point which he was fond of stating, that "The labors of a manager are chiefly mental, and consist in the choice of agents and looking closely after them. This would be nothing more than a pleasant occupation to a successful retired merchant. In Massachusetts, lawyers not unfrequently occupy such positions, and they make capital agents." (p. 6.)

[31] *Ibid.*

[32] *Ibid.*, pp. 6-7.

[33] *Ibid.*, pp. 7-8. "If we had the water-power at Graniteville, and were going to erect three or four such factories there, I would consider it the interest of the proprietors to make no other size thread than No. 14, which we are now making. It might be advisable to make some change by weaving cloths of different widths." He advised against a cloth mill putting up yarn; it was better to sell it in cloth.

[34] *President's Report,* 1854, pp. 9-10; cf. p. 15.

[35] *Ibid.,* p. 11.

[36] *Ibid.,* pp. 12-13. One who is familiar with the picturesque old ruins on the Saluda River above Columbia is impressed by Gregg's account of its downfall. The company commenced with a capital of $50,000 a work which required $400,000. They built a factory to hold 10,000 spindles, and looms to weave the yarn. After a few years of sickly existence the plant was sold, and the company could not pay its debts. The location, just the right distance from the city, was magnificent; had the company built an inexpensive village with a good school and a church or two, after the fashion of Graniteville, as they might have learned how to do by looking to New England, they need not have had to purchase Negroes to run the machinery, and the establishment would have grown in size and profit. Within the last twenty years, if I am not mistaken, a few of the poor shacks occupied by these slave hands were still to be seen under the spreading trees in what was once the mill yard.

[37] *Ibid.,* p. 13. For a gloomy view of the prospects of southern mills in 1852, see *Plough, Loom and Anvil,* IV. 636-7.

[38] *President's report,* 1854, p. 14. The people would be much more benefited by the free school fund when drawn together in villages. "As manufacturers, they will in a few years become a regenerated people, and do more for our State than all the cotton planters have yet done; for the prevailing policy of the planter seems to have been to exhaust the soil as rapidly as possible, with a view of abandoning the country. . . . Aside from the all-absorbing profits which should be the pole star with those who expect to thrive in any branch of business, there is a charity in the matter, which will attract many good men who have been fortunate enough to become retired capitalists."

[39] See James L. Quinby, "The Graniteville Boys. What They Have Done and What They are Doing, in *Horse Creek Valley News* (Warrenville, S. C.), Nov. 16, 1907. Mr. Quinby for years had a store at Graniteville and was a lover of the traditions of the place.

[40] *Op. cit.,* pp. 15-16; another large Graniteville investor had recently moved permanently to New York, and Gregg believed that his capital would soon be lost to home enterprise. Cf. *Plough, Loom and Anvil,* I, 761.

[41] *President's Report,* 1854, pp. 17-18. The average cost of labor, stock and materials, per yard, was now 5.20 cents, as against 5.636 for 1851. Cotton in 1854 cost an average of 8.87 cents per pound, as against 10 cents in 1851 and 10.21 in 1853.

[42] *Ibid.*, pp. 19-20. Drayage on the wheel and fitting it up cost $107.82. Graniteville was back in the saw mill business, a new one being built this year; a grist mill, of which there is no previous record, was rebuilt; a railway was constructed, evidently that of which some sills remain in the factory yard.

[43] *Ibid.*, p. 21.

[44] *Ibid.*, p. 22; not more than half of the $198,000 subscribed for new stock was to be called for in 1855, and the balance in 1856.

[45] *Minutes*, Mch. 14, 1855.

[46] See *ibid.*, Apr. 24, 1856, Apr. 23, 1857, Apr. 24, 1858.

[47] *Ibid.* Apr. 24, 1848.

[48] *Ibid.*, June 22, 1859.

[49] *Ibid.*, May 27.

[50] *Statutes at Large*, S. C., XII, 602.

[51] *Minutes*, Apr. 21, 1859. Allen, Beach, Blackwood, and Taft composed the directorate; Mills had served for the one year of 1858.

[52] *Ibid.*, June 22, 1859; Apr. 24, 1858.

[53] *Ibid.*, June 22, 1859. References in the next succeeding pages are to the minutes of this date, unless otherwise indicated.

[54] Gregg was at great pains to explain from this time forward that the functions of the treasurer were the most vital in the whole undertaking.

[55] William, when the directors refused to raise his salary, "engaged in the hardware business and could not be obtained at any price." (*President's Report*, Apr. 18, 1867.)

[56] The arrangement with Mr. Taft, made at the outset in 1848, whereby he received 2 per cent on all sales in Charleston and 1 per cent on goods sold through commission agencies away from Charleston, he incurring no risk in the shape of guarantees, "was a matter of necessity at the time, and proved to be a judicious one, but has continued much longer than it would have done had we been able to secure the right man at Graniteville." Taft's commissions on sales away from Charleston amounted in 1858 to $1,670.78; the freight on goods to agencies amounted to $22,000, of which $10,000 was freight to Charleston. Gregg informed Taft that inasmuch as William was receiving a salary from the company, this expense should be saved; so they entered into an agreement by which, after January 1, 1859, Taft was to receive no commissions on sales west of the Savannah River. The carrying out of this plan might now be very much embarrassed.

[57] Gregg had recently had a visit from Mr. Bigelow and two other Boston cotton manufacturers. Bigelow had written a book in which the embarrassed state of the manufacture in America as compared with England was ascribed to long credits, "the sale of goods through com-

mission houses and their consequent control of prices, and their power to control the destinies of large manufacturing companies. . . . Mr. Bigelow observed more than once, that we [at Graniteville] were happily situated and came nearer to individual enterprise, than any Company he knew of and thought it a most fortunate thing, that the stockholders should give the entire control to one individual, a large stockholder, who with ordinary intelligence and enterprise could not fail to realize profits. I know how to appreciate such views, and could not but feel proud of our success and that nothing had occurred to jostel us in our quiet progress." (*Ibid.*)

[58] All that is known of the careers of his sons points to the success of his program for them. "I consider myself fortunate that my sons should be willing to forego the pleasures of gaiety and dissipation, to prepare themselves by toil for usefulness in life. . . . I have always impressed on my sons, the importance, when engaged in the labor department, of setting a good example to those around them, and have invariably given instructions to the overseers in the factory, not to regard them in the light of a rich man's sons, but require them to be at their post at daylight, and work the hours that were required of others, and to allow them just such wages as their work was worth and not a cent more." The directors' principal objection to raising the salary of his son William, he said, had been that it would savor of favoritism to pay so young a man, being his son, $2,000. He believed that youthfulness was not the true ground of opposition. William owned some thousands of dollars of the stock of the company, was 25 years old, married and settled at Graniteville. His school associates were in banks in Charleston and receiving as much for their services. Rather, the directors, in ignorance of the nature of the treasurer's difficult duties, sought to guard the company against undue exactions.

[59] Two weeks before this meeting Gregg had written Hammond of his satisfaction at the prospect of building up, through his sons, a great and permanent manufacturing interest in the Horse Creek Valley, and continued: "James has given a new impetus and I now feel that in my failing years, the business which I have reared will go on with vigour. We are now fitting up Vaucluse that James may make a display of the knowledge he has obtained in Europe. If he succeeds as I think he will, we will extend that establishment to the full extent of the water power there. (Kalmia, Jan. 7, 1859. *J. H. Hammond Papers*, XXVI.)

[60] Knowing that the point might be brought up, Gregg explained the three breaks which had occurred in the Graniteville dams, two of which cost the company $5,000 each. The first break was owing to the careless-

ness of the man in charge at the time, who failed to see the danger. The second, caused by a freshet and dams breaking above, might have been forestalled with one man's work if taken in time. As it was, Gregg was sent for at Kalmia and, despite pushing his horse to top speed, he arrived fifteen minutes too late to save the dam. The third break was in August, 1856, just after William Gregg, Jr., entered the service, and would have been prevented by the experience he acquired later. Could he himself have been present, Gregg was convinced none of the breaks would have taken place.

[61] Gregg's description of the function of the treasurer resulted in a decision to change that officer's title to "treasurer and general agent."

[62] *Daily South Carolinian*, June 4, 1864.

[63] *Minutes*, Apr. 19, 1860.

CHAPTER VII

[1] Merritt, *James Henry Hammond*, pp. 61-62, 84-85.

[2] The articles were printed in pamphlet form in 1848 with the title "The Railroad Mania, and Review of the Bank of the State of South-Carolina, a Series of Essays by Anti-Debt. . . ." Then there appeared "Anti-Alarmist and Charleston in Reply to the Objections to Railroads by Anti-Debt. Originally published in the Charleston *Mercury*" (1848); also "Reply to Anti-Debt on the Bank of the State of South Carolina, in a series of articles originally published in the Charleston *Mercury* and *South Carolinian* by Fair Play." (Columbia, 1848.) See also "Speech of Mr. C. G. Memminger on the Question of Rechartering the Bank of the State of South Carolina, delivered in House of Representatives, Dec. 9, 1848." (Columbia, 1849); "Reply of Mr. C. G. Memminger to the Various Speakers on the Question of the Propriety of Rechartering the Bank of the State"; "Speech of Benjamin C. Yancey, Esq., of Edgefield, in Relation to the Bank of the State of South Carolina, delivered in committee of the whole House, December session of the Legislature, 1848." (Printed at Hamburg, S. C.) All of the foregoing, with others, are in the collection of August Kohn, Esq.

[3] Merritt, *op. cit.*, p. 85.

[4] Gregg to Hammond, *J. H. Hammond Papers*, XIV. As showing his opinion of the South Carolina Railroad, Gregg said that much of the stock had been sold at $16 per share after $75 had been paid for it. He parted with 100 shares at $15. He calculated that the real capital of the company had been $2,650,000, from which the purchase of the Hamburg road represented a loss of $1,400,000 and the building of the Columbia branch another $1,300,000; this left $50,000 (Gregg made a mistake in his figures somewhere), which was at most $16 per share.

[5] Nov. 17, 1847. ". . . as for the cabbage, turnips, &c., the Rail Road thus far have had their hands too full to accommodate the staple commodities of the country, and it is a subject of universal complaint that small matters receive so little attention by the agents of the Road that persons are deterred from shipping. . . ." He gave interesting evidence of the dependence of a cotton producing region: ". . . it is a singular fact, that the Rail Road Board on reducing the freight of Hay to 20 cts. per hundred to encourage its growth in the upcountry and transit to the Seaboard, the opposite result was the effect. The Columbia and Hamburg stables were supplied by this cheap rate of freight with Eastern Hay through our City."

[6] Written from Charleston, Nov. 30, 1847. And he proceeded to give Hammond more ammunition. He was informed that the Wilmington Road had not paid any dividends; he would get the report for Hammond. The Raleigh and Gaston Road was a total failure and did not sell for enough to pay more than half of the State loan, and the same was the case with the Portsmouth Road. Carroll (later to be Gregg's political opponent in Edgefield), having been employed to drum up subscribers for the Greenville Road, was bitter over losing so large a subscription as that of the State. Ker Boyce must have shared Gregg's views on these matters, for he wrote Hammond, Dec. 4, 1847, cheering him on in his war on the Bank.

[7] Charleston, Nov. 16, 1848, *Hammond Papers*, XV. No Bank report had been published that month, and Gregg took this to indicate collusion to hide the real condition of the institution.

[8] Appleton's *Cyclopædia of American Biography*, I, 378.

[9] Merritt (*op. cit.*, p. 85) ranks Hammond's promotion of industry more highly than the present writer would. He was not able to see, as Gregg did, that the political differences between North and South were grounded in dissimilarity of economic pursuit, and that nourishing a spirit of disunion was not the way to industrial advance in the South. Gregg advised Brisbane that Cheves would not serve as one of his sponsors, as proved to be true.

[10] Gregg to Hammond, Charleston, Dec. 1, 1848. *Hammond Papers*, XV. The reader interested in comparing Hammond and Gregg finds significance in a memorandum in Hammond's handwriting belonging to this period (*ibid.*, XVI) setting forth that "It is the duty of the State to Educate its Citizens, and the Manner of Doing It. . . . The first point I propose to consider is how far a State, organized—as I should desire all States to be organized,—on Republican principles, with complete Religious Toleration, Free Trade, Free Press, and the *Laissez Faire* system to the utmost extent short of disorganization and anarchy, is

never the less bound to take care that its citizens shall be educated."
In his mind, the political justification was the first thing to be settled.
With Gregg it was a question of contact between master and children
in an industrial community; indeed, all progress in public education
waited upon the progress of economic production. Hammond looked to
theoretical matters, Gregg to practical. Here was the distinction over
again between Jefferson and Hamilton.

[11] Charleston, Sept. 27, 1849. *Hammond Papers*, XVI. The letter is
instructive on several points, particularly the aversion of Charleston to
mechanical improvement, and the obstacles which financial speculations
placed in the way of industrial progress. Brisbane wrote: "When
you . . . come down I want the *State* to be present, and this could not be
before . . . the session of the Legislature so that the members of that
body could be present, as the most important." Hammond might be surprised that Brisbane's articles in the *News* (Charleston *Evening News*)
had not been appearing of late; it was because his "mechanical move
was soon found too dangerous to go at large," and he must get up
something better suiting the state of the controversy between capital
and labor. "The 'Carolina Institute' was consequently organized and went
into operation handsomely patronized." He no sooner began to bring the
subject of machinery before the State than the *News* protested that if
it continued to back his cause the paper would be ruined. Other papers,
however, had taken the question up favorably. "But, my dear General," he
asked, "what can be done to concentrate the capital of the State, while
our friend Elmore and the Bank stand at the door, while they are suffered to stock-job at the cost of the State? Nothing, nothing. . . .
The bank is in the way of our introduction of machinery, and this must
be got rid of before the least thing can be done. Look at our 'machine
shop' for example [the repair shops of the South Carolina Railroad,
probably]. Every body was satisfied that it should be constructed in
Charleston, but who would come forward with capital? Not the merchants, for they had none; not the money brokers, for they could sit at
the bank door and make more by usury; not the planters, for they
wanted to get into the funds, as they call 'bank stock.' Nobody." Gregg,
knowing all of this, perhaps congratulated himself that he had launched
his subscription for Graniteville four years earlier. Another letter of Brisbane to Hammond (dated 8 Feb., 1849, but apparently, from the context,
should have been 1850) goes over much the same ground, complaining
of the clique which made united effort for the public good impossible
in Charleston, and asserting that the directors of the Bank had effectively
threatened the papers against his industrial propaganda. By this time

it was known, said Brisbane, that General Hammond was the champion of the manufacturing cause; if he took it up in earnest it would add to his force against the Bank, and this would be popular with the majority in Charleston. Brisbane was afraid that he had affected the planting interest against the manufacturing move which "requires so much care in Charleston and on our Seaboard. They see in it the development of white labor, and they fear it; they call it the *mob*. They cannot see that if we do not *develope it here,* where it must be friendly, *knowing* that it depends on black labor, *it will develope at the North,* where it will not know its dependence on black labor, and therefore be the fanatic enemy of the latter."

[12] *Address Delivered before the South Carolina Institute, at its First Annual Fair, on the 20th November, 1849,* pp. 12-13. It appears from a letter to Quattlebum that he had intended conceding less to manufactures. Merritt, *ibid.,* p. 87, note.

[13] *Address before S. C. Institute,* p. 13.

[14] *Ibid.,* p. 26.

[15] See Merritt, *op. cit.,* p. 87.

[16] See DeBow's *Review,* XI, 123 ff. (Aug., 1851). In the preceding March, in connection with a sketch of Gregg's life, DeBow mentioned having received the text of the address before the Institute, and promised to publish it the following month, but waited until August, when he prefaced it by saying "Mr. Gregg is . . . one of the most practical and valuable citizens of the South, and has done more . . . than any man in it towards exciting a spirit of broad and liberal manufacturing enterprise. . . . Will not such men be raised up in Louisiana, Mississippi, Texas, Arkansas and Tennessee?"

[17] Almost a decade afterwards, he wrote an explanation to Hammond in which he betrayed—as he seldom did—resentment against the North: "My essay was intended to show what a powerful and independent people we would be, if we were to add to our great staples, such a diversity of occupation as to embrace the manufacturing arts so as to avail ourselves of all the elements of national wealth that we have so profusely scattered around us, and how perfectly independent we would render ourselves of a people, who since the delivery of that address have proved themselves to be our most bitter enemies." (Mch. 31, 1858. *Hammond Papers,* XXIII. Cf. Gregg in DeBow's *Review,* XXIX, 77 ff.)

[18] This same lesson was preached most graphically two generations later by D. A. Tompkins; in his *Cotton Values in Textile Fabrics* he resorted to an actual exhibit of cloths, with a contrast of the price of the raw material and the value added by manufacture.

[19] Machinery making and the housewrights' arts would be stimulated by the cotton manufacture and all "the small manufactures common to cities, and which can accommodate themselves in the cellars and garrets, holes and corners, by-ways and alleys, will cluster around us in Charleston, and add their charming influence to the spirit of onward progress in remodelling our old-fashioned city." This was a dream of Gregg's patterned after what he had seen in Philadelphia, but Charleston's becoming a warren of industry was indeed a thing of the imagination.

[20] "Some people seem to think . . . that our entire system of agriculture is to be revolutionized, our rice and cotton-fields turned into potato-patches, and that we are to give up our cotton bales for wooden clocks and Yankee notions. Any change for the better must be gradual, the result of enlightened public opinion, or it will not be permanent. In attempting to introduce manufactures, no doubt but many improper things will be done, and much capital will be wholly lost to its owners, by injudicious investments in machinery. Those who are engaged in . . . [agriculture] must be contented to look for their advantages in the general prosperity which will be brought around them—a home market for all their products, increased value of real estate, good roads . . . increased population, good common schools, and the example of a working class of white people around their children." Some saw eye to eye with Gregg in the conviction that industry would benefit the Poor Whites. Thus J. H. Lumpkin, of Georgia: ". . . I am by no means ready to concede that our poor, degraded, half-fed, half-clothed, and ignorant population, without Sabbath-schools, or any other kind of instruction—mental or moral—or without any just appreciation of the value of character, will be injured by giving them employment. . . . After all, the most powerful motive to good conduct, is to give suitable encouragement to labor. . . ." (DeBow's *Review*, XII, 49.)

[21] DeBow's *Review*, XI, 132-133. Gregg amplified this in a letter to Hammond (*Hammond Papers*, XXIII) from Kalmia, Mch. 31, 1858: "I of course intended to include male and female, old and young, as well as those who receive their subsistence from the soil in such a small way as to produce no surplus. I also intended to include the middle and educated class, that have little or no employment for the want of diversity of industrial pursuits; in this class are included my sons, the hundreds of young men who study law and medicine and crowd those professions to overflowing, also that large class of young men who are educated at our military schools to fit them to carry on the arts and commerce of our country and who have to emigrate to other States

to seek employment. Were we engaged in manufacturing, as well as agriculture, there would be a thousand occupations springing up for that class of men."

²² In connection with the annual meeting of the South Carolina Institute, a fair was held. The report of the committee on premiums of the first year is bound in with Hammond's address. Almost ten pages are given to listing the various awards. It is probable that many entries taking prizes, usually silver medals, were the only exhibits of their particular sort, as, for instance, the best engraving on a cocoanut shell. Many of the items were of ladies' manufacture; others were of no importance whatever, as for example: best specimen of a dressed hickory stick; basket of palmetto and Carolina grass; best silk embroidered banner; best peacock fly brush. More interesting are awards to the Graniteville Manufacturing Co. for second best 7-8 brown shirtings, a diploma; for best 4 qr. brown shirting, a silver medal; for best cotton drilling, a silver medal. The silver medal for the best 7-8 brown shirting went to the Charleston Manufacturing Co. (James H. Taylor, agent.) Medals for osnaburgs, cotton bagging, and yarns went to the Troup Factory, Ga., the Rockingham Manufacturing Co., N. C., and the Bowenville Manufacturing Co., Ga., respectively.

In a list of the members of the Institute, William Gregg's name stands first, though he was not a life member. From four double-column pages of names, the following may be mentioned as especially connected with Gregg: A. H. Brisbane, J. H. Taylor, Ker Boyce, W. E. Howland, Geo. Buist, H. S. Hayden, Otis Mills, Edward Sebring, R. Yeadon. Others of his friends were life members, such as H. Hutchinson, J. H. Hammond, W. Aiken, E. M. Beach, C. Kerrison, A. R. Taft, James Jones. The Second Annual Report of the Board of Directors of the Institute, Nov., 1850, says the exhibits had been well attended; there were still some willow baskets and cut paper letters, but also there were awards for the best jewelry to Gregg, Hayden & Co., Charleston; best cotton yarn, to D. McCulloch, Fairfield; best shirtings, sheetings, drills, to Graniteville Co., with the Charleston Factory taking second award. An item indicating the practical interest being aroused in cotton manufacturing at the South is the award of a diploma to Jos. Baldwin, of Nashua, New Hampshire, for an exhibit of looms, shuttles, and bobbins.

The 1851 fair, at which Gregg made the address, had on display more articles of a useful nature than ever before, albeit along with Southern-made brogans went "socks knitted from the fur of wild cat." Graniteville received no award; the Charleston Mill showed the best shirting and a Huntsville factory the best gingham. (DeBow's *Review*, XII, 113.) Gregg in 1860 deprecated the policy of the Institute in favoring northern exhibitors with premiums and he thought fripperies should be subordinated to important manufactures. (*Ibid.*, XXIX, 499-500.)

²³ See Merritt, *op. cit.*, p. 113.

²⁴ Gregg to Hammond, Kalmia, Feb. 16, 1857. (*Hammond Papers*, XX.)

²⁵ Cf. Merritt, *op. cit.*, pp. 120-121 on Hammond's eagerness at this time for disunion.

²⁶ Kalmia, Jan. 7, 1859. (*Hammond Papers*, XXVI.)

²⁷ "No Englishman would engage to furnish the customers who consume the Graniteville goods with a similar amount without a bonus over what we get of $50,000 a year. . . . The English cheat the whole world; they make good articles for home consumption, [and] inferior for every other people. Such goods in appearance as the Graniteville are loaded with clay sizing until 25 per cent is added to the weight of cotton." These goods were sold all over the world alongside honestly made American goods, and Gregg threatened to bring the chalk hills on the Graniteville land into requisition to stuff up his cloth bound for China and South America.

Gregg in 1860 gave explicit statement to his adherence to the protective policy in DeBow's *Review*, XXX, 103.

²⁸ "Let our South Carolina friends unite in the measures requisite for bringing about absolute freedom of trade, by repudiating incidental protection, adopting the policy of *protection for the sake of protection*." (*Plough, Loom and Anvil*, II, 197 ff.) Cf. *ibid.*, I, 47-8; IV, 636-7. For a brief discussion of the controversy over the tariffs of 1842 and 1846 as they affected the cotton manufacture, see F. W. Taussig, *The Tariff History of the United States* (5th ed.), pp. 119-20, 139 ff.

CHAPTER VIII

¹ See the excellent summary in Wilbur C. Plummer, *The Road Policy of Pennsylvania*, pp. 54-56.

² Delivered before the Literary Club of Charleston, 1851.

³ *Essay on Plank Roads*, p. 3. Gregg's plan for this road had evidently expanded since December, 1849, when the legislature incorporated the Graniteville Plank Road Company (*Statutes at Large*, S. C., XI, 598-603). Gregg's name came first among the incorporators, the others being F. W. Pickens, James Carroll, and Ker Boyce. The company was for the purpose of constructing timber, plank, or hard roads from Graniteville to some point on the Savannah River, and from Graniteville to Abbeville, or so far in these directions as might be determined. The capital was $50,000, but might be increased to $250,000. Five years were allowed

for the completion of the roads, but when three consecutive miles were built, tolls might be collected; toll rates were not specified, but the dividends of the company must never exceed 14 per cent. The road must be smooth and permanent and so constructed as to allow vehicles to pass on and off at intersections with other roads. The company might take land at commissioners' valuation. The charter was to continue in force for thirty years. Another act of the legislature, signed the same day, chartered the Hamburg and Edgefield Plank Road Company (Josiah Sibley being among the incorporators). This company had the privilege (not mentioned in the charter of Gregg's project, though in his speech he stressed this feature of plank roads) of building branches from the main line. (*Ibid.*, pp. 583-587.) This road was actually constructed, but proving unprofitable, the legislature in 1861 allowed the company to tear up any portion of the road it saw fit. (*Ibid.*, p. 804.) An act of 1850 provided for the incorporation of plank road companies generally, and specifically for the building of one on Sullivan's Island and the chartering of the Greenville Plank Road Company, (*Ibid.*, pp. 16 ff.)

⁴ *Plank Roads,* p. 3.

⁵ *Ibid.*, p. 4.

⁶ *Ibid.* With a lively sense of the economic value of coöperation, Gregg remained in some respects persistently individualist. Thus he said that "The travelling community will . . . move without being subject to the rules and regulations of others, as to the time, speed or equipage in which they may desire to travel."

⁷ Gregg acknowledged his indebtedness for information to W. M. Gillespie, *A Manual of the Principles and Practice of Road-Making,* etc., published in New York, 1847; I have not been able to find copies of the other works to which he referred—by Wood and Leslie, and by A. A. Dexter, of Montgomery, Ala., of which last he used the figures and language freely. There was abundant material published before this date which he might have consulted: *The Western Journal and Civilian* had carried at least six articles, but he was more likely to have seen those in DeBow's *Review* and *Hunt's Merchants' Magazine,* to which he subscribed. Philo White's *Report to the Council of Wisconsin* had appeared in 1848. A work very similar to Gregg's own, which, however, he did not mention, is Robert Dale Owen's *A Brief Practical Treatise on the Construction and Management of Plank Roads* (1850). George Geddes' *Observations on Plank Roads* was published in 1850 also; the author was engineer of the first plank road in the U. S., and prepared his pamphlet in response to the shower of questions that came to him.

[8] *Plank Roads,* pp. 4, 5, 6.

[9] *Ibid.* It was surprising to learn how little of the railroad mileage of the country yielded a profit commensurate to the capital invested; there was a fatal error in exhausting the resources of the community to construct works which, "however gigantic in their conception, will not prove sufficiently useful to pay for keeping them up." It was significant that private capitalists were not quick to project railroads, and it was economic unwisdom to start them by exciting appeals to patriotism. (pp. 6-7.) Though in Iowa (see Brindley, *History of Road Legislation in Iowa,* Chap. iii) plank roads were looked upon as merely auxiliary to railroads, Gregg thought of them as effective competitors with steam.

[10] It is to be remembered that for a number of years at the outset of the Graniteville enterprise Gregg worked in several capacities for nothing.

[11] *Plank Roads,* p. 9.

[12] *Ibid.,* p. 10. Three years before he had written: "Since the establishment of the Charleston and Hamburg Road, I have mingled constantly with railroad men—have been a Director, and have kept myself posted as to the movements and designs of railroad projectors. . . . I am a railroad man, and would like to see such works spreading over the State, and will help to build them, but I am afraid of their combined power." (*Letter to Thornton Coleman, Esq.,* p. 9.)

[13] *Plank Roads,* pp. 11-12. He was careful of common economies. With a little additional strengthening of the axles of an ordinary road wagon, it would carry 15 to 20,000 pounds on a smooth plank road. "It is not the weight usually put on them that racks them to pieces, but the strain to which they are subjected from running on steep sideling declivities, and from being dragged over roots, stumps and ruts." A bale of cotton might thus be carried a hundred miles for 37 cents, a rate which railroads would find it hard to equal. (pp. 13-14.)

[14] *Plank Roads,* pp. 16-17. The question arises whether, on the completion of the plank road, Gregg would have built a branch running from Graniteville to join it, thus hauling the factory's supplies and products by wagon. The company at one time, toward the end of Gregg's life, had a difference with the South Carolina Railroad, but this was probably inescapable. The railroad was obliging in running special trains to Graniteville for the convenience of stockholders at the time of annual meetings. During the war, when track of the railroad was torn up, the Graniteville teams hauled long distances, but this was of course immediately discontinued when the track was relaid.

[15] *Ibid.,* p. 19.

[16] *Ibid.,* p. 20.

[17] Edward Ingle, *Southern Sidelights*, pp. 220-261, gives an understanding account of the trend of these conventions. Dr. Herbert Wender, who has made a full study of the movement, has obliged me by allowing me to examine his manuscript, and has supplied me, besides, with particulars of Gregg's part in several of the meetings.

[18] DeBow's *Review*, XII, 429-430. As may be seen in other places in his writings, he did not contemplate a break with the slave system. "God speed the change," he said, "which shall produce such a revolution as will fill every department of our commerce, manufactures, &c., with our own people! In such a state of things, with the aid of the African race to drain our swamps and speed the plow, we may become the thriftiest people on earth." With some who did urge the claims of industry upon the convention, hardly better than a plantation manufacture was contemplated, and the proposal was principally a scheme to benefit agriculture. Thus Governor Aaron V. Brown, of Tennessee, hoped the meeting would appeal to planters to go in for cotton manufacturing. Their slaves could erect the buildings. "Two or three, or half a dozen can unite in one establishment. They can select from their own stock of slaves the most active and intelligent ones for operatives, without the necessary advances in money to white laborers. The cost of machinery, and the expense of one or two others of practical experience to superintend the rest, will be nearly the only outlay of actual capital for the business. I earnestly desire to see one-fourth of southern slave labor diverted from the *production* to the *manufacture* of cotton. [This] would give a steadiness and elevation of prices to the raw material, which would better justify its cultivation." And he prayed for—the action of a strong committee! (*Ibid.*, p. 429.)

[19] *Journal of Proceedings*, Memphis, 1853, pp. 16-23.

[20] *Ibid.*, Charleston, 1854, pp. 49, 98, 100.

[21] The first peach bloom opened Mch. 15. From day to day during this month he was at work beautifying the Graniteville cemetery, or planting elms and walnut trees. He noted with pleasure that on the day of the annual meeting, roses were blooming in the mill yard, though the first had appeared two weeks earlier.

[22] The early York Troths were being shipped by the 11th of the month, and the 25th was a "great peach picking day," with 45 men employed in gathering and shipping "240 boxes [and] 43 baskets of fine fruit."

[23] The diary mentions putting guano in his orchards (he had learned of this at Beach Island probably), and a list of addresses at the end includes a firm in New York from which he could get potash, phosphate, and lime; commission merchants in Northern markets, and

nurseries in New Jersey and Maryland from which he secured his young trees, were also noted.

He was persuaded, however, of the superiority of Southern nursery stock, and urged planting of native peaches. Some of these trees in his orchards were still bearing after 23 years. (DeBow's *Review*, XXIX, 775.)

²⁴ On this trip (one of several which the family made to the North) visits were made at Saratoga, Niagara, New York, Philadelphia, Baltimore, and Washington. In Philadelphia the Greggs were guests of families of Webbs, relatives of Mr. Gregg's mother.

²⁵ This almanac-diary has printed pages giving rather full information of the personnel of financial, commercial and other institutions in South Carolina, particularly Charleston. The names of men prominent in the Graniteville enterprise are constantly appearing. Thus, to select only a few, Thos. D. Wagner, sometime Graniteville director, was at this time first vice-president of the Charleston chamber of commerce; J. H. Taylor, treasurer and director, was commissioner of one of the free schools in Charleston; Richard Yeadon was a magistrate for St. Philip's and St. Michael's parishes; John F. Blacklock and Otis Mills were directors of the Charleston Gas Light Company; Mr. Mills was an alderman of the city, and director of the Union Bank; G. A. Trenholm was director of the Bank of Charleston and of the South Carolina Railroad, and A. R. Taft of the State Bank; J. J. Blackwood was a director of the Bank of Hamburg; E. M. Beach was a director of the South Carolina Insurance Co.; Gregg himself does not appear at this time in any of the lists except that of the trustees of the Charleston Savings Institution. Both Trenholm and Wagner were officers of the Blue Ridge Railroad. It is clear that Gregg could not speak in the legislature of either banks or railroads without touching the interests of his Graniteville associates.

CHAPTER IX

¹ *Minutes*, June 22, 1859.

² Several of Gregg's friends were candidates for the legislature in this election; Richard Yeadon took a prominent part in the session, but E. L. Burckmyer was not elected. (See Charleston *Courier*, month of Oct., 1856.)

³ The act of Congress of 1846 provided that they should be appointed on the Tuesday after the first Monday in November, and the regular session of the legislature would not take place until the fourth Monday in the month. (*Courier*, Nov. 5, 1856.)

[4] *Ibid.*, Nov. 6. Gregg returned to Graniteville the same day of the adjournment. (*Diary*, 1856.) When in Columbia Gregg regularly stopped at the old Wright's Hotel.

[5] He went down from Graniteville, to which he had just returned from Charleston, where he attended the sixth annual fair of the S. C. Institute.

[6] *Courier*, Nov. 26. The introduction of white laborers "must lead to' that conflict between labor and capital, 'which makes it so difficult to maintain free institutions in all wealthy and highly civilized nations where such institutions as ours do not exist.' . . . My hopes and fortunes are indissolubly associated with this form of society." The legislative correspondent of the *Courier* dissented vigorously from "his Excellency's views, as to the desirableness of a slave monopoly of every department of laboring industry, in preference to a further infusion of foreign population."

[7] *Ibid.*, Dec. 1.

[8] The *Courier* correspondent was absent from the hall when Gregg spoke. (*Ibid.*, Dec. 6.)

[9] See U. B. Phillips, *A History of Transportation in the Eastern Cotton Belt to 1860*, p. 171.

[10] *Ibid.*, pp. 174-184.

[11] *Ibid.*, pp. 188-197.

[12] For a succinct sketch of this undertaking, see *ibid.*, pp. 375-380.

[13] Gregg wrote (*Speech on Blue Ridge Railroad*, p. 2) that "the work is to be carried out by four separate corporate Companies, each Company under a separate Board of Directors, having entirely separate and distinct interests, and connected only by the bonds of mutual concern in the general operations . . . of all the roads which form the general line." Phillips, however, says: "Each of the other three companies, upon organization, promptly assigned their franchises and resources to the South Carolina Blue Ridge company, [called by Gregg 'The Blue Ridge Railroad of South Carolina'] and had little more than a nominal existence. The South Carolina company, further, had a chartered control of the route as far northward as the North Carolina boundary, and completely merged the Georgia company's stock and franchises into its own." (*Ibid.*, p. 376.) This statement is probably covered in Gregg's notation that citizens of Charleston, in order that the Georgia charter might issue, took $549,000 of the stock of the Georgia company, the subscription later being assumed by the City of Charleston; he further said that the South Carolina company subscribed $940,000 to the capital of the Tennessee company. Gregg particularly stressed the point that the first State subscription of South Carolina was made without warrant. To the

South Carolina company the City of Charleston subscribed $500,000, and the citizens of Charleston $52,000 more, "making the sum total of subscription, to the Blue Ridge Railroad Company in *South Carolina*, six hundred and four thousand dollars. . . . By some misapplication of figures the Comptroller General was led to believe that *The Blue Ridge Railroad Company in South Carolina* had complied with the requisitions of the State by obtaining a subscription of a million of dollars." In this belief he issued bonds and subscribed to $400,000 of the company's capital. (*Speech on Blue Ridge Railroad*, p. 3.) Phillips has not regarded this point, saying "The City Council of Charleston . . . had already subscribed $1,049,000 to stock for the route in South Carolina and Georgia; and accordingly the company had met the conditions of the first state subscription beforehand." (Phillips, *op. cit.*, p. 377.)

[14] Phillips, *ibid.*, p. 378.

[15] *Ibid.*, pp. 378-379. C. G. Memminger, B. F. Perry, and others aided Frost's advocacy, while "a voluminous newspaper contributor signing himself 'Nolumus' " joined Gregg and others in opposition.

[16] The chairman of the committee was his friend B. F. Perry (*Courier*, Nov. 27, 1856).

[17] *Ibid*. It was referred to as "that great problem of connecting the great lake basin of the North West with this city—a problem which, after a quarter of a century, seems approximating a solution."

[18] Dec. 15. 1856.

[19] Gregg had tried to have the debate take place on Dec. 8, but his motion was not carried. (*Journal of the House of Representatives of the State of S. C., 1856*, p. 158.)

[20] *Blue Ridge Railroad*, pp. 5-6.

[21] *Ibid.*, pp. 6-8.

[22] *Ibid.*, pp. 8-9. The Greenville and Columbia Railroad was chartered in the winter of 1845-46. After great difficulty in getting subscriptions, and further difficulty in holding subscriptions from districts disappointed in the routing of the road, the company, in order to take advantage of the prevailing low price of rails, appealed, jointly with the Charlotte and South Carolina Railroad, to the State to take stock. It was this to which Gregg referred when he said the legislature furnished the Blue Ridge the equivalent of ready money while it offered "pitiful sums to useful internal improvements . . . we have going on in our State, to be paid in depreciated stocks. . . ." The State subscribed to each of the local roads $250,000 and paid in bonds of the South Carolina Railroad, which stood at a 10 per cent discount. Completion of the line from Columbia to Anderson and Greenville by 1853 was accomplished

only by a 20 per cent assessment of the stock, an assessment which the legislature finally refused to pay. (See Phillips, *op. cit.*, pp. 339-345.)

[23] *Blue Ridge Railroad*, p. 10.

[24] The whole cost of this road, Phillips reports, stood in 1885 at $13,414 per mile. "At such a cost, with a route through broken country, and with three river crossings, the road was necessarily of the flimsiest." (*Op. cit.*, p. 345.)

[25] *Blue Ridge Railroad*, pp. 11-14.

[26] *Ibid.*, pp. 14-19.

[27] "It was nothing but the $3,000,000 of individual subscription," he said, "that saved the State at that time from . . . total loss." (*Ibid.*, pp. 20-21.) The State in 1845, when the shares came back to par, began to urge establishment of a sinking fund to liquidate the $2,000,000 loan from English bankers which the company had got on the State's endorsement of its bonds. The private stockholders refused year after year. (Phillips, p. 207.)

[28] *Blue Ridge Railroad*, p. 22.

[29] *Ibid.*, p. 23. See Phillips, pp. 174, 211-212. The controversy over the Camden branch precipitated the crisis in the company's affairs in 1849; the administration, however, won out.

[30] *Blue Ridge Railroad*, pp. 23-24.

[31] He threw in a remark here which is very interesting to the student of Gregg. He exclaimed: "Boston! that city which has of recent years run mad on an abstraction, and clings to niggerdom closer than even to the almighty dollar!" He was always profoundly annoyed by dogma, but this does not explain his tone in this fling. With all his good sense, he was not entirely immune from the slavery "defense mechanism" which was so rapidly maturing in the South. Though his every advocacy led away from slavery, Gregg nowhere gave evidence that he thought slavery as an economic system incompatible with fully rounded economic and social development. After all, and in a way that is easily understood, he belonged to his times.

[32] *Ibid.*, pp. 23-26.

[33] South Carolina, which had "a great deal to do internally, without cutting roads through the mountains to foster the commerce of cities," should complete the lines already started within the State, which would "all work themselves into permanent and profitable investments. We want rest and repose from this eternal ding-dong on the State for aid. . . ." (*Ibid.*, pp. 26-29.)

[34] *Ibid.*, p. 30. The directors had engaged in "building a new inclined plane, and other expensive works almost as bad, and had turned

upside down the affairs of that Company." (But see Phillips, pp. 214 ff.) Gregg had certainly been in the faction which opposed Gadsden's administration in 1849, and he had not relinquished his views when outvoted.

[35] *Blue Ridge Railroad*, pp. 29-31. It was found on the death of two of the principal movers that they had transferred their capital to New York; these were instances of a general drain of capital away from South Carolina which Gregg constantly lamented.

[36] The freight on a hundred bales of domestics shipped shortly before from Graniteville to St. Louis had cost $640. The same goods might have been sent to St. Louis by way of New York, Philadelphia, or New Orleans at charges ranging from $500 down to $275. (*Ibid.*, pp. 32-33.)

[37] This was the Nashville and Chattanooga Railroad, organized in 1848 and connecting with the Western and Atlantic.

[38] *Ibid.*, pp. 33-34. The Memphis and Charleston road, to which Charleston had also subscribed, would absorb more of the business which the old seaport badly needed. And if trade went to Savannah, it was not the Georgia State Road which accomplished it, but Georgia's enterprise in affording markets better than Charleston.

[39] He was reëlected in the closing session (*Courier*, Dec. 22, 1856.)

[40] *Ibid.*, Dec. 19, 1856.

[41] *Diary*, 1856.

[42] Governor R. F. W. Allston in his message to the legislature made guarded reference to the banks of the State; he believed they were solvent, and inclined toward a liberal policy in dealing with them. (*Journal of House*, 1857, p. 26.)

[43] See *Mercury*, Nov. 26, 1857.

[44] *Ibid.*, Nov. 26, 1857.

[45] *Journal of House*, p. 53.

[46] *Ibid.*, p. 74.

[47] Nov. 28, 1857.

[48] The Richmond *Examiner* thought it suicidal in time of inflation to limit the bank rate; by such an act Virginia had driven capital from the State. (Quoted in *Mercury*, Nov. 30, 1857.)

[49] *Mercury*, Dec. 3, 1857.

[50] Dec. 3, 1857.

[51] *Ibid.*

[52] He was followed by Mr. William Whaley, who supported his main contentions. In the Senate on the same day the debate on the bank question was far less thoughtful than in the House, Mr. Dudley speak-

ing sentimentally and ignorantly in support of the usury laws, and Mr. Mazyck replying almost contemptuously. (*Ibid.*, Dec. 4, 1857.)

[53] *Speech in the Legislature of South Carolina on the Bank Question,* p. 5.

[54] *Ibid.,* p. 6. He had just put into a business in Charleston (it is not possible to determine what) the sum of $100,000. One of his partners had returned from Europe with a large stock of perishable goods. They borrowed from the banks $130,000 to make good the falling off of their sales; this tided them over a difficult interval, and they were soon able to return the money.

[55] *Ibid.,* p. 7.

[56] *Ibid.,* pp. 9-10. If the bank capital of the country were divided among the sufferers from the suspension, it of course would not cover the loss. At $25 a bale, the cotton States would lose $82,500,000. (p. 8.)

[57] *Ibid.,* p. 11.

[58] *Ibid.,* p. 12. Lessons of adversity were soon forgotten. Expansion and speculation followed hard on the recovery from the revulsion of 1840. In the decade beginning in 1847, 678 new banks were created in the United States; from 1843-51, bank circulation increased from $58,000,000 to $155,000,000, and by 1854 was $204,000,000. Only gold from California had kept up confidence in the banks.

[59] *Ibid.,* p. 13.

[60] *Ibid.,* pp. 13-14.

[61] *Ibid.,* pp. 18-19; he may have been speaking more especially of the South, in which case his disregard of industrial development would be explained.

[62] *Ibid.,* pp. 18-19.

[63] *Ibid.,* pp. 19-20. A sliding scale of interest was a great regulator of monetary affairs in England through the Bank of England, he reminded his South Carolina hearers. All of the American States would do well, he thought, to abolish laws against usury so that the danger signal of rising interest rates might be clearly apparent. As it was, the banks got around the laws. He reflected that "laws made by men are utterly inadequate to regulate the value of money any more than any other commodity, and . . . supply and demand will govern, as certainly as . . . water will find its level." (pp. 21-22.) He would repeal the usury laws so as to give money a permanent and profitable home in Charleston "and thus enable us to disenthral ourselves of a childish dependence on that ever-inflated, bloated and speculative city, New York, where we go to purchase more than half of our supplies, and

where the best merchant's paper is often sold at from 12 to 40 per cent discount." (pp. 23-24.)

⁶⁴ *Ibid.*, p. 21.

⁶⁵ *Bank Question*, p. 26. To show how little use there was for banks in country villages, except to profit-seeking stockholders, he supposed himself at the head of a bank in Sumter. He described vividly how he would avail himself of the full privileges conferred by his State charter, put out his notes, get New York or Charleston exchange for them, and shave home borrowers by charging what would amount to 12 per cent. In quiet times he would get from 12 to 18 per cent, and when money was tight, up to 30 per cent. His hearers could not have missed the mockery of his closing remark. "In crises, like the one just passed through," he declared, "I would use all the appliances in my power to prevent the necessity of a suspension, and when I found such an event inevitable, I would act like a general besieged in a strong fortress, hold out until the merchants and people around sent me strong petitions to suspend and relieve the community. I would then close the vaults and refuse to pay the bank's debts, in order to 'save the people and the country at large from bankruptcy and ruin,' which I had helped to bring upon them." (pp. 27-29.)

⁶⁶ *Ibid.*, p. 31. "If ever there were a bank-ridden people, they may be found here." The humblest individual was forced by public opinion to become the creditor of the banks. If a huxter-woman had a dollar in her pocket, "a hundred to one if it be not the indebtedness of a bank." (p. 32.)

⁶⁷ *Bank Question*, pp. 33-36. "I have felt personally and sorely, the evil, in the management of a large cotton manufacturing establishment, which by the dint of close economy and good management, has paid 10 per cent per annum, while, all our advantages considered, I am confident that in such times as we had from 1842 to 1846, that establishment would have returned its cost, $350,000, to its owners every five years." And he went on in a brief description that applies strikingly to the textile industry in years of depression since the World War: "It has paid a good interest to its proprietors, while many similar establishments in the Northern and Eastern States have been compelled to stop, and now stand a tax to the owners; and I feel a confident hope that Graniteville will ride the storm, and be a beacon light to the whole South, and a nucleus around which a great branch of industry is to grow up." (p. 36.) South Carolina would be much better off had her excessive bank capital been employed, not in tempting inflation and speculation, but "in improving the agriculture of our State, and pushing forward manufacturing enterprises." (pp. 37-38.)

[68] *Letter to Thornton Coleman, Esq.,* p. 3. Banks were not at this time auxiliary to industry, as now, but were viewed, in the best light, as assistants to commerce, and, in a worse interpretation, as mere money-changers. Gregg had been a bank director off and on for thirty years.

[69] *Ibid.,* pp. 4-5. "Besides that, we want to punish you; you have acted badly; you have shaved the people by exacting usurious rates of interest. The State is in needy circumstances, and ought to relieve taxation. . . ." (p. 5.)

[70] *Ibid.,* pp. 6-7.

[71] *Ibid.,* p. 8. He devoted the rest of the letter to a blast against instances in which the State had been "cheated into debt and consequent taxation." The projectors of the Blue Ridge Railroad were still confident of fastening that incubus on South Carolina. The scheme had been conceived in extravagance, and would run, in cost, even beyond his estimates of 1856. He had kept himself posted on the designs of railroad promoters and State bond speculators. "There are men who live, and live luxuriously, by watching the outgoings of public funds." Gregg was a particular scourge to the commissioners who built the State House. This capitol represented in his mind South Carolina's obsession with politics. Factory buildings were more to his taste. As things have turned out, few today could agree with Gregg's words 75 years ago in calling it "the most magnificent monument of folly, which was ever commenced by a sensible people. The interest, on the outlay for that building, over and above what ought to have built a splendid State house, will amount to . . . $150,000 a year, which, added to our school fund, would educate every child in the State for all time to come." (*Ibid.,* pp. 9-10.) The constitution ought to be amended so that the State could not become involved in expenditure for any public work without the consent of two-thirds of both houses of two legislatures. The want of such a safeguard was simply impounding taxes which would soon of necessity be loosed on the unsuspecting people. City writers were proposing to tax improvements on country lands. Gregg's own share of increased taxes under such a system would amount to hundreds of dollars a year, and he felt sensitive on the subject. (*Ibid.,* pp. 11-12.) "Our large real estate at Graniteville and Vaucluse is now regarded by law merely as a plantation, and pays a land tax accordingly."

[72] *Mercury,* Dec. 15, 1857.

[73] *Ibid.,* Dec. 14, 1857.

[74] *Ibid.,* Dec. 22, 1857. The section of the 1840 act imposing a tax on the issues of suspended banks was to be inoperative until Jan. 1, 1859; if after Jan. 1, 1860, any bank had notes outstanding to a value more

than three times that of the gold and silver in its vaults, a penalty was to attach for each day over thirty successive days during which this condition continued; and after the same date no bank was to issue a note under $10 denomination. The *Mercury* approved the act, which "left the banks free to aid the community, and rectify their own disorders, until the resumption of specie payments. . . ."

[75] Mch. 31, 1858. *Hammond Papers*, XXIII.

[76] *Minutes*, June 22, 1859.

[77] *Letter to Coleman*, p. 1.

[78] D. A. Tompkins, *Cotton Mill, Commercial Features*, p. 205.

[79] *Letter to Coleman*, pp. 1-2.

[80] *President's Report*, Apr. 18, 1867, p. 9. "In many instances they have been abandoned in inclement weather in our streets, destitute of food and clothing, and we have been obliged to minister to their wants and to send them back to the neighborhood from which they came, with our own teams. Some times they come by railroad, a poor woman with four or five helpless children, sent here and the passage paid by charitable people, under the presumption that Graniteville is a sort of charitable hospital. We pay the railroad to carry such people back to their friends. This looks uncharitable, but is absolutely necessary to avoid being over-run with such people."

CHAPTER X

[1] DeBow's *Review*, XXIX, 77, 225, 494, 623, 771; XXX, 102, 217. Rhodes did not put the case too baldly when he wrote: "Twenty-two million people confronted nine million, and of the nine million three and a half million were slaves. . . . The Union had much greater wealth, was a country of a complex civilization, and boasted of its varied industries; it combined the farm, the shop, and the factory. The Confederacy was but a farm, dependent on Europe and on the North for everything but bread and meat, and before the war for much of those." (*History of the United States*, III, 397.) For a sketchy account of the industries in the South during the war period, see J. C. Schwab, *The Confederate States of America*, pp. 267-283.

[2] The motion for the election of James J. Gregg was put by Mr. Allen and seconded by Mr. Taylor. President and treasurer were to receive each $2,500 in salary. To judge from the stockholders' minutes, Gregg was mistaken in saying, in his report in 1867, (p. 7) that James became treasurer in 1860.

[3] *Annual Cyclopædia*, II, 13.

[4] Schwab, *op. cit.*, Appendix 1.

[5] "With prices constantly rising, it seemed impossible to lose by any venture, and all seemed to grow rich by investing their notes in commodities, and selling these at an advance. The mania affected old and young alike, and extended to every kind of commodity. As one observer put it: 'Every man in the community is swindling everybody else.' " (Schwab, *ibid.*, p. 231.)

[6] See Rhodes, *op. cit.*, pp. 193-194.

[7] Address before Manufacturers' Association of the Confederate States, *Daily South Carolinian*, (Columbia) June 4, 1864. Thus Gregg had had a special occasion for extending his policy of direct sales; "the demand for our goods was not equal to their production, and I paid a visit to Nashville, Memphis and New Orleans, and also Richmond, Virginia; at which places I took large cash orders and made many valuable customers, so that we had from that time forth, orders in advance of all we could make, deliverable at our door." (*President's Report*, Apr. 18, 1867, p. 7.) In December 1861 (1860 price equaling 1), the currency price of cotton had not risen, Irish potatoes stood at 1.7, rice 1.2, oats 2, wheat .9, butter 1.9, lard 2.2; bacon in November was 2.1. Gregg must have been mistaken in saying prices of most agricultural products had not risen. By the time of the April 1862 meeting, cotton was down to .8, but there had been a general rise in other commodities. (Schwab, *op. cit.*, Appendix 1.)

[8] *Minutes*, Apr. 24, 1862.

[9] *Daily South Carolinian*, June 4, 1864. Gregg is speaking of cotton manufacturers in the South generally.

[10] *Minutes*, July 15, 1862. It would soon be possible to declare an extra dividend which would permit shareholders, if they chose, to pay for new stock. Gregg's policy looked toward conservation, and never exploitation.

[11] J. L. Quinby in *Horse Creek Valley News* (Warrensville, S. C.), Nov. 16, 1907; Aiken *Journal and Review*, Sept. 29, 1920.

[12] Augusta *Constitutionalist*, Apl. 13, 1862, quoted in Putnam's *Record of the Rebellion*, IV, 85.

[13] *President's Report*, Apr. 18, 1867. Sometimes Gregg had to make contributions in advance of authorization; thus the stockholders' meeting on Dec. 13, 1862 provided that his donation to the Soldiers' Relief Society should be regarded as made in his official capacity and that the company assume payment. A more important appropriation was that of

$10,000, which was added to the fund left in the will of Ker Boyce for the education of the children of Graniteville; it is certain, of course, that the whole fund was invested in the stock of the company. (*Minutes.*)

[14] *Hammond Papers,* XXXI.

[15] Gregg wrote to Hammond June 14. Six weeks later Hammond wrote to W. G. Simms complaining of the practices of the impressment commissioners, whom he had denounced in the Beach Island Club. As usual, he had a surplus of corn unsold in June. He informed the government purchasing agent that he would be ready to shell and deliver the next week, offering him 6,000 bushels at $10. "I thought I had about 15,000 surplus on hand," Hammond said. "But Gregg alone wanted 6,000 as absolutely necessary for Graniteville, and as soon as it was known that I had corn to sell at $10, the country people for 30 miles around sent their wagons to take it on the ear. . . ." The government agent declining to pay Hammond's price, he at once contracted with others, whom he had kept in abeyance, to take his corn "selecting those who like Gregg were exempted from impressment, and contracting for payment as soon as the corn was shelled and sacked and deposited in my warehouse, to be held at my weights and their risk of all sorts." He could have disposed of 100,000 bushels in ten days, he said, for corn was selling in August at $15 to $18. Quartermaster officers representing Jackson's Branch Barn came to Hammond's plantation of Redcliffe on July 9. He told them he had sold all his corn to persons whom they could not impress and offered to show his contracts. Two of the officers were satisfied, but the third wrote out for Hammond a notice of impressment notwithstanding. Much angered, Hammond next morning tore up the notice in the officer's presence, and felt like kicking the fellow out of his house. (*Hammond Papers,* XXXI.) However, a new order was issued, July 18 (it is preserved in *ibid.*) impressing all of Hammond's surplus corn for the army at $5 in new currency per bushel. Hammond's attitude in this vital matter of supplying food to the starving Confederacy seems strange in one who was such a fiery patriot a few years earlier.

[16] Only one copy of this handbill survives; from a notation on the back, in old ink and a contemporary hand, it was used to wrap some Graniteville correspondence of the month of October, 1862, from which it may be thought the appeal was made prior to that date.

[17] *Minutes,* Dec. 13, 1862. The old matter of examination of the company's books came up again; two stockholders were appointed to perform this duty quarterly, the company paying their traveling expenses.

[18] *Ibid.,* Apr. 23, 1863. A proposal to erect a hotel for travelers did not meet with favor. (The old hotel, which had been conducted for a time at least by G. W. Henderson, burned to the ground shortly before.

It stood in an oak grove near the site of the first stables before these were moved to what is now called "Battle Row"; Aiken *Journal and Review*, Sept. 29, 1920.) Application of one Kelly for a lease on water power at Bridge Creek was referred to the directors. T. D. Wagner was elected a director, due to the absence of Perrin in the army.

[19] On the regular day for the 1864 meeting, Apr. 21, there was no quorum (the first time in the history of the company); so the meeting was called for June 1. Earnings for the year 1863 (in currency) were $1,986,645.30, which, added to $155,299.41 "surplus profits" on hand Jan. 1 of that year, made a total of $2,141,944.71. From this had been paid Dividend No. 24, Apr. 1, 178,500; No. 25, Sept. 1, $357,250; transferred to cash capital, $50,000; paid to (illegible) & Co.'s account, $1,620; paid in State tax, $454,598.55. The next figures are for gold values: the capital stock was now, with a small scrip dividend, $717,250; of this $75,788.99 representing buildings, $186,050.62 machinery, $11,-320.93 canals and dams, $94,801.03 real estate, $3,332.17 gas works (gas had recently been installed in the mill, due doubtless to the need for running longer hours; see Gregg's statement in *Daily South Carolinian*, June 4, 1864), $3,631.07 water works, leaving for surplus capital $342,325.19. Gold was worth 17 to 1 of currency at this time. During the year 1863 the mill had turned out goods as follows: 4-4 sheeting, 1,125,393 yards; 7-8 shirting, 1,470,369 yards; 3-4 shirting, 644,807 yards; 7-8 drills, 469,288 yards, a total of 3,709,857 yards, which represented 3,146 bales of cotton consumed. The treasurer (William Gregg, Jr., who had returned to the company in his old post, succeeding his brother) reported that the factory had been running smoothly along, keeping up about its usual production.

[20] *Minutes*, June 1, 1864; *President's Report*, Apr. 18, 1867, pp. 13-14 At this 1864 meeting the number of the directors was changed from four to six. Officers' salaries were lowered; from July 1st, the president's salary was to be the currency equivalent of $1,500 in gold, the treasurer's $1,000, and those of superintendent and secretary $800, all subject to alteration by the directors monthly. In the month intervening before July 1st, the currency estimate was to be at the rate of 15 for 1, which was rather better than the rate, 17 for 1, in the Confederacy as a whole at this date. The value of the currency was fluctuating violently; in February it had taken 23 currency dollars to equal one of gold, and by the end of the year 38 were required. (See Schwab, *Confederate States*, Appendix 1.)

[21] *President's Report*, Apr. 18, 1867, pp. 14-15. Gregg's quotation from the minutes of the board of directors is the only bit of those records which has survived, so far as I have been able to discover.

NOTES TO CHAPTER X

[22] See *Daily South Carolinian*, June 4, 1864.

[23] *Public Laws of the Confederate States of America*, passed at the third session of the first Congress, 1863, James M. Matthews, ed. p. 117.

[24] Cf. Schwab, *op. cit.*, pp. 203 ff.

[25] "The shoemaker who formerly purchased his leather at twenty-five cents per pound, and paid his journeymen one dollar a day, was poorly paid for the use of his shop, tools and material at seventy-five per cent on the cost of production; but when he had the good luck to see leather advanced to ten and twelve dollars a pound, and wages to five or eight dollars a day, the case was very different. Under this conscript law, it was the interest of all such producers to pay high for everything his manufactory consumed, in order to enhance the first cost of his products, and enlarge his profits." Sections III and VI of the act contributed to the same end; a progressive tax of from 10 per cent to 16 2-3 per cent was laid upon the earnings of manufacturing enterprises, rents and the cost of labor and raw material, to be deducted from gross earnings. (*Public Laws of the Confederate States*, pp. 120, 121.)

[26] Nassau and St. George were the ports used by the Charleston blockade runners. From July, 1862, to June, 1863, it was said, 57 steamers and 91 sailing vessels left Nassau for Confederate ports, 51 of the former and 55 of the latter landing their cargoes, and in the same period 44 steamers and 45 sailing vessels reached Nassau from the Confederacy. Until the last of the war the trade was carried on from Charleston by the Importing and Exporting Co. of S. C., with 23 vessels. Most of the capital risked in the trade from this port belonged to Charlestonians. (See Theodore D. Jervey, in *Annual Report American Historical Assn.*, 1913, I, 169 ff.)

[27] He never forgot the benefit to the population: "And what adds great importance to it, homes would have been provided for, and lucrative employment given to thousands of women and children—the families of absent soldiers, who are now receiving a scanty support from State and private charity."

[28] "Some claimed correctly that high prices were a stimulus to Southern industries, and that any attempt to forcibly lower prices would lessen production, as had been the result of impressing goods at government prices." (Schwab, *op. cit.*, p. 184.) Gregg instanced further the unwillingness of the Augusta Company to add 5,000 spindles to the mill; the members of the corporation, as individuals, had invested in blockade runners. "Why have they not filled their mills to the utmost capacity with additional machinery? The question is easily answered, and the answer should be obvious to every one. It is the want of sufficient encouragement and the prospect of profits."

320

[29] Aiken *Journal and Review*, Sept. 29, 1920.

[30] See *War of the Rebellion, Official Records of the Union and Confederate Armies*, series I, XLVII, part I, p. 1151, giving references to the reports; the most important are those of Generals Atkins, Sherman, Wheeler, and Kilpatrick, and Col. Jordan. Both sides claimed success in their operations. General Sherman wrote (*Personal Memoirs*, II, 274-275) that "On the 10th I rode up to Blackville, where I conferred with Generals Slocum and Kilpatrick, became satisfied that the whole army would be ready within a day, and accordingly made orders for the next movement north to Columbia, the right wing to strike Orangeburg *en route*. Kilpatrick was ordered to demonstrate strongly toward Aiken, to keep up the delusion that we might turn to Augusta; but he was notified that Columbia was the next objective, and that he should cover the left flank against Wheeler, who hung around it." Kilpatrick's account may be quoted, in part: "February 9, moved to Windsor and thence to Johnson's Station, destroying portions of the railroad. Up to that point I had moved from Blackville in such a manner and had so maneuvered my troops as if I was the advance of the main army moving on Augusta. On the morning of the 11th I found that the movement was a success. Wheeler had left the Edisto unguarded, uncovered Columbia, and by marching all day and night reached Aiken at daylight on the morning of the 11th with his entire command. To make certain of this, General Atkins, commanding brigade, was directed to move out of my works at Johnson's Station and make a reconnaisance in the direction of Aiken. His advance, without opposition, entered the town and a moment afterward was most furiously attacked by Wheeler's entire command. General Atkins fell back, fighting gallantly, disputing every foot of ground, to my position at Johnson's Station, giving me sufficient time to make all necessary dispositions to check the enemy's further advance. At 11 a.m. Wheeler, with one brigade, feinted upon my left flank and charged, mounted, with his entire command. He was handsomely repulsed with a loss of 31 killed, 160 wounded, and 60 taken prisoners. He made no further attack, but fell back to his old position at Aiken. I remained at this point, destroying track as usual, constantly demonstrating in the direction of Augusta, till the night of the 12th, when I left Wheeler's front." (*War of the Rebellion*, series I, XLVII, part I, pp. 858-859; see also part II, pp. 449, 455, 1170, 1295.)

[31] See, e.g., *War of the Rebellion*, series I, XLVII, part I, p. 865.

[32] An old resident of Graniteville, who knew the teamsters, gave their names as follows: Tolliver Hearn, Oscar Sentell, Tom Sentell, John Hunter, Bill Parker, Frank Tuey, Jim Bryan.

CHAPTER XI

[1] *Minutes,* Apr. 20, 1865. This policy had already been in force. On Feb. 1, 1865, there had been a dividend in cloth valued at $556,659; on Mch. 2, a dividend of 100 per cent, $715,500, had been paid in cash; on Apr. 7, $7 per share was paid in gold. At the close of the war William Gregg, Jr., declined to serve longer as treasurer, and Gen. James Jones was elected to the office (May 30, 1865). This old partner of Gregg's, an experienced manufacturer and "systematic business man," stood the company in good stead while the president was away, in New England and abroad, purchasing new equipment. Gen. Jones died, however, a few months after his election, Oct. 18, and B. C. Hard became treasurer pro tempore. (*Minutes,* May 22, 1866.)

Greenbacks were worth 75 cents in gold on the day of the report. They had fallen to 69 cents by the date of Gregg's death. (Wesley C. Mitchell, *Gold, Prices, and Wages under the Greenback Standard,* pp. 301, 305.) Money figures in the Graniteville reports after the war must necessarily refer to greenbacks. At the end of the war there was a spectacular fall in prices, though there was a recovery in the second half of 1865. From January, 1866 "until the autumn of 1871 the general trend of prices was strongly downward. . . ." (*Ibid.,* p. 26) Brown sheetings in the first quarter of 1866 fell from 31 cents to 23 cents (wholesale) and middling cotton at New York from 51 cents to 39 cents. (*Ibid.,* pp. 346, 344.)

[2] *Minutes,* May 22, 1866. "The Mill was not fairly started before first January, 1850."

[3] *Ibid.* This policy of diversification was in opposition to his earlier preachments, as well as his earlier practice. It is impossble to say what changed Gregg's mind; perhaps it was the optimistic reports received from home, of which he spoke; perhaps it was the finer goods mills which he saw in Europe, or perhaps he thought Graniteville could thenceforth take the whole South for its special province and manufacture every kind of goods that the section needed. Later, in justifying this course, he explained to the stockholders that when operations were commenced in 1848, the machinery was adapted particularly to making sheetings and shirtings from yarn, of which there were 14 hanks of 2,520 feet each to the pound. "The consequence was that in dull seasons we necessarily accumulated heavy stocks and had on hand at times from two or three thousand bales of cloth." Still, the superior character of the article manufactured gave it a lead in all the markets of the country. (*President's Report,* Apr. 18, 1867, p. 11.)

[4] When Gregg went to England, he expected to retain the mill's old looms—336 of them—and purchase only 250 more. At an auction where a large mill of new machinery was sold, he bought 258 fine looms, at $28 a loom, and afterwards had 20 specimen looms made, at £7 each. (*President's Report*, Apr. 18, 1867, p. 10.)

[5] This letter to his daughter shows that the population of Graniteville in the back-wash of the Civil War was not faring well without the kindly ministrations of its master. In Europe he was doing all he could to bring prosperity back to the town. "I don't take pleasure," he wrote, "of hearing of suffering and want at Graniteville but think it is time for that people to realize that they had a faithful and watchful friend in me." Perhaps the strain of war years had done something temporarily to destroy their old appreciation of William Gregg.

His constant insistence upon real work comes out in his advice for a clergyman friend: "If I were in his place, I would seek a situation where labor of a more profitable kind would secure bread and clothes for a family of children, but he may be fishing for some of the rich girls that occasionally visit Aiken. But I think that a bad chance—big whiskers don't always win fair ladies, and it isn't every lady that is ready to fall in love with a parson, particularly a poor one with a dozen children."

Though no one in the South had been more nationally minded than Gregg, the tocsin of the war gave him some prejudice against the North, which comes out in a playful remark in this letter. "We were all rejoiced to hear of the birth of your boy and expect to see him walking about when we get home. I intend to buy him a pair of breeches, and if you want him well fitted, send his measure in haste. It will get here in time—state color &c., for if left to my choice, it will be black or drab. I hope he will carry a Gregg to his name. I know he will be a busy little fellow and a saucy chap. You must not send him to any Yankee college. He must be brought up in the faith, a true southerner and a Reb every inch of him."

[6] *President's Report*, Apr. 18, 1867.

[7] One of these married a girl of Graniteville and remained there. An old operative still vividly remembers helping to unload the machinery at Warrenville. He believes the shipments contained cards and mules, besides looms.

[8] *President's Report*, as of May 1, 1866; contained in *Minutes*, May 22, 1866. Gregg contemplated no withdrawal from active supervision at Graniteville, for, against his old design, it was decided that the new treasurer, to be elected, should not necessarily be required to reside at the mill. The number of the directors was reduced to five, including the

president. The company was to proceed against the United States government for the value of 119 bales of goods taken from the mills in April and May of 1865 by a Federal officer.

[9] *President's Report* Apr. 18, 1867, p. 8. However, at some future time such an engine might well be installed to take care of shortages of water or the break-down of the large wheel, since, when in full operation, the loss of a day would be equivalent to $1,000. (*Ibid.*, pp. 9-10.)

[10] *Ibid.* "In the month of August the removal of these obstructions was dangerous to health, and required many hundreds of days' work and the supervision of an experienced eye. The consequence was that I traversed the bed of the creek, with my water-proof boots, more than a mile down, a half dozen or more times, and finally brought the bed of the creek to where it ought to be, and where it may be kept at small expense if properly attended to."

[11] When Confederate soldiers were discharged in North Carolina without a dollar, and were walking homeward by way of Graniteville, Gregg would try to give them work about the village. Many remained in Graniteville, married, and have descendants there now. (Interview with Mr. Gideon Perdue.)

[12] There is no reference to this in the 1866 minutes, but Gregg's report in 1867 speaks of his previous announcement.

[13] He had sent around a circular in advance of the special meeting, stating that he would not be a candidate for reëlection, thus giving the stockholders time to choose his successor.

[14] *President's Report*, Apr. 18, 1867, pp. 3-4.

[15] MS letter.

[16] Though the previous production of a staple article made it necessary in dull times to accumulate heavy stocks, even so the mill "made a superior article that took the lead in all the markets of the country, and gave us vent for our products, while other similar establishments could makes sales only by sacrifices. Our cloths took the premium at all the great fairs in the United States, as well as at the World's Fair in London." He had begun making prize goods at Vaucluse, indeed. Mr. August Kohn has in his possession a silver medal of the American Institute, New York, bearing on one side the figure of a woman, and a spinning wheel, plow, and ship, and on the other the words "Awarded to Gregg & Jones for superior cotton Osnaburgs, 1845."

[17] "This enhanced value," he said, "is the accumulation of profit, not a dollar having been contributed by the Stockholders since the first capital Stock was paid in—three hundred and sixty thousand dollars." In the treasurer's report for this year, bound in the same pamphlet, p. 24,

H. H. Hickman valued the property at a million in gold. I find a contemporary penciled note on the margin of Gregg's report, probably in the hand of Mr. Quinby, for years a store keeper at Graniteville, calculating that the 27,000 spindles, at $35 each, including $55,000 of cash capital, brought the value to $1,000,000.

[18] As an evidence of the possibility of enormous profits, he cited the case of a Manchester man (doubtless one whose acquaintance he had made on his recent visit to England), who in twenty years had risen from $1.50 a day as a mule spinner to the ownership of 300,000 spindles. Indeed, Graniteville's example, he reminded them, was a case in point. An old gentleman in Charleston, whose memory covers nearly the whole period of Graniteville's history, exclaimed to me with enthusiasm: "My dear sir, there never *was* such a mill!"

[19] Due to the resumption of cotton planting in the South following the war, European stocks accumulated and, with the crop annually increasing, prices fell till the end of the decade. (See James L. Watkins, *Production and Price of Cotton for One Hundred Years*, pp. 14, 15.) The sooner the mill disposed of the cotton, or used it, the greater would have been the profit, of course.

[20] Wesley C. Mitchell, *Gold, Prices, and Wages Under the Greenback Standard*, pp. 6, 7.

[21] *President's Report*, Apr. 18, 1867, pp. 13-15. James P. Boyce and James H. Taylor obtained permission to enter the following protest in the minutes of this meeting in 1867: "The undersigned, members of the Board of Directors of the years 1864 and 1865, being present at this meeting and having heard the report of the President, desire in the matter personal to themselves to protest against its statements and inferences. We think a full statement of the facts would show the incorrectness of the positions taken and inferences made by Mr. Gregg."

[22] See the writer's *Rise of Cotton Mills in the South*, pp. 250 ff.

[23] Gregg's whole preachment of "domestic industry" would be compromised by subservience to Northern selling agents. It has been seen how he objected to making even Charleston agents distributors for the mill's goods. "The jobbing trade of Charleston," he said now, "may be supplied by sending orders to the factory. I am satisfied that a good business man, properly sustained with cash capital, will soon find customers in the West to absorb all our goods, and I can see no good reason why they should be sent to New York to supply customers in Nashville, Louisville, St. Louis, Memphis, New Orleans and Mobile, and even Augusta. Our goods sold at home pay no commissions, and no city taxes, and these expenses saved will pay four times over the salary of a high-paid

325

Treasurer. . . ." The Southern cotton manufacturing industry is now
notably turning to the policy of direct sales which he advocated, having
suffered under every one of the disabilities which Gregg specified so
long in advance. "Any bargain, on our part, to yield to another the
control of our goods for the sake of low rates of interest," he declared,
"will necessarily place a master over the establishment that will render
your Treasurer powerless. . . . He [this commission agent] would
direct that such goods only should be made as would suit the New
York market, having no regard to the Southern trade, and would dictate
to what points the goods should be sent for sale, with no other interest
at stake but that which would prompt him to make the speediest possible conversion of our goods into ready money, in order to make his
loan as small as possible. His interest would of course prompt him to
avoid making goods peculiarly adapted to the home sales and all those
profitable Western markets where time would intervene between the
departure of the goods and their arrival in New Orleans or other Western
points. The goods would naturally be sent to the nearest cash market,
and forced at times on temporarily dull markets, at ruinous sacrifices."
His next remark applies as well to selling agents who, later on, became stockholders in Southern mills. "Do you suppose that you will find
a house that will be so honest as to work for your interest while it will
be positively against its own? Could you expect such an agent to send
five hundred or a thousand bales of your goods to New Orleans, even
for an advance of two cents per yard, which would be equal to about
$18,000 gained to us, while it might cost him, under this money arrange-
ment, the necessity of making an additional advance of one hundred
and fifty thousand dollars." Besides, those who proposed raising funds
in this way, were not aware, Gregg thought, of the expense of selling
goods through commission firms. If the mill should produce 6,600 bales,
it would cost to sell them in New York $66,000 more than if sold at
the door of the plant; it would cost about as much to sell in Charleston;
and to this sum should be added an equal sum to cover losses on forced
sales. Cf. Gregg in DeBow's *Review*, XXIX, 81 ff.

[24] *President's Report*, Apr. 18, 1867, p. 16, note.

[25] He believed the reconstituted Augusta Company (near at hand and
therefore likely to strike the stockholders as a forceful example), would
consider this industrial fealty nothing short of ruinous.

[26] He had taken office July 1, 1866.

[27] Commissions would amount to $10 a bale—$65,000; loss in price
would be 3-4 of a cent a yard—$43,875; and interest would amount to at
least $7,000 on $100,000 borrowed—a total of $115,875. "I submit if it

would not be better to pay a high rate of interest for the capital you require, and keep in your own hands the control of your splendid mill."

[28] The board of directors was enlarged to contain the president and seven others, was to meet monthly, and at least six times a year the meetings were to take place in Charleston. The secretary of the company was to send detailed cost sheets and statements of operation to directors monthly and quarterly.

[29] *Minutes*, Apr. 23, 1868.

[30] *President's Report*, Apr. 18, 1867, p. 6.

[31] *Minutes*, Apr. 23, 1868.

[32] An old lady, a resident of Graniteville, wrote out at the time of Gregg's death an *In Memoriam*, which is now in the possession of Mrs. Chafee. It represents what must have been Graniteville's sense of loss, "which never could be made up again." The writer recorded that "he rose up to meet our common foe," and so died at his post. One who knew Gregg well wrote that he had been moved by wise forethought to set his house in order. "Within the past year, he had entirely refitted the Graniteville Mills, and started them upon a new and more extensive course of usefulness; he had portioned off his children, he had gone to see his relatives in distant States . . . and the few personal enmities that no one could have escaped exciting in so long and active a life, he had seen to, and settled amicably. . . ." (Dr. Cook, at a meeting of the Beach Island Farmers' Club, Nov. 2, 1867, quoted in Edgefield *Advertiser*, June 5, 1879.)

[33] *President's Report*, Apr. 18, 1867.

[34] *Ibid.* By Mch. 1, 1868, the loan debt, with interest added to Jan. 1, had been reduced by $56,536, standing now at $100,208. Gregg had borrowed toward the last at 12 per cent, but Hickman had been able to pay off most of the obligations contracted at this rate, and 7 per cent was the highest he had given in New York. In addition to this liquidation, the company had been able to pay two dividends amounting to $14,330.

[35] *Minutes*, Apr. 23, 1868. Few of Gregg's original associates in the Graniteville enterprise were left at the time of his death. A. W. Thomson and W. H. Gilliland, two of the oldest members of the company, had passed away within the year. A page of the stockholders' minute book, after the custom, was ordered to be set aside as a memorial to Gregg, but, as a matter of fact, this was forgotten.

The fate of James Gregg is properly a part of this story. The bad boy of the village was Bob McAvoy. One who knew him described him:

327

"He would mold nickels, and it was said he would take Confederate money and raise its denomination by pasting a 2 on top of the 1 of a 10-dollar note." Playing about a freight car at the Kalmia station, Bob got a severe injury to his left leg. When Mrs. Gregg knew of it and learned that the wound was infected, she went to the McAvoy home and bathed and dressed the hurt. The leg had to be amputated, and Mrs. Gregg nursed the boy and took him to Kalmia to convalesce. When he was well he had a crutch, in the use of which he was remarkably dexterous. He would go hunting all day through the swamps, and could climb a tree like a cat.

One April day in 1876, nobody knows why, he appeared at the door of the mill office in the main factory building, where James Gregg, then superintendent, was working at a desk. He shot Gregg, fled through the passage-way, and swung round the jamb of the door toward the canal, across which he disappeared with uncanny swiftness. One may still see the hole in the door frame torn by the bullet which Gregg sent after him. Gregg died a few days later in Augusta. Mrs. Gregg recorded it in the family Bible that her son was murdered in cold blood.

Bob McAvoy hid in the attic of his father's house in the village. Planning his escape, he employed his handiness with tools to make a wooden leg to replace his tell-tale crutch; he devised a wig, donned woman's clothing, and was accompanied by his sister to the train at Aiken. In indiscreet solicitude for his safety, his sister cautioned him as he stepped on the platform, "Now be careful and don't let them catch you"; the conductor overheard this remark, telegraphed ahead, and McAvoy was captured by officers at Columbia. He was brought back to Aiken, tried, and hung. Many Graniteville people witnessed the execution. One villager, now an old man, told me of seeing Bob's father drive back to the town sitting on his son's coffin. He buried the body in the corner of his yard where he could watch over the grave—this out of fear, so the story goes, that doctors would disinter it to dissect the brain, which was admitted to be "a powerful one." "After times and times," my informant concluded, "the mound disappeared—old man McAvoy had moved the body himself, nobody knew where to."

[36] See *Augusta Chronicle*, June 20, 1926.

INDEX

331